CLASSIC WALKS IN
The Pyrénées

by Kev Reynolds

The Oxford Illustrated Press

The Oxford Illustrated Press

© 1989, Kev Reynolds

ISBN 0 946609 62 4

Published by:
The Oxford Illustrated Press Limited, Haynes Publishing
Group, Sparkford, Nr Yeovil, Somerset BA22 7JJ, England.
Haynes Publications Inc., 861 Lawrence Drive, Newbury
Park, California 91320, USA.

Printed in England by:
J.H. Haynes & Co Limited, Sparkford, Nr Yeovil,
Somerset.

British Library Cataloguing in Publication Data
Reynolds, Kev
 Classic walks in the Pyrenees.
 1. Europe. Pyrenees. Visitors' guides
 I. Title
 914.6'520483
 ISBN 0–946609–62–4

Library of Congress Catalog Card Number – 89–83555

All photos by the author.

CONTENTS

ACKNOWLEDGEMENTS

My sincere thanks are due to all those who have at one time or another wandered with me in the Pyrénées, and in so doing added much to pleasures gained. They are: Michael Adams, Nigel Fry, Alan Payne, Pete Smith, Keith Sweeting and Hugh Walton; and my ever-forgiving family: Claudia, Ilsa and Linda Reynolds who have shared not only many of the best days in the valleys, but also their home, with thousands of Pyrénéan photographs, books and maps.

I should also like to thank Peter Derbyshire and Jude Lock of Barèges for their hospitality, and Ken Rawlinson of Phoenix Mountaineering Ltd for the best tent I've ever used whilst doing the final research for this book. Ian Anderson of Redhill, Surrey printed all the black and white photographs for me, and I am indebted to him for his patience. Colour photographs were taken on Kodak film.

Thanks also to all those fellow enthusiasts at home and abroad who for many years have involved me in their adventures through a lively correspondence.

Kev Reynolds

DEDICATION

This book is dedicated to my wife, who made it all possible.

INTRODUCTION

The principal charm of the Pyrénées consists in the unrivalled scenery
CHARLES PACKE 1826-1896

Comparisons between mountain ranges are invidious; each has its own characteristic, its own essential quality that will either attract or repel the advances of man. For nearly thirty years it has been my good fortune to walk and climb in a variety of highland regions of Europe and North Africa, and in each one I have found landscapes of such great beauty that ambitions fulfilled merely led to others being formed and dreams stirred for a return. Yet it is to the Pyrénées that I find myself drawn with greater frequency than to any other area. Why? This book, I trust, will give an answer to that question and lead others to an enthusiasm for this delectable range of mountains.

True, there are areas with higher mountains. There are bigger glaciers, more impressive snowfields, steeper and more imposing walls to be found in the Alps where even among non-climbers, certain peaks have a recognised notoriety, while you can spend half a lifetime climbing in the Pyrénées and still find no-one back home who has heard of the mountains that have been the focus of your attention. And the valleys and passes crossed on some of the finest treks to be experienced anywhere in the world, will be dismissed by others with the question—'Where?'

Until recently the Pyrénées were Europe's unsung mountains, known and loved by only a comparatively small band of enthusiasts. Now, however, their peaks, passes and valleys are growing in popularity as each year more and more walkers and climbers turn their sights to the south in search of a fresh challenge and the reasonable certainty of good weather. Few will be disappointed with the experience.

This book is an introduction to Europe's second major range west of the Caucasus; a preamble to a selection of walks that lead into landscapes of splendour. These walks are among the very best out of hundreds of possibilities. They range from a single day's outing that would be acceptable to almost any active person, to seven-or-eight-week long expeditions that should only be attempted by strong and experienced mountain trekkers. There are walks in each of the three National Parks, walks on paths trodden by many hundreds of pairs of boots every summer, and routes that are devoid of trail or waymark, other than the occasional discreet cairn, leading through true wilderness areas where weeks of high summer go by with barely a visitor—save for the birds and isard and marmots.

The majority of these outings are circular and require several days to complete. They would suit equally holiday makers with their own transport and those who journey to the mountains by air or by train. A few are linear routes and each of these start and finish near a town with access to public transport. Every walk is a gem in its own right, and although there are others that could arguably have been included, a limitation of space has necessitated their omission. Some routes overlap and several have been chosen in close proximity to one another in order to give walkers based in one area a holiday full of worthwhile outings.

I know of tourists who have gone to the Pyrénées by car and returned a little disappointed. They fell into the trap of making comparisons with the Alps, and because they remained on roads throughout, failed to discover the essential qualities that make this range rather special. The Alps, of course, reveal themselves quite openly so even the aged and infirm may revel in their beauty from the comfort and safety of the valley. One can gaze at huge glaciers from the warmth of a village hotel, and almost touch the crags of instantly-recognised peaks from either car or train. Not so in the Pyrénées. You can drive into and out of the foothills here with one line of mountains hiding another. You can cross from north to south over a tortuous pass with barely a gimpse of the magnificent peaks accompanying some of the walks in this book. Here you have to pull on your walking boots and work for your visual pleasure, albeit sometimes with only minimal effort. In so doing you will be introduced to some of the loveliest landscapes in all of Europe.

Wandering through these landscapes the discerning walker will experience the multi-dimensional rewards that only an untamed country can give. It's not only the visual impact, although that is stunning enough. There is also the empty peace that borders silence. Valleys where few have ventured and even today you can share in the pleasures of pioneering—in a land that is only twenty-four hours from London by public transport. And the senses of sight and sound are not alone in being aroused in the Pyrénées—the hills and valleys are, from spring through until autumn, awash with a fragrant scent as aromatic plants respond to the drawing power of the sun and the breeze. Flowers and shrubs carpet pasture and remote cliff-face alike with an extravagance rarely seen in other ranges, and among their number are more than a hundred species that will be found nowhere else in the world.

Wild flowers are at their best in June. Among the higher mountains snow still lies deeply and most years some of the more adventurous walks will be out of bounds until the end of the month because of the threat of avalanche. But tarns will be clearing their winter burden of ice and instead filling their waters with the upturned mirror of neighbouring peaks. There are tarns everywhere. Hundreds of them. It has been estimated that in the region of the High Pyrénées alone (the area in which most of these walks are to be found), there are more than a thousand such tarns left behind by the last Ice Age. They lie in many instances like jewels in a tiara of peaks. Collections of tarns of all shapes and sizes are scattered among the raw inner recesses of hanging valleys. Others at the head of valley systems are remote and known only to a few determined climbers and trekkers. But wherever they are found, these tarns and pools and larger lakes are an important feature of many of the multi-day treks, and will highlight any walker's day.

Perhaps it is the existence of so many tarns, streams and

cascades that contributes to the marvellous quality of light in the Pyrénées. Certainly there is a purity, a clarity of atmosphere that I have not experienced elsewhere. Other writers in the past have attempted to quantify its brilliance, but it is beyond description. Go and experience it for yourself and you'll appreciate it too.

A few years ago one noted authority called the range: 'Europe's last great wilderness.' That wilderness is not so wild or extensive now, but this book points you into some remote corners where you may still discover a land seemingly untouched; a Genesis country with mystery and romance in memorable proportions. It is a land of Alpine stature, but without the crowds. There are 11,000ft (3353m) summits; huge canyons of multi-coloured limestone; big bald granite massifs draped with little glaciers; fantastic spires rearing out of the pastures; pastures a-dazzle with the richest flora in all of Europe. There are vultures and buzzards in the air, bears in the forests and a million crickets to leap away from your boots. Isard, the Pyrénéan chamois, are as agile and shy as their Alpine cousins. Mouflon, with their immense goat-like horns, are increasing in numbers. Marmots, introduced fom the Alps, are found in most high valleys, and there is an amazing assortment of butterflies drifting among the flower heads of summer.

National Parks

There are three National Parks; one in France, two in Spain—Ordesa in Aragon, Aïgues Tortes in Catalonia. Each one is unique in its own right. The *Parc National des Pyrénées Occidentales* (PNP) is the largest and with some of the finest peaks: Pic du Midi d'Ossau, Balaïtous, Vignemale, and the *cirques* of Gavarnie, Estaubé, Troumouse and Barroude. Adjacent to it in the east is the *Réserve Naturelle de Néouvielle,* and a number of walks are described that explore the very best of this extensive region.

South of the frontier and backing the Cirque de Gavarnie, the *Parque Nacional del Valle de Ordesa* occupies one of the most dramtic corners of all. A narrow, steep-walled canyon, it is the oldest Pyrénéan National Park, having been created as long ago as 1918. recently its boundary has been extended to include the neighbouring Anisclo Canyon, and this magnificent region is, of course, included here with some challengine walks.

The *Parque Nacional de Aigues Tortes i Sant Maurici* covers a large area of semi-wilderness in Catalonia. The best known peaks here are the twin Encantats which rise above the lake of Sant Maurici. But the lesser-known, tarn-glittering, granite wasteland at the head of the Riu Malo, with the long Besiberri ridge on the west and the jagged Travessani pinnacles on the east, is even finer. An outing is suggested here for experienced mountain trekkers that will do much to show the wilder aspects of the Pyrénées, offering perhaps the best illustration of what our pioneering predecessors would have faced.

Pioneers

The pioneers, naturally, came mostly from France or Spain. They were military surveyors or geologists, academics and a few adventurers. The first outstanding name was that of Ramond de Carbonnières, a politician caught in pre-Revolution intrigue when he made his first visit in 1787. He was a tremendous walker who initially based himself at Barèges, and then covered a great deal of country in a short space of time, crossing Port d'Oô and the Port de Venasque, and making an attempt on the Maladeta's summit. On subsequent visits he made the first crossing of the Brèche de Tuquerouye and, in 1802, the second ascent of Monte Perdido after sponsoring the first ascent a few days previously.

In 1817 Dr Frédéric Parrot walked from the Atlantic to the Mediterranean in fifty-three days, and still managed to climb a few peaks on the way. It was clearly a period when strong walkers were ten-a-penny, for during the nineteenth century there are several accounts of epic walking feats without any suggestion that they were at all unusual. Two of these strong walkers were Charles Packe and Count Henry Russell who, either singly or together, explored almost everywhere in the High Pyrénées and gained for themselves a certain reputation for Pyrénéan devotion that remains to this day. Packe was a wealthy Leicestershire landowner who had a penchant for Pyrénéan mountain dogs and a passion for wild flowers. His first visit was made in 1853, and by 1862 he had amassed enough information to be able to produce a detailed mountaineer's guidebook to the range. Three years later he concentrated on the Maladeta massif and drew a remarkably accurate map as a result.

While Packe was studious, Russell was a true romantic and one of the greatest mountaineering eccentrics of all time. As a young man it is said that he would dance all night and set out at dawn on a thirty mile walk. He also climbed, often alone, and with a poet's eye for the caprices of nature, wrote about the Pyrénées in the very fondest of terms. His love affair with the Vignemale is unrivalled in mountaineering history, and the degree to which he expressed that passion is unlikely to be equalled. One night he had himself buried in a shallow grave on the very summit, with only his head remaining free. Then he excavated a total of seven caves (or grottoes) in the walls of the Vignemale in which he lived for weeks at a time. There he held dinner parties, and even celebrated Mass with a congregation of thirty kneeling on the ice outside. Eventually, in 1889, the *syndicat* of the valley at Barèges leased the four summits of the mountain to him 'without right to forbid access' for a ninety-nine year term—at the sum of one franc per year. As I write, this lease runs out, but several of the grottoes remain.

In the century since Russell and Packe wandered the mountains, the band of enthusiasts has steadily increased. Yet unaccountably, and happily, they have never matched the numbers attracted to the Alps. Some have been introduced to the mountains in less peaceful times than today. During the Spanish Civil War in the late thirties, for example, a regular flow of refugees crossed into France by night, fleeing persecution and the bitterness of a nation torn by brother fighting brother. A few years later this tide was reversed when Germany overran France, and the Resistance included a number of volunteers who knew the Pyrénées well enough to lead escaping servicemen over the mountains to safety.

After lecturing on the Pyrénées recently, I was approached by an ex-RAF bomber pilot who told me that he had been shot down over Belgium in 1941, and how, after many months of travelling south through France, a Basque shepherd was contacted by the Resistance to take him in winter, by night, across the frontier and on the road to freedom. The Pyrénées have always been a barrier—*la frontière sauvage*—but this is part of their appeal.

Frontier Crossing

There are several walks described in the following pages that trespass from one side of the international frontier to the other. It should be stressed that walkers ought always to carry their passports with them on such expeditions, although in practice it is most unlikely that any frontier officials will be seen. In more than twenty visits to the Pyrénées, involving probably fifty or so frontier crossings, I have only twice been asked to show my passport—once in the Esera Valley in Spain, and once on the Port de Rat leading into Andorra. However, a couple of friends and I were stopped by Spanish frontier guards one day below the Puerto de Gistain whilst tackling the High Route. They were armed and admirably equipped with superb mountaineering gear, including two-way radio. We were more than a little disconcerted, wondering what we had done wrong. But we need not have worried, for the guards were lost, and asked if we could tell them exactly where they were!

Accommodation

A small handful of these walks can be tackled from a valley base. As for the rest, you must put your home upon your back and take it with you. There are huts *(refuges)* in most high mountain areas, which do provide shelter for the night. On the French side these huts are owned usually by the CAF (French Alpine Club) or the National Park authorities. In Spain they may belong to a climbing club like the Catalan Mountain Club (CEC) or to private individuals. A few belong to commercial organisations, but all have one thing in common; they are open to anyone, irrespective of club membership. Some have a warden (or guardian) in residence during the main summer season, which is usually taken to be from late June to the middle of September. When these *refuges* are manned, meals are nearly always available.

Hut accommodation is not hotel-standard. Communal bunks are almost universally found, although some huts do have a few individual bunks and the occasional bedded room. Meals are often basic but plentiful, and it is usually possible to buy wine, beer or soft drinks.

Outside the more remote areas *gîtes d'étape* are becoming far more numerous in France, often inspired or sponsored by the Randonnées Pyrénéennes organisation. These *gîtes* are run along the lines of a Youth Hostel, very much on a self-help philosophy. Accommodation will usually be in dormitories, and although meals are available in most, you may find it necessary to cater for yourself in some. Practically every *gîte* has cooking facilities regardless of whether meals are available from the guardian.

Camping

The Pyrénées offer Europe's finest wilderness campsites and over the years I have pitched my little tent in some of the most idyllic spots imaginable. Backpacking brings an enormous sense of freedom, for you can stop virtually wherever and whenever you like and in a few short moments have a home erected around you. With your back to the good earth you can become very much a part of the natural world. Without bricks and mortar separating

The Pyrénées provide some of the finest wilderness camp sites in all of Europe. The Phoenix Phalcon seen here is ideal for a backpacking trip.

you from nature you know at once when there's a change in the weather, or wind direction; you can still hear the stream chuckling a few paces away, know when the moon is shining, hear birds singing first thing in the morning and respond to the first rays of sunshine.

This freedom must, however, be balanced by an awareness of one's responsibilities to the wilderness. Wilderness is a fragile gift. Those who respond to its call must be determined that it remains so for future generations. Pitch your tent, by all means, and draw strength from the world about you. But leave no signs of your stay. Light no fires (take your own cooking stove). Leave no litter. Do not pollute the water. Then it will be possible to return again and again to enjoy the untainted glories of these peaks and valleys.

Advice for Walkers

All the walks contained in this book are designed for tackling in summer and autumn. Some may be in a suitable condition during the spring, but much depends on the amount of snowfall the previous winter. Summer in the Pyrénées is a delight, the weather more settled than in the Alps. But sudden storms are not at all uncommon, and should your walk take you onto an exposed ridge, keep alert to any change in the weather. If a storm approaches, descend quickly to the valley.

It is always preferable to begin your walk early in the morning. This will not only give you the opportunity to walk at a leisurely pace, but you can take advantage of the coolest part of the day and relax by a tarn or stream at the height of the sun's power. Drink plentifully on the walks. In my experience most streams found high in the mountains are perfectly safe for drinking. Obviously you should avoid any water supply found below pastures where animals are grazing.

Clothing suitable for summer walking in Britain ought to be

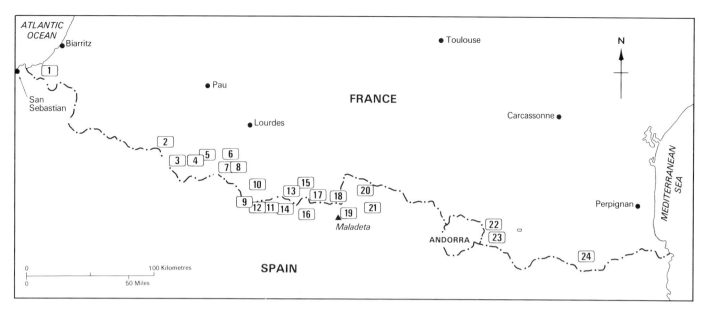

Above: **The location of the twenty-four classic walks.**

adequate in the Pyrénées. Shorts and a light shirt are ideal wear on most days, but wind and waterproof clothing should be carried in a rucksack. A wide-brimmed hat will shade your head and neck from the bright southern sun, and a high-factor sun cream should be used liberally, certainly at the start of a walking holiday. Sunglasses will no doubt be found essential to all those with sensitive eyes, for the light can be extremely bright in summer.

Light boots will be ideal footwear. On only two walks will an ice axe be necessary (the High Route and the Maladeta Traverse), and on the Maladeta Traverse crampons and rope must also be taken. All other routes are normally free from the snow and ice that make these items essential.

It goes without saying that a first aid kit is an important item of equipment, as are map and compass—*and the ability to use them correctly*. Unlike most walking areas of the Alps, the Pyrénées have an air of being remote and uncharted. This is especially true in parts of the Spanish Pyrénées where a simple mishap could have severe consequences. There are no well-developed rescue services here, although having seen the mountain gendarmerie in action on a rescue call on Pic du Midi, it is clear that the French have some highly skilled members in their rescue team. In Spain, things are very different, and as a result, wilderness walks there take on an additional degree of seriousness. Go prepared, and go in company.

Maps and Guidebooks
In 1978 I wrote *Walks and Climbs in the Pyrénées* (published by Cicerone Press). This guidebook is regularly updated and many of the routes contained in this present book are based on outings walked on research for that earlier work. Where other guidebooks would be helpful for specific routes, details are given in the fact

sheet accompanying each chapter.

Map details are also given in the fact sheets. IGN, the French national survey maps, are the best available for use on the northern side of the frontier, and they also stray widely into Spanish territory on certain sheets. These maps, under the general heading of Cartes de Randonnées, have been overprinted in red with major walking routes. They also indicate the position of a number of *gîtes* and mountain huts. The scale of these maps is 1:50,000, which will be sufficient for most needs.

Spanish maps are published by Editorial Alpina of Barcelona. They are not totally reliable but used with discretion they will prove adequate. Their scale varies from sheet to sheet. Published with them is a slim guide, in Catalonian.

I have gained immense pleasure from every day spent walking in the Pyrénées and consider myself amongst the most fortunate of men for having had so many magnificent experiences there. Sharing these mountains and valleys with you, the reader, is also a great joy but it is tinged with a nagging concern. The Pyrénéan environment is a delicate one, and by enticing others into it I am adding to its burden. My plea comes from the heart: love and respect all you find there, and make sure no-one has reason to curse your passage. May generations yet unborn be able to explore for themselves Europe's last great wilderness among the Pyrénées. As Packe himself wrote more than a hundred years ago:

'Learn all you can beforehand of the places you are about to visit, and then trust to yourself and your own emotions, and your soul shall have a feast.'

WALK 1: GR10—The Pyrénéan Traverse

Distance: About 700kms (400 miles).
Time Required: 7-8 weeks.
Type of Walk: A long-distance walk *par excellence*. Not particularly difficult, other than in its length, it follows mostly a middle-mountain course along the French Pyrénées using a combination of footpath, farm track and short stretch of road. It is waymarked throughout with varying degrees of efficiency.
Start: Hendaye-Plage (Atlantic coast).
Finish: Banyuls-sur-Mer (Mediterranean).
Accommodation: Mountain huts, *gites d'étape*, village pensions. There should be no necessity to carry a tent, although a small camping stove could prove useful.
Maps: IGN Cartes de Randonnées Nos 1-11, all at 1:50,000.
Guidebooks: *Walking the Pyrénées* (Robertson McCarta). This book is a translation of the 4 French Topo Guides. In preparation *GR10— Across the Pyrénées* by Alan Castle (Cicerone Press).

700 Kilometres from Ocean to Sea

The GR10 *Sentier des Pyrénées* can rightly claim to be one of the great walks of France, not only on account of its length, but also for its scenic grandeur, its ever-varied landscapes and cultural diversity.

Between the Atlantic and the Mediterranean there lies a broad stretch of country, and the wanderer with seven or eight weeks to spare will experience on this walk numerous contrasts and contradictions in architectural styles, in language (not simply the regional vagaries of *patois*), in vegetation, in the geography of valleys, in rock structure and in the overall impact of the mountains themselves.

There are two main walking routes across the range; GR10 and the High Route *(Haute Randonnée Pyrénéenne)*. A third route has

Above: **Wandering across the pastoral landscapes of the French Pyrénées, the trekker on GR10 passes many such granges, or haybarns. On the Spanish slopes they are called** *bordas*.

Right: **Pic du Midi d'Ossau appears suddenly above the deep forests of the Ossau Valley near the little village of Gabas.**

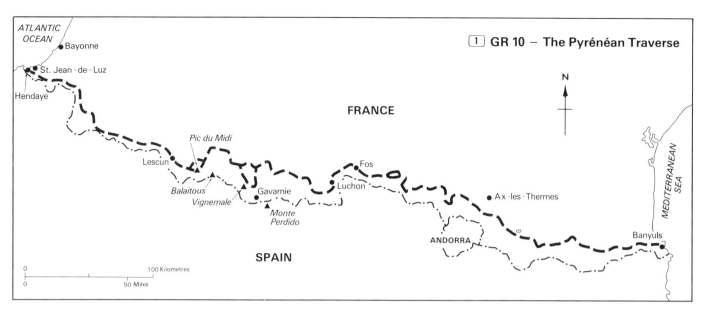

recently been established, the *Sentier de Piémont,* but this strays some way to the north of the main frontier peaks and does not enjoy quite the same charismatic quality of the other two. While the High Route sometimes trespasses into Spain, is in places devoid of an actual footpath and calls at times for basic mountaineering skills, *Grande Randonnée 10* remains throughout on French territory, is waymarked and signposted and follows a series of footpaths, tracks and minor roads from Hendaye to Banyuls, almost doubling as it does the actual crow-flying distance of 400-odd kilometres (250 miles). Under normal conditions it presents no difficulties at all for those with sufficient stamina and the necessary time to devote to it.

The first recorded traverse of the range was made by Dr Frédéric Parrot, a Russo-German professor who, in 1817, walked from the Atlantic to the Mediterranean in 53 days and managed to climb several peaks on the way. In more recent times the activities of the *Fédération Française de la Randonnée Pédestre-Comité National des Sentiers de la Grande Randonnée* (a mouthful usually abbreviated to CNSGR) have brought about the development of numerous long distance footpaths throughout the country. The GR10 along the length of the Pyrénées happens to be one of the longest and more challenging.

Happily one has no need to consider backpacking for such a lengthy journey for there are village hotels, *gîtes d'étape* and mountain *refuges* all along the route to provide overnight accommodation and, almost everywhere, meals. The walker can set out relatively lightly laden, able to concentrate on the full glories of the way ahead.

Few will, of course, have sufficient time available to tackle the GR10 in one single expedition. However, there are several towns and villages conveniently situated along the route where access to public transport enables it to be broken into manageable sections. Overall it is divided into about 60 one-day stages (this number may be considerably reduced by the fit and experienced long-distance walker), but is easily divisible into three or four separate two-week trips. With numerous *variantes* and circular tours sprouting from the main route, the prospect of a succession of attractive walking holidays based on the GR10 becomes apparent.

Section 1: Hendaye to Lescun (10-12 days)

The GR10 begins where the High Route begins, in Hendaye on the banks of the Bidassoa with Spain a very short step away across the river. This is Basque country, a region of wooded hills and lush, vegetated valleys watered by the mild Atlantic mists and rain. There's no real frontier crest here. Indeed, local people steadfastly refuse to acknowledge any distinction between the Basque lands of Spain and those of France. The seven Basque provinces, they argue, belong to them and should be governed by them. They are a proud people who guard their own individuality with a stubborn resolution.

Hendaye is a seaside resort as well as an international frontier. It has a fishing harbour, a good beach and avenues shaded with laurel and mimosa. There are palm trees, magnolias and eucalyptus shimmering in the westerly breeze—an incongruous setting for the start of a long mountain walk. But at once the GR10 turns its back on the ocean and wrestles with housing development as far as Biriatou before heading properly, and with some relief, into the true hill country. These Basque lands roll green and fresh in every direction. They are hills not mountains, and the route wanders among them via colourful villages whose architecture is unique to this corner of France. It follows shepherds' trails over misted cols, crossing a soft landscape with dolls' houses neat among the meadows.

At the end of day two you come to Ainhoa, seen by many as the perfect Basque village with its white-washed walls, its projecting roofs, its

vines and flowers and broad sunny street. Between Ainhoa and Bidarray in the valley of the Nive, the country is dominated by Pic du Mondarrain and Artzamendi, both easy summits offering lovely views. Two days of walking from Bidarray brings you to St-Jean-Pied-de-Port, a justifiably popular little town and one-time capital of Lower Navarre. South of the town a road heads up to the Col de Roncevaux with its stirring memories of Charlemagne and Roland, rich in folklore and legend.

The extensive Iraty forest is one of the major features of the Basque country. It spreads to both sides of the frontier south and east of St-Jean-Pied-de-Port and colours the land with its deep, almost liquid greenery. There are woods and forests out of Larrau too, but then you come to a jaunty land of rock ridges, open pastures and the spectacular gorges of Kakouéta. This is limestone country, and both peak and valley leave you in no doubt as to the power of water upon it. There is another gorge beyond Ste-Engrâce. This, the gorge of Ibarra, signals the end of the Basque country, and is passed on the climb to the Col de la Pierre-St-Martin and beyond that to the ski resort of Arette la Pierre-St-Martin, a wasteland of modern buildings and mechanical ski apparatus, but a handy place for restocking with food for the days ahead.

Above the ski resort rises Pic d'Anie (2504m/8215ft) as a marker to denote the start of the High Pyrénées, and a day's walking

Above: **The welcome sign at the end of a day's walking. There are now scores of *gîtes* throughout the Pyrénées offering simple accommodation for travellers.**

round its northern edge, with lovely views ahead to a growing landscape, leads to the pastoral tranquillity of Lescun slumbering with its glorious backdrop of mountain, forest and meadowland; the Cirque de Lescun.

Section 2: Lescun to Cauterets (6-7 days)

This section makes an effective and memorable introduction to the bigger mountains of the National Park, and is one of the most scenically spectacular of them all. Being limited to only one small portion of the GR10, I'd plump for this one and make a full two-week holiday of it by straying here and there to tackle the Tour of Pic du Midi, or wandering into the Marcadau Valley to sample its many delights. (These options are outlined elsewhere as separate walks in their own right.)

Treading Lescun's meadows and entering its neighbourhood forests, the route continues at first heading south before climbing over a minor ridge to the scattered hamlet of Lhers. There follows a stiff haul over a steep but heavily forested hillside to gain Col de Barrancq, beyond which an equally steep descent is made to the ancient village of Borce. From here you can gaze over a balcony into the Aspe Valley where Etsaut stands astride the road and offers comfortable *gîte* or hotel accommodation before tackling the next stage leading to Pic du Midi d'Ossau.

This is a splendid day's walk. It takes you alongside the Somport road for a short spell, then on the mule-path of the *Chemin de la Mature* and up to Col d'Ayous for a surprise view of Pic du Midi d'Ossau rising out of the soft Bayous pastures ahead. A short descent from the col takes you to a land of tarns, sloping pastures, streams and ragged peaks; and the PNP-owned Refuge d'Ayous with the lovliest outlook of any hut in the Pyrénées.

This is the place to rest for a day or two, given sufficient time. I can think of few more attractive sites in all the Pyrénées—but you won't have it all to yourself. Pic du Midi is surely the most popular of all the range's many peaks; the paths that surround it are invariably well-trodden throughout the summer, and the Lacs d'Ayous draw countless visitors to their shores whenever the sun shines. Sample the area for yourself and you'll understand why.

Leaving the hut the path goes down into the valley of the Gave de Bious with Pic du Midi in full view almost every step of the way. Lac de Bious-Artigues is dammed, and from it a road winds through forest to Gabas in the Ossau Valley where overnight accommodation prepares you for the long day's trek through rugged country to the ski resort of Gourette on the far side of Pic de Ger.

A sharp climb to Col de Tortes makes a rather cruel start to the day on leaving Gourette, but once over this the walk becomes much less hectic as you wander down through a hanging valley to the Aubisque-Soulor road. Round the Cirque du Litor, followed by a short ascent to Col de Saucède brings you to a long view through the Val d'Auzun stretching far off into the summer haze. You walk across high rolling pastures grazed by ponies, down farm trails and tree-enclosed tracks with isolated barns and farmhouses scattered in a gentle green countryside, all the way to Arrens-Marsous.

Two more days of walking through lush, flower-bright valleys and over Col d'Ilhéou (visited on The Marcadau Circuit), and you come down out of the high mountains to the little town of Cauterets—a base for so many enticing walks.

Section 3: Cauterets to Luchon (8-10 days)

Luz St-Saveur nestles in the valley of the Gave de Pau, next valley to the east of Cauterets. To reach it GR10 has two options. The first, and shorter route, involves crossing Col de Riou (1949m/6394ft) in the ridge midway between the two valleys, and will demand about seven hours of walking.

The other, main route, will occupy about three days. Initially it takes you through the Val de Jéret to Pont d'Espagne, then by way of Lac de Gaube to the Refuge des Oulettes de Gaube with the North Face of the Vignemale demanding constant attention at the head of the valley a short distance away. From the hut you cross Hourquette d'Ossoue and descend below the Vignemale's glacier (longest of all in these mountains) towards Gavarnie. Although the route actually avoids entering Gavarnie itself, most walkers new to this corner of the range will no doubt feel compelled to make a short diversion to see what it is that makes this the most visited place (other than Lourdes) in all of the Pyrénées. In truth, it is not Gavarnie itself that attracts, but the cirque rising so magnificently to the south of it. Ten minutes in Gavarnie will probably suffice!

GR10 wanders north of Gavarnie, along the mountainside in a steady traverse of the left bank of the Gave de Pau, coming down on the outskirts of Gèdre, but then continuing along

the valley—still on the left bank—as far as Luz-St-Saveur. Luz has plenty of accommodation and shops and a regular, typically French market in its maze of back streets. At first glance it has no remarkable features, but take the time to wander its streets and alleyways, its fortified church and National Park information centre, and you will soon discover that Luz has much to commend it.

Behind the town the Col du Tourmalet road cuts through the valley of the Gave de Bastan, while GR10 climbs the steep southern hillside and works its way, laboriously at first, over high pastures, through woodlands and past a number of isolated farm buildings en route to Barèges. This historic little one-street village has only recently woken up to its great potential as a walking centre, formerly seeing itself only as a spa and winter resort. But Barèges has the Néouvielle lakeland on its doorstep, and mountains and minor valleys abundant in alpine flora within easy reach. Our route merely gives the opportunity to

pause overnight, but on leaving it heads across the Néouvielle massif in a delightful west-east traverse, amongst tarns, beside crystal streams and over one or two passes, sharing a section of The Néouvielle Lakes Circuit (Walk 15) as far as Refuge du Bastanet. (An alternative crossing of the Néouvielle region takes in the Lac d'Aumar and Col d'Estoudou. Those who choose this option would spend the night in the Chalet-Hotel de l'Oule.)

From Refuge du Bastanct you work your way south for a while, then skirt hillsides above Lac de l'Oule before branching off to the east to leave the Néouvielle and wander across the ski terrain of St-Lary-Soulan, a sad experience of naked pylons invading the bald slopes of summer. Below stretches the Vallée d'Aure and after making a high-level traverse way above it, the path then drops briefly into the valley bed. Through Vieille-Aure, you cross the Neste d'Aure and follow the course of the Col de Peyrelit road up the eastern hillsides. There are several villages on the way to the col; Bourisp,

Above: **This steep hillside forms the north-eastern slopes of Montvalier around which the GR10 works a devious route**.

Estensan and Azet, and as you head up the hillside so long views draw the eye north towards the foothills, and south and westward to the higher peaks ranged along the frontier with Spain.

East of the col you look onto another long and fairly straight valley patterned with villages and farmsteads. This is the Vallée de Louron. At its head rise Pic Schrader and the crests of the Aygues-Tortes in a great bowl of an amphitheatre within whose secret embrace there lies a magic land of pools and tarns and craggy peaklets. GR10 is not tempted by this, however, for you cut straight down the grassy slopes to Loudenvielle, head south along the valley to the granges (barns) of Ourcibats, then begin the climb to Pas de Courat by entering the little Val d'Aube. You must part company with the Aube stream at the Cabane d'Ourtiga for the final steep stretch leading to the pass which is on the ridge breaking north from Pic de Leytarous.

The descent from Pas de Courat leads into the flower-rich Val d'Esquierry, which in turn takes you to the Val d'Astau upstream from the village of Oô. Here you bear right and follow a much-used trail past the Granges d'Astau and through woods to the classic and much-loved Lac d'Oô, one of the loveliest and most accessible sites in the neighbourhood of Luchon. The path continues above and beyond the lake, and although GR10 actually forks away from the main trail shortly before reaching Refuge d'Espingo, this is an idyllically situated hut in which to spend the night, and worth a short diversion.

A day's walk separates Refuge d'Espingo and the bustling town of Luchon. It's a day of complex panoramas, a day of breezy ridge-walking and one on which you can often see hang gliders and *parapente* enthusiasts taking off from Superbagnères.

From the hut it is necessary to backtrack a short distance on the path to Lac d'Oô, then break away on GR10 which heads off to the right and crosses Hourquette des Hounts-Secs.

Soon after another, neighbouring, ridge is crossed to give views over the curving Vallée du Lys and up to a fine wall of peaks in the south, most of which are over the 3000 metre (9843ft) mark and offering a stark contrast to the deep abundance of vegetation seen in the valley below. The path cuts across the mountainside to avoid Pic de Céciré (there is a route to it from the ridge, for those who like to collect such summits along the way), then regains the ridge to the east of it. The ridge then takes you to the hotel at Superbagnères where you look down on the sprawling mass of Luchon below to the north.

Section 4: Luchon to Mérens-les-Vals (14-16 days)

By the time the route enters Bagnères de Luchon one senses the back of the journey to the Mediterranean has been broken. East of the town the Spanish border projects northwards to contain the anomoly of Val d'Aran, so the GR10 makes a northward loop too, then skirts the heady, prominent mass of Mont Valier and stutters its way eastward. *Haute Arriège* has some of the wildest and least-known mountains of the range. There are deep valleys tangled with forest and swept by fast-flowing streams. GR10 crosses by way of convenient passes, drawing on the flavour of the land and resting up at quiet *gîtes* between days of activity.

For those who shy away from the bustle of towns, three hours beyond Luchon the quiet hillside village of Artigue has a *gîte d'étape* which puts the walker in a good position to tackle the ridge route to Pic de Bacanère the next day. From Bacanère you overlook the Val d'Aran, one foot in France the other in Spain, with a glimpse of the Pyrénéan giants off to the south rising above other frontier summits. There, shining in the morning sun, are the snows of the Maladeta. Beckoning. Alluring.

Following the international frontier you maintain a rough northerly course until all slopes fall away from Pic de Burat (2145m/7067ft). Now you descend to the forest-clad eastern flanks of the mountain, passing the *cabanes* of Courraus, d'Artigue and d'Artiguessans, and into the Garonne's valley for a night's rest in the village of Fos.

It is a green land again. Forested slopes, small pastures, moss-coloured mountains rising all around. From Fos a good day's exercise brings you to Refuge de l'Etang d'Araing, a CAF hut with room for 53 in its dormitories. Another hut nearby, Cabane de l'Etang d'Ara-ing, is unmanned and can only accommodate about twenty. The lake is dammed and is visited on one of the High Route *variantes*. Rising from it to the south the Pics de Crabère and Canejan form part of the frontier, and send out ridges to enclose the lake in a deep bowl. In order to escape, GR10 climbs over the eastern ridge, known here as the *Serre d'Araing*, and makes a determined effort to avoid the stern upper reaches of Pic de Mauberme by going straight down to the Vallée du Biros. (One of the circular tours mentioned in the introduction to this Chapter, the Tour du Biros uses this stretch of the GR10. This is a five-day walk that visits villages, peaks and pastures, with overnights spent in a variety of *gîtes* and *refuges.*)

The route maintains its easterly course, crossing cols and dipping into valleys where streams flash in silver spray and sheep cluster on far-off slopes like so many maggots. It's a peaceful land, save for the rumble of mountain torrents and the bleating of ewes and their lambs. Mists often hang in the upper corries and come tumbling of an evening to cast doubt on the next day's journey. But it's all good walking here, and soon Mont Valier dominates the scene and forces the path to make a more northerly trend round its lower flanks. On the eastern side, however, the route offers another *variante*.

Having made an extensive loop around it, the main path tucks itself against Mont Valier's south-eastern slope, then breaks away to cross Col de Pause on the way to Couflens on a junction of minor roads. By now the frontier ridge has made a more southerly sweep while GR10 tackles less demanding hillsides thick with woods and mastered here and there by groups of buildings. The valleys grow less wild and become patchworks of agriculture, while small communities hug the banks of mountain-born rivers. The walk takes on a different character. It becomes civilised.

Aulus-les-Bains is the largest village since leaving Luchon and, in common with Luchon, is a spa whose waters were known to the Romans. But of more immediate interest to the long-distance walker is its *gîte d'étape* and a variety of shops giving the opportunity to restock with food or to replace worn-out items of clothing for the continuing trail. From Aulus you make a steady climb to Port de Saleix, then cut south-eastwards into some interesting hill country noted for its tarns, and down to another *gîte* in the hamlet of Mounicou.

Above: **Ainhoa is one of the most attractive of all Basque villages and is visited on both GR10 and The High Route.**

After Mounicou the route marked on the map looks like a hospital temperature chart as the GR10 heads first north-east, then south-east, then northward again in a series of valley and hillside traverses. Long ridges here project northward from the frontier, imposing their will on the GR10 surveyor, but then, a little south of Vicdessos the path's trend is somewhat less frenetic, and a few more days of minor col, ridge and valley brings you down to Mérens-les-Vals on the road to Andorra. (Perhaps more importantly for walkers tackling the GR10 in sections, it should be noted that Mérens also has access with Ax-les-Thermes for a rail link with Toulouse and Paris.)

Section 5: Mérens-les Vals to Banyuls (8-9 days)

After crossing the Carlit massif to the south-east of Mérens, you can feel the change of atmosphere as you come under the influence of the Mediterranean. The route takes you out of the Carlit and down to the Cerdagne at Col de la Perche, wanders along the slopes of the frontier mountains that form the southern wall of this broad sunny valley, and gains momentum as the sea is clearly drawing near.

Only Pic du Canigou holds its head up in this far-eastern corner. It is a grand yet easy mountain, and one that was considered for a time to be the highest in all the range. This, of course, was due to its regular sighting from the plains where it would appear much higher than all its neighbours. From its summit the sweeping bays of the Mediterranean are clearly seen over a roll of shrinking hills. GR10 picks a way over its northern flanks.

There are orchards and vineyards and historic villages in the valley defended by stout walls where swifts race shrieking of an evening. But you must also face a summer stream of traffic on Col de Perthus where you become almost homesick for the sanctuary of the high mountains far behind you.

A final day's walk brings you down to the Mediterranean from an unmanned hut close to the frontier ridge. It is a memorable stage with wonderful views of the Côte Vermeille drawing you along an easy ridge. Roussillon lies to the north, the Costa Brava to the south. Both worlds have little to do with that other, higher, more austere but splendid world of the wild peaks that were constant companions so many days and weeks before.

Contrasts have become a feature of this lengthy walk. Now there are forests of cork and beech, there are vineyards and aromatic plants, the smell of the sea, a sprawl of caravan sites, hotels and restaurants, a scuffing of sand and, boots off, a welcome paddle in the dazzling warmth of the Med.

Savour it.

WALK 2: The Cirque de Lescun

Location: West of the Vallée d'Aspe. Lescun is reached by road from N134 (the Col du Somport route), with a turning 3.5 kms south of Accous.
Distance: 46kms (28 miles).
Time Required: 3-4 days.
Type of Walk: Strenuous in places, with several passes to cross. Mostly on good paths, but with one particularly notorious stretch on the Spanish side leading to Col de Pau or Col de Burcq. It is a very scenic walk with a great variety of mountain landscapes.
Base: Lescun.
Accommodation: Uncertain at the Cabanes d'Ansabère—possibly nothing available and camping (or bivouac) will be necessary. Mountain hut at Arlet; *gîtes d'étape* at Borce, Lhers and Lescun. Hotel and campsite also at Lescun.
Map: IGN Carte de Randonnées No. 3: *Béarn* 1:50,000.

Astride the Frontier Ridge

Lescun is a magical village set in a delectable landscape. Grey stone-built houses huddle alongside steep and narrow cobbled alleyways. Their windows look to the sun, out to a view that will catch your breath and hold you steady with wonder. Soft green pastures are tilted towards the south, down to a great bowl of meadow and woodland. Scattered amongst them, drystone walls or ragged hedgerows mark the boundaries of these meadows. There are haybarns and cattle byres, isolated farmsteads, small groups of trees and fields patterned with drying stooks of hay.

But as a backcloth to this pastoral wonderland there rises a jagged wall of peaks out of an apron of forest; not particularly high, as Pyrénean peaks go, but shapely, enticing,

Above: **The Aiguilles d'Ansabère on which a number of extreme climbs have been made by those committed to the Pyrénées.**

Right: The first pass of the walk has no name and is merely a slight dip in the frontier ridge. Pete Smith stands in the bright Spanish sunlight while French valleys remain lost beneath a cloud-sea.

Right: Near Col de Saoubathou this soft and level promontory offered a scenic pitch for the tent—until a cloud of mosquitoes emerged from the pool and sent us scurrying away.

challenging. They have an undeniable allure. This is the Cirque de Lescun.

To the west rises Pic d'Anie, first of the High Pyrénées and beyond which stretches the Basque country. Guarding the valley that leads to it are the twin Pics Billare, and peeking over a shoulder of the southerly of these is a knife-blade of rock—one of the Aiguilles d'Ansabère. Then, sweeping across one's field of vision, comes peak upon peak of weathered upstanding limestone along whose summits runs the Franco-Spanish frontier.

As an introduction to the Pyrénées it is one of the finest panoramas imaginable. It is both accessible and friendly, its impact immediate and lasting. Yet unfortunately it tends to hug the mists and only rarely out of several visits have I been fortunate enough to capture that glorious view in its entirety. But when the mountains have revealed themselves it has been a moment to savour, and to store away in memory.

These frontier peaks are climbers' peaks. On the aiguilles are some of the most difficult rock climbs in the range, but walkers' routes lead over and along the ridges, through pastures and forests and out of France into Spain. The High Route runs along the frontier; GR10 traces the lower meadowlands and crosses the wooded subsidiary crests. Shepherds' trails wind elsewhere. As a base for a walking holiday Lescun takes a lot of beating. The following route gives a flavour of the good things it has to offer.

The Route

From Lescun head south-west across the pastures and through forest to reach an inner sanctuary of peaks, the Cirque d'Ansabère. Then up onto the frontier ridge to the south-east of the needles on the path of the Pyrénéan High Route, and over into Spanish territory for a traverse of the southern slopes. Return to France by way of either Col de Pau or Col de Burcq, and take a splendid belvedere of a path running a little below the actual crest, as far as Refuge d'Arlet.

Next day skirt the Montagne de Banasse and descend northwards into the valley of the Gave de Baralet on a National Park footpath, and over a col to the parallel valley of Belonce, which you then follow almost as far as the medieval village of Borce. Here you break away on the GR10 to climb west over the projecting mountain wall by way of Col de Barrancq. Steeply down through forest and open meadows you then come to the hamlet of

Lhers, with its *gîte* and fine views overlooking Lescun and its pastureland.

The final short day's walk takes you back to Lescun along the path of GR10 among more pasture and woodland.

There is one accommodation-related problem with this route. The first stage from Lescun to Refuge d'Arlet is really too long to be achieved in one day, and would ideally be broken at the foot of the Aiguilles d'Ansabère. At present there is only a shepherd's *cabane* there, and although it is sometimes possible to arrange to spend a night in it, this should not be relied upon. Plans have been voiced for some years about building a trekker's hut in the vicinity, but to date this has not come to fruition. So either take a tent or be prepared to bivouac for this first night.

Elsewhere, accommodation is in a National Park *refuge* and *gîte d'étape* in either Borce or Lhers.

Days 1-2: Lescun to Refuge d'Arlet

Lescun itself is reached by a narrow road that twists for several kilometres out of the Aspe Valley. There is hotel accommodation to be had here, and a *gîte d'étape* on the outskirts. There is also a small campsite with admirable facilities situated a short distance to the south, on a grassy shelf facing the village. A small grocery store in the village will be able to supply provisions for the trek.

A GR10 signpost near the little general store in Lescun directs you out of the village and onto a narrow lane heading across the pastures, but you soon trade this for another lane along haybarns and grazing cattle; a lane that becomes a forest track with the mountains hidden by a screen of densely growing trees. The track plunges deeply into the woods—the Bois de Landrosque—and finally emerges at the Pont Lamary where you cross the stream and begin to climb along the edge of woods on a narrow, root-handicapped path. Then you top a rise and a green basin lies before you.

But eyes are raised above that pasture and wood-rimmed basin to the magnificent sight of the Aiguilles d'Ansabère on the far side, lifted from a pedestal of screes and stabbing at the sky. It is very much a sight to stop you in your tracks and to set a climber's fingers itching.

Tearing yourself away you descend into the basin of pasture, over a stream and up the southern slope among trees again. Trees, this time, that drape their branches and threaten to

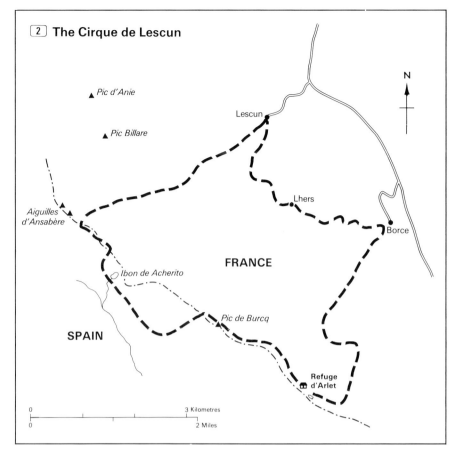

2 The Cirque de Lescun

eye can see there is nothing made by man. A huge panorama of green hill and hazy sierra, of empty valley and moulding ridge. A sense of peace and tranquillity; an air of calm washes from that ordered view.

Cutting down the grass-covered hillside you cross a minor craggy ridge and descend to Ibon de Acherito, a sparkling lake embraced by a horseshoe of cliffs. There is a stream flowing from the southern end and it is advisable to top-up water bottles here.

A clear path continues from the lake, heading south-east and descending slightly. When you come to an area of shrubbery, with a number of box trees growing beside the path, you must leave it to climb through a white limestone 'gully' and into a shallow combe. Above it the hillsides are broad, rolling and featureless. You scramble north-eastwards over these vast pasturelands and come to the frontier again, either at Col de Pau or Col de Burcq—the two separated by Pic de Burcq. As you pass through either of these cols you come onto a wonderful belvedere of a path that cuts round to the south-east a little below the actual crest. Beckoning from the east, some distance away, is the unmistakable form of Pic du Midi d'Ossau, and far beyond that you can make out the topmost cone of the Vignemale.

The path leads easily now round the head of two valleys and over Col de Saoubathou in the ridge that projects between them, and finally up into the green scoop of hillside lit by Lac d'Arlet, to the PNP-built Refuge d'Arlet. (There is a guardian in residence during the main summer season, and meals are provided during this period.)

Days 3-4: Refuge d'Arlet to Lescun

From Arlet two options immediately become apparent. The first, and the shorter of the two, is to backtrack a little towards Col de Saoubathou, but then cut down into the valley of Belonce and walk through it almost as far as the village of Borce, before turning west on the path of GR10 to gain Lhers. The alternative is to take the next valley east of Belonce, that of Baralet, and halfway along it to cut over Col de Lagréou into the valley of Baralet and then pick up the route from there. This second option allows the opportunity to explore two valleys rather than one.

The Pyrénéan High Route heads eastward from Arlet, down to the Vallée d'Aspe and on to Pic du Midi d'Ossau. Our route follows this

hold onto your rucksack. Above them a rough tussocky area gives way to screes and there, at the base of the Petite Aiguille (2271m/7451ft), huddle the shepherds' *cabanes*. Here, or a little lower, will be the place to rest for the night.

The first time I spent a night here I was camped a short distance below the *cabanes*. On the walk in, mist had denied all views, and rain had been falling intermittently. Darkness brought no respite from the weather, and I was resigned to another poor day ahead. But I awoke to the glory of sunrise, to find all the valley below lost beneath a cloud-sea while the Petite Aiguille caught the glow of morning, and I watched from the tent as the red dye of dawn washed down that tremendous pinnacle and brought life to the lifeless screes.

Leaving the *cabanes*, a narrow trail makes a rising traverse of the steepening slopes round to the south-east, and brings you to a tiny tarn, Lac d'Ansabère. From here a short steep pull brings you to the frontier ridge where a very different view is presented. Gone are the bold outlines of the savage aiguilles, and in their place, a vast sweep of smooth hillside rolling far off to a blue wash of distance. As far as the

path for a short distance. It goes beyond Lac d'Arlet and round into the modest cirque of Montagne de Banasse, which is littered with a curious pudding stone. Halfway round this you leave the High Route to cut away northward on another path which descends into the glacier-cut valley of Baralet.

After passing the shepherds' huts of Gourgue Sec and de Larrecq, the path becomes rather steep on the initial descent from the upper cirque to the lower, more wooded, reaches of the valley. Then on the left bank of the valley, in and out of woods, and working a steady route northward until, after following a short stretch of narrow road that has come from the Aspe Valley, you bear away on a crossing of the left-hand hillside. This crossing is achieved by way of Col de Lagréou (1454m/4770ft), and is followed by a descent through woods into the Vallée de Belonce.

Now heading down-stream the valley becomes narrower, but the path remains clear and brings you out onto hillsides overlooking the little medieval village of Borce. There is a *gîte* here, should you prefer to spend a night in this archaically pleasant village rather than continue over the next pass to Lhers.

The GR10 strikes away up the steep hillside above Borce on a thousand metre climb to gain Col de Barrancq, then down again, mostly through woods, to find the scattered hamlet of Lhers where once more there is a *gîte* with 15 places.

A short distance below Lhers one gains a classic view across the pastures to Lescun, but another fine view is offered as you come out of the woods west of Lhers on the continuing GR10 that winds down through the meadows, passing barns and farms and onto the lane that climbs the final twists to Lescun itself.

A lovely place to begin a walk, Lescun makes an even finer destination.

Above: **From the scattered hamlet of Lhers you catch a fine view down to Lescun.**

WALK 3: Tour of the Vallée d'Aspe

Above: **Refuge de Larry is a small PNP hut with only minimal facilities. The fence around it is not to keep walkers in but sheep out.**

Location: Western Pyrénées, entirely in France, on the route of the Col du Somport.
Distance: 50kms (31 miles).
Time Required: 4 days.
Type of Walk: A moderate walk on good paths nearly all the way. Some cols to cross, some valley stretches with a mixture of forest and pasture, and a splendid section of ridge-walking on the last day.
Start/Finish: Etsaut, Vallée d'Aspe
Accommodation: Mountain huts owned by the National Park authorities, one of which is unmanned. At the end of the second day one must either camp or make a diversion of some kilometres to the nearest village (or Col du Somport) for hotel accommodation.
Map: IGN Carte de Randonnées No. 3: *Béarn* 1:50,000.
Guidebooks: *Walks and Climbs in the Pyrénées* by Kev Reynolds (Cicerone Press). *Detours Pyrénées No.1: Pyrénées Occidentales* (Randonnées Pyrénéennes/FFRP).

A Moderate Four-Day Circuit of a Lush Green Valley

The long glacier-carved trench of the Vallée d'Aspe in the *département* of *Pyrénées-Atlantiques* is a classic assembly of open fertile basins and narrow, rock-girt defiles, with lush rolling pastures and forests to east and west and the Col du Somport making a low saddle at its head. A little west of the Somport rise the neat limestone peaks of the Cirque d'Aspe.

Providing an easy and important route to (and from) Spain, the valley has been washed by the tides of history for two thousand years or more. In 79 BC under the youthful Pompey the Romans pushed a road from Spain over the Somport which, alone in Pyrénéan legend, rivals the Basque pass of Roncevaux. After the legions of Pompey came Saracen hordes on a whirlwind campaign, but as the dust settled after their departure, there followed more peaceful times with centuries of valuable trade being conducted between the Béarnais and their counterparts of Aragon, and with the passage of religious pilgrims bound for Santiago de Compostela. (The hospice of Santa Cristina on the Somport was built by Viscount Gaston IV of Béarn in 1108 to cater for the needs of these pilgrims. A few ruins of the hospice remain to this day.) More than eight centuries later a sad procession of refugees crossed the col in the opposite direction and descended through the valley in search of exile during the time of the Spanish Civil War. Today, however, it is the crowds of French skiers who take advantage of the Somport's year-round accessibility and drive a short distance across the frontier for winter sport on the slopes of Candanchú, while mountain trekkers, following either one of the great Pyrénéan traverse routes, the GR10 or the High Level Route, cross the valley bound for bigger and more rugged country towards the heart of the range.

The Aspe Valley itself has some fine walking country on its very doorstep. There are green summits sending out green ridges, with green cleft valleys in between and lovely, if modest, limestone peaks carved in attractive cirques at their head. There are trails leading along some of these ridges with huge vistas to lift the spirits; others that traverse little-known peaks, some that wander among forests, tread pastures ankle deep in wild flowers and look onto quiet villages basking in a pastoral landscape as though untouched by the passage of time. This is walking country with so much to commend it, and the Tour of the Vallée d'Aspe takes the trekker on a circuit that explores some of the very best parts, mostly along good paths that are either sections of the GR10 or the High Level Route or marked by the National Park authorities.

The Route
Initially the circuit begins by aiming towards the head of the valley in a devious south-easterly direction in order to explore a side glen topped by a tight wedge of peaklets. Beyond them stands hidden Pic du Midi d'Ossau. Over the first pass, Col de la Hourquette de Larry, the path drops to an unmanned *refuge*, then veers away on a long traverse of hillsides way above the Aspe, full of ups and downs towards the Somport. We do not reach this ancient pass, but instead cross the valley to delve through forest and over rough pastureland, climbing north-westward along part of the

High Route to find the PNP hut, Refuge d'Arlet. The final stage treads a long north-projecting ridge with big views before dropping eastward in forest and across green hillsides once more to the valley of the Gave d'Aspe.

It is not a difficult walk, but it is an ever-interesting one despite the fact that it never properly looks on any of the major peaks of the Pyrénéan chain. There is no great rock face to draw one's attention, other than that along which the *Chemin de la Mature* has been carved. There are no glaciers nor permanent snowfield nor jagged crest. But instead you wander through a soft and almost feminine landscape, dressed with turf or tree or flowering shrub. There are gentle glens reaching out below green spurs where sheep graze in slow-moving specks of white cloud. There are two or three remote shepherds' huts isolated from the modern world, and a hillside speckled with lumps of pudding-stone.

Along the route there is one manned *refuge* in which to spend a night and another that offers only shelter and fresh spring water, but you will have to make your own cooking arrangements. Unfortunately, there is nothing suitable on the actual route for the second night's lodging, so one will be left with either a short diversion up to the Col du Somport where hotels are found on the Spanish side, or a hitch down-valley some ten kilometres to Urdos for accommodation. Alternatively, carry a tent and camp somewhere discreet away from the Somport road.

Day 1: Etsaut to Refuge de Larry
Etsaut squats on the right bank of the Gave d'Aspe, a village popular with mountain walkers on account of its situation—astride the GR10—providing plenty of accessible trekking country to east and west. The Cirque de Lescun is not far away, and there are side glens and broad rolling hills inviting closer scrutiny. It has a *gîte d'étape*, an invariably-busy hotel, a couple of restaurants and the opportunity to stock up with provisions for the trail ahead. This convenient little village can be reached by SNCF bus from the railhead at Bedous.

From Etsaut to Col de la Hourquette de Larry the route follows the same path as that used on the initial stage of Walk 4. It first treads the Somport road for nearly two kilometres, then takes GR10 among trees on a steady climb towards Pène de Lamounedère which guards the northern entrance to the steep gorge of Baigt de Saint-Cours where rock climbers can often be seen in action from the

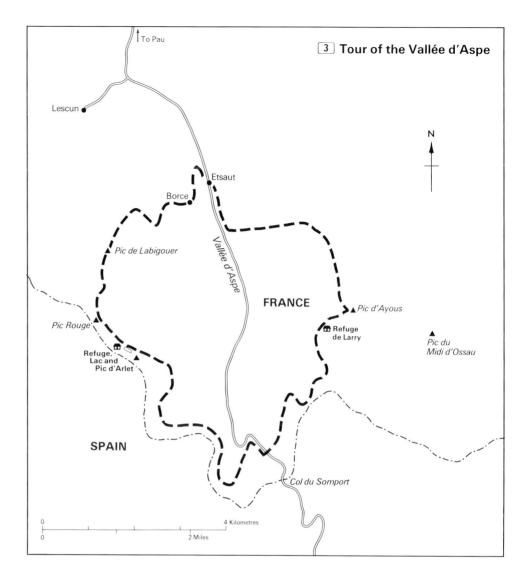

pathway. The dramatic so-called *Chemin de la Mature* traverses the very steep face of this cliff for some distance before easing itself across a broader hill slope. For those who are a little nervous about such exposed, though safe, paths such as the *Chemin de la Mature*, an alternative route leads directly from Etsaut, links one or two farms and crosses the hillside above the cliffs of Pène de Lamounèdère at Col d'Arras to join the GR10 farther to the east.

The route curves away in a clockwise direction over pastures and along the edge of woods, passing a few barns and into the protected realms of the National Park, climbing steadily to a tight clutch of peaklets in the south. The GR10 path is abandoned near the head of the cirque, and an alternative trail taken off to the right. Within a few minutes, Col de la Hourquette de Larry (2055m/6742ft)

is crossed after almost six hours of walking from Etsaut, and a descent of about forty minutes or so on the western side of the pass brings you to the little PNP hut of Refuge de Larry.

The hut is a simple shelter fenced around to keep the sheep out. (There are two farms a little below the hut on the approach path from Urdos, and sheep are often found grazing nearby.) Within its compound there's a good water supply, and inside the hut officially has space for ten trekkers, though six would be quite enough to make it 'cosy'.

Day 2: Refuge de Larry to Peyranère

All of this stage of the circuit follows paths used on the High Level Route. It is a short day's journey down to the valley, requiring

little more than four hours of walking, but since there is no certainty of accommodation there and a diversion is likely to be required, a short day is perhaps no bad thing. A trekker's hut, or *gîte,* has been planned for some time in the region of the Peyranère pastures, but to date no precise details are available. Only the backpacker at present can enjoy the certainty of a night's shelter.

From Refuge de Larry the path climbs roughly westward among rocks to cross Col de Gouetsoule (1845m/6053ft) within the first half-hour or so of the day. The path then changes direction to head south along an open hillside with a dark band of trees way below folding into the valley. There is forest beneath and forest ahead. There is forest too on the far side of the valley, but for some time the path remains above the treeline, although you continue to make a steady descending traverse of the bare hillside and must be thankful, on a bright summer's day, that this section of the walk is tackled in the morning rather than the afternoon when the lack of shade can be rather cruel.

Across the Gouetsoule stream, you enter the shade of beech trees on a short uphill pull before wandering still among trees into the knuckle valley of Arnousse where you pass a shepherd's *cabane* that is nostril-evident long before you actually see it. This little glen is a strange hidden place of rough grass slopes, shrubs, streams and the mire of too many sheep. Fortunately it does not take long to walk through it, and the path soon crosses the main stream and wanders uphill among trees to gain Col de Lazaque on a prominent spur of hillside with good views to the north.

Now you cross the so-called Plateau de la Gentiane, an open shrub-and-flower-bright stretch of level walking, with peaks ahead that form the frontier ridge. The head of the valley is drawing near. Across the valley you can see tomorrow's route, and as the path eases round the western end of the Plateau de la Gentiane, so the lovely forms of the limestone peaks that make up the Cirque d'Aspe show themselves in all their splendour. Bilberries and wild raspberries grow in some profusion on the hillsides, and the final hour's wandering down the

Above left: **The Chemin de la Mature is a dramatic path cut into the steep wall lining a gorge. This wall is very popular with rock climbers and the climber here is abseiling to the foot of his climb. Walkers must take care not to trip over ropes belayed across the path!**

Above: **At the head of the gorge, beyond the Chemin de la Mature, the path enters a region of lush vegetation and provides some lovely views back towards the west.**

Right: **Etsaut, nestling in the Aspe Valley below Borce, makes an important stocking-up point for trekkers on GR10 and is the starting place for several fine walks.**

Far right: **Flowers brighten a window in the grey, medieval village of Borce.**

pine-fragrant path to the Somport road is one that is both rich in scenic pleasures and in the variety of plants smiling on either side.

Day 3: Peyranère to Refuge d'Arlet

Another day spent following the path of the High Level Route, this is among the more taxing stages of the walk with a fair amount of altitude to gain. The path is mostly clear, although some confusion may occur where the route tackles the Espélunguère Forest if recent felling has taken place. It is, however, way-marked.

Wander down the road for about 1500 metres as far as a parking bay and picnic site, marked as Sansanet on the map. The river comes boiling through its rocky bed, forest on either side, the walls of the Cirque d'Aspe rising out of them high above, but distorted from this angle. Two or three paths go up to the ridge and off into a little-known Spain where large empty sierras make a bald land-scape of sunshine and shadows. The path crosses the river on a sturdy bridge and winds uphill through forest heading roughly north. There is a *cabane* in an untidy clearing, a stark contrast with similar 'alps' found in Switzer-land or Austria where no doubt the grass would be cropped short, rather than pig-

churned as here, and there would be a hewn log with spring water gushing instead of a length of plastic pipe spewing water unchecked onto the jungles of dock. But the views are fine, especially to the south and below in the valley can be seen the Forges d'Abel and the road stretching off to the north towards Urdos and, unseen, Etsaut.

For another hour and a half forest trails lead in an anti-clockwise direction, invariably muddy after rain or recent clearing work, towards the indent of Pla d'Espélunguère, a green pastoral coomb with mountains curving in a steep protective wall on three sides. Through it dashes an undisciplined stream which is crossed by a footbridge. On its far side snakes a road that has come from the electricity works at les Forges d'Abel.

The path takes to woodland shade once more and rises steeply northward to a little col which marks the end of the forest. To the left is yet another coomb, or minor cirque, with the Couecq stream digging its way through a narrow channel. Two or three simple *cabanes* inhabit this back-of-beyond, while the path makes a belvedere ledge away from it, slanting uphill beyond the stream along a spur of mountain that creates the coomb's northern wall.

Along this corner of the mountains numer-ous spurs project from the frontier ridge. Some of these spurs themselves splay out with other fingers of ridge like gigantic swastikas, so that the path is forever rising and falling to cross them on the hesitant route to Arlet. After crossing Col de Lapachouaou (1891m/6204ft), the route swings westward round the pudding-stone littered cirque formed by the Montagne de Banasse. Marmots occupy the stony slopes of this cirque, and their high-pitched warning whistles will often be heard as you cross. Keep alert for signs of these furry creatures that live in deep burrows beneath the rocks.

The Baralet Valley makes a deep trench off to the north and it is interesting to speculate on the glaciers that scooped out that lovely vale long ago. Between the cirque and the valley proper you can clearly see the former glacial sill, and gazing northward it is not difficult to decipher where the moraines spilled out. Just below the path, in the bed of the cirque, stands a small shepherd's *cabane* beside a pool, and another PNP path leads down past it to follow the course of the one-time glacier. Our route continues to cut across the cirque, turns a bluff and duly arrives on the bank of Lac d'Arlet. Above the tarn, and overlooking it from a grass slope stands Refuge d'Arlet, another of those huts provided by the National Park authorities. It has room for thirty-six in its dormitories and a guardian who provides meals during the main summer season.

Day 4: Refuge d'Arlet to Etsaut

Refuge d'Arlet occupies a grassy bowl of mountain in pleasant walking country. Using it as an overnight stop, several two, three or four-day walks are possible; short tours from Lescun, Lhers or Etsaut; a combination of frontier-hugging High Route, and long north-projecting ridge as here, or through a deep green valley as on Walk 2. Opposite the hut Pic d'Arlet rises to the south-east, forming the cornerstone of the Banasse cirque and also that of Arlet itself. An easy route leads to its summit from which broad vistas overlook much of the country traversed by this circuit and give a preview of the last day's journey down to the valley.

Yet again you set out along the High Route path, but for less than an hour this time before straying from it at Col de Saoubathou. Shortly before coming onto the saddle you pass a good clear spring gushing out of the ground beside the path. (It came as a life-saver on one of my first long walks in this region one drought-ridden summer long ago, and it would be churlish not to take advantage of its cold, pure gift.) There is a small pool nearby set in a levelling of turf and marshy ground with a long view north, but the water in this pool is often rakish and breeding midges, though it makes a good foreground for a photograph. Once on the col turn right, leaving the High Route path to continue its journey round the head of the Vallée du Labadie hugging the frontier crest.

Col de Saoubathou (1949m/6394ft) lies a little north of Pic Rouge on a ridge that extends for almost eleven kilometres (6½ miles) as far as the junction of the valleys of Aspe and Lescun. Our route follows along the crest of this ridge for more than 3½ hours. A delightful stroll high above forest-draped valleys, enjoying magnificent views all the way.

To begin with it is necessary to skirt along the eastern slopes of Table de Souperret, but as you do so it is worth pausing now and then to study the frontier mountains falling away behind to the south and south-east. Avoiding a spur cutting north-east, you then gain the crest of the main ridge as it heads almost due north towards Pic de Labigouer (2175m/7136ft). The route goes right over the summit (a path actually cuts westward round the peak from Col de Souperret to Col de Labigouer), and there are more huge panoramas to enjoy from here. A splendid place to rest awhile, to soak in the views and to appreciate the health and strength that allows you to reach such places. And be thankful.

The walk continues along the ridge. Off to the left, beyond the western wall of the Vallée du Labadie, pastures roll into the great Cirque de Lescun. Fine grey limestone peaks rise from the meadows. At the back, unnecessarily shy, stands Pic d'Anie, first of the High Pyrénées. Beyond it, all the hidden country to the west is Basque land—all the way to the Atlantic.

The ridge slopes steadily downward. There follows a succession of cols separated by a succession of summit knolls. Below to the east fingers of forest creep towards the ridge, and when those fingers manage to curl onto it and spread down the other side, you know it is time to leave the crest. Col de Barrancq signals a parting of the ways. The GR10 crosses here. If you were to descend to the left you would come to the village of Lhers, but the route lies in other directions and you drop down to the right, following the trans-Pyrénéan footpath in a series of long sweeping loops for a good two hours or more before coming to the picturesque and historic village of Borce.

Etsaut is only twenty minutes' walk away and the Tour of the Vallée d'Aspe is complete.

WALK 4: Highlights of the National Park

Above: The entrance to one of Russell's Vignemale caves. Although several of Russell's caves have since been swallowed by the glacier, this and two others remain. A heavy iron door secures the interior from the excesses of the weather. The view from its entrance is dramatic.

Location: Western Pyrénées, France. From the Vallée d'Aspe eastward.
Distance: 80kms (50 miles).
Time Required: 7-8 days.
Type of Walk: A mixture of soft valley and rugged high mountain terrain. Many passes to cross, some of which could be problematic for inexperienced trekkers. Mostly on good PNP paths or with cairns to waymark the route. A varied walk with superb scenery.
Start: Etsaut, in the Vallée d'Aspe.
Finish: Gavarnie.
Accommodation: Mountain huts throughout. Mostly PNP or CAF owned.
Maps: IGN Carte de Randonnées No. 3: *Béarn* and No. 4: *Bigorre* 1:50,000.
Guidebooks: *Walks and Climbs in the Pyrénées* by Kev Reynolds (Cicerone Press).
Pyrénées High Level Route by Georges Véron (Gastons-West Col).

A Week-Long Traverse of the National Park of the Western Pyrénées

Between the cirques of Lescun and Barroude the *Parc National des Pyrénées* (PNP) follows the Franco-Spanish border for approximately 110 kilometres (68 miles). It is essentially a narrow, irregular strip of country no more than 15 kilometres (9 miles) wide at its broadest point, yet within it are to be found more than 100 gleaming tarns, delightful flower-laden valleys and some of the finest individual peaks north of the watershed; Pic du Midi d'Ossau, Pic Palas, Balaïtous, Vignemale, and the cirques of Gavarnie, Estaubé and Troumouse. Only two roads at present cross the international frontier from within the Park's boundaries. These are Col du Somport at the head of the Aspe Valley, and Col du Pourtalet a little south-east of Pic du Midi. A toll road goes as far as the Port de Gavarnie

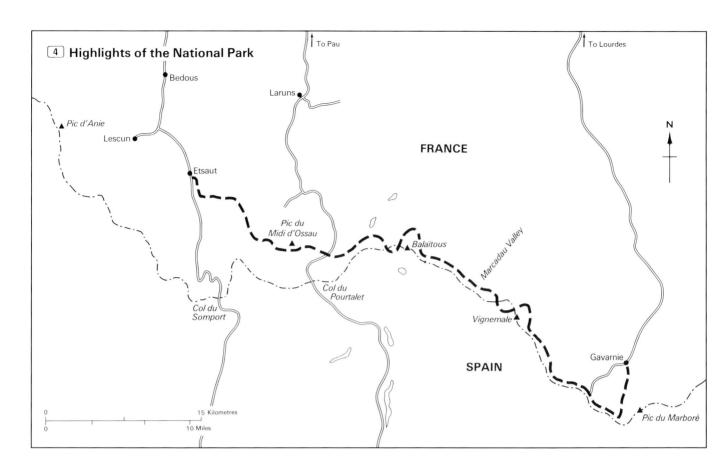

4 **Highlights of the National Park**

(Col de Boucharo), but this has yet to be joined by a linking route from Spain.

The National Park was created in 1967 by an Act of the French Parliament with the aims of preserving the natural beauty and wildlife of this unique area, and to promote its enjoyment by the public—mainly by providing facilities for mountain walkers such as the creation and waymarking of paths and the construction of a number of mountain *refuges* in formerly remote areas.

As well as protecting this spectacular region from development by officially discouraging industrial and commercial activities within it, the authority's policy is to aid the rural population of outlying areas by actively promoting tourist development on the peripheral, or *Préparc,* zone of its northern boundaries. Thus it is that apart from the anomoly of a small ski run and chair lift at Pont d'Espagne above Cauterets, ski tows will be found lacing a number of slopes right to the Park's very limits, but remaining outside them. National Park Information Centres have been established in several villages on the edge of the Park, and large rustic notice boards erected at

roadheads and parking places to inform the general public not only about the specific attractions of the surrounding area, but also of the bye-laws governing activity within it.

Running through the Park there are more than 400 kilometres (248 miles) of waymarked trails, and linking some of these in a partial west to east traverse would make an attractive week's walking holiday, providing an introduction to specific peaks and valleys that are among the true highlights of the PNP. Some of this route is shared by the GR10, some by the High Level Route. Part of it is included in the much-loved Tour of Pic du Midi, so that those who have the time and energy available could easily divert from the main traverse for a day or two in order to make this classic circuit before continuing eastward towards Gavarnie.

There are *refuges* at strategic points along the way, so camping will be unnecessary. (Camping is now officially forbidden in the vicinity of some of the huts anyway.) Some of these *refuges* have been provided by the PNP authorities, others are either owned by the CAF or Touring Club de France, but they are of course open to all visitors. In the main

Above: **Sunrise over the shoulder of Pic du Midi d'Ossau is one of the unforgettable experiences gained by a night in Refuge d'Ayous.**

summer season most have guardians who provide meals where required, but some food should be carried in the event of emergencies. There are no villages or hamlets along the route, and any community large enough to warrant a shop will be found only by a long walk down valley, occupying several hours of additional exercise.

The Route

In *Classic Walks in Europe* (edited by Walt Unsworth, 1987) I contributed a chapter on a ten-day walk through the PNP starting from Lescun and heading eastward to Gavarnie. The route described below is based on a variation of that walk. It begins in the deep Vallée d'Aspe and heads south-eastward along the route of the GR10, climbing to a craggy pass that brings you in full view of Pic du Midi d'Ossau. Measured in kilometres it is only a relatively short stage, but with a considerable amount of height gained between the valley and Col d'Ayous this will be sufficient for the first day of a walking holiday.

From Refuge d'Ayous a second short stage leads over Pic du Midi's shoulder and down to the popular climbers' hut, Refuge de Pombie.

From this base an extra day could be well spent, by those with sufficient experience, making an ascent of this attractive peak via its normal route, or tackling the classic standard circuit of the mountain (see Walk 5), before moving on once more, this time to explore the great granite wilderness area of the Balaïtous massif.

There are two routes to choose from on the way round Balaïtous to the Marcadau Valley, one of which, with its crossing of a high rugged pass, is really for experienced mountain trekkers only, while even the alternative southern route makes for a hard day's travel.

The Marcadau's pastures come as a welcome respite after the uncompromising sterility of the Balaïtous, but after this you are faced with the crossing of at least two, and possibly three, high passes, each one separated from the last by a substantial loss of height. It takes you beside the great North Face of the Vignemale and on towards Gavarnie. But instead of dropping straight down the long Ossoue Valley to the village, stray towards the frontier ridge and come to a hut perched within the embrace of the walls of the Cirque de Gavarnie, putting off the descent to reality among the crowds until the next day.

Days 1 and 2: Etsaut to Refuge de Pombie

Roughly halfway along the Vallée d'Aspe, Etsaut is a small village of old grey stone houses on the right bank of the river, about 20 kilometres (12¹/₂ miles) north of the Col du Somport. From its base a number of interesting excursions into the mountains are possible. (See Walk 3 for an example. The initial part of this walk shares a passage of the Aspe Valley circuit.) By virtue of its easy access from the railhead at Bedous, Etsaut makes an ideal start to a traverse of the National Park, for the overnight train from Paris via Pau conveniently delivers the walker to the Aspe Valley with sufficient time to complete the initial stage at a leisurely pace.

Leaving the village you head up-valley along the Somport road for almost two kilometres, as far as the Pont de Cebers which takes the road across the river. The GR10 footpath then breaks away, still heading up-valley among trees until it swings left and with a surprise, brings you to a steep wall of rock along which a path has been skilfully carved. This is known as the *Chemin de la Mature*, a safe but exposed touch of drama below the Pène de Lamounèdère with the Sescoue stream dashing below through a gorge.

Beyond the *Chemin de la Mature* the valley begins to open out and a couple of hours later you enter the National Park by a shepherd's hut nestling in the mouth of a minor horseshoe of peaks, with a view north to a crest of mountains containing the celebrated little aiguille of Capéran de Sesques, on whose northern side some hard climbs have been achieved.

The path continues into the narrowing cirque over pastures, and up, then, to a craggy bowl with Pic d'Ayous on the left sending out its ridges to the north and to the south-west. Two alternative paths break away to the right bound either for Hourquette de Larry or Col de Larry—routes that lead back to the Vallée d'Aspe.

Having gained almost 1600 metres (5249ft) of altitude since leaving Etsaut, it is with a sense of relief that you come onto the rock-guarded pass of Col d'Ayous and gaze eastward to the lovely shape of Pic du Midi d'Ossau rising on its pedestal of stone from the hidden green luxury of the Bious meadows. In that vision there is plenty of promise of good things to come. It is a classic view of a classic mountain; one to savour for a few minutes, but it could be worth leaving rucksacks at the pass

for an hour or so to stroll up the crest to the left as far as the easy summit of Pic d'Ayous (2288m/7507ft) where the views are more extensive.

Twenty minutes below Col d'Ayous you come to the National Park hut which occupies a truly idyllic site, with Lac Gentau spread before it to give double value to views of Pic du Midi. It is one of those places of which dreams are made, and it presents the perfect opportunity to transform those dreams into living memory. If the day's walk to reach Refuge d'Ayous has demanded only a few hours of exercise, make an early finish and spend some time exploring the immediate countryside around the hut. You will be well repaid for it.

The next day's stage leading to Refuge de Pombie is full of interest, full of colour, full of variety and an ever-growing acquaintance with Pic du Midi. This stage is part of the Tour of Pic du Midi described elsewhere in this book. It takes you beside tarns, over a minor saddle behind Pic Casterau, then down through a pitted scoop of a little glen to the head of the valley of Bious. To the left a stream winds in lazy ox bows through the most delectable pastures, but the route to Pombie resists the temptation to stray amongst them and climbs steeply onto a grass, tree and shrub-softened bluff to enjoy a sudden revelation of Pic du Midi rearing ahead and giving a passable impression of Mount Kenya.

Soon pastures are left behind to be traded for a maze of huge boulders, followed by screes and rocks and a winding zig-zag path that leads to the pass of Col de Peyreget and a view into the wild South Cirque of Pic du Midi. On the descent from the pass to Refuge de Pombie there are more little tarns and long views ahead towards tomorrow's mountains, dominated as they are by the Balaïtous.

Days 3 and 4: Refuge de Pombie to Refuge de Larribet

The Pombie hut makes an ideal base for rock climbers, situated as it is beneath the vast south and east walls of Pic du Midi d'Ossau. It is also a good starting point for tackling the *voie normale*, while those who wish to make the standard walking circuit of the mountain, would be advised to arrange to spend two nights here. The tour, crossing Col de Suzon into the Magnabaigt Valley, through the Bious pastures and over Col de Peyreget, would occupy about six hours.

The next massif east of Pic du Midi is that of the Balaïtous, first of the 3000 metre (9843ft)

Above: **The Ossoue Glacier flowing from the Vignemale is the largest of the Pyrénéan glaciers. The path to Gavarnie descends below it.**

summits to be met when travelling from the Mediterranean. But what a contrast with Pic du Midi! Whilst Pic du Midi is surrounded by soft pastoral valleys, Balaïtous stands head and shoulders above a stark and uncompromising landscape of bare rock and icy tarns. The vegetation is poor and basic. Deep clefts of mountainside hold the echoes of falling stones. There are long ridges bristling with *gendarmes*, and gullies with screes fanning below them. On the nothern slopes hang excessively steep little glaciers. On the south side, in Spain, a great well of tarn and scree punishes the boots of all who stray there. While Pic du Midi stands alone, a solitary figure in shades of rust, the Balaïtous is guarded by rank upon rank of neighbouring peaks, each one sending out its own ridges in a bewildering maze of rocky walls. To traverse this massif is one of the challenges of Pyrénéan trekking; it is not for the weak of heart, nor for the weak of knee; a two-day scramble to test your fitness. Early in the season, snow or ice could make the crossing of one or two of the passes a distinctly hazardous undertaking, and poor visibility may well create problems in locating Port du Lavedan, to say nothing of its descent on the northern side. But for all that, it is a superb traverse, with an easier option on day four for those with insufficient experience to tackle the northern circuit. Even so, the southern option is still hard enough.

Leaving Refuge de Pombie, a clear path plunges eastward into the Vallée d'Ossau, a deep valley cut by the Brousset stream. There are woods on the lower slopes and rough pastures in the valley bed, and once over the stream a short steep haul brings you to the

Pourtalet road. Beside the road, to the left of a couple of buildings shown as *Soques* on the map (*Cab de Soques* on some editions) there stands a basic little hut which, when open, serves drinks and snacks and, on occasions, even provisions for the journey ahead. But do not count on it being open when you arrive. Instead, treat anything you can buy there as a bonus.

From Caillou de Soques there follows another woodland section, steep in places but with a clear path leading through. Beyond the woods continue into a narrow climbing wedge of a valley with the Arrious stream dashing down to the right, and a number of boulders and rocks littering the poor grass slopes. In its upper reaches isard are sometimes seen, and as one goes higher into the valley towards the pass at its head, so the views behind of Pic du Midi's east face grow in stature. There is a constant temptation to keep pausing for yet another photograph.

Col d'Arrious, nine hundred metres (2958ft) above the Ossau Valley, looks onto a deep hollow containing the large Lac d'Artouste, whose northern shore is reached first by cable car from the valley, then along a rack railway. (The National Park boundary runs down the untouched eastern shore, thereby avoiding this pre-Park development.) There is a path leading down towards this lake from Col d'Arrious, then it swings to the right and climbs to Refuge d'Arrémoulit. For the heavily-laden and those with no nerves for too much exposure, this is the route to take. But there is an alternative, more interesting, section leading south-east from the col to a pleasant teardrop of a tarn, Lac d'Arrious, then round a safe but narrow ledge of a path carved in the wall of Pic du Lac d'Arrious. The *Passage d'Orteig* has a sobering drop beneath it with the waters of Lac d'Artouste waiting far below. At the far end of this exposed pathway climb onto a whale-back graniteland and follow a few cairns and paint flashes down to Refuge d'Arrémoulit, a neat little hut on the shores of yet another tarn and with Pic Palas rising behind it.

It would be feasible for the experienced mountain walker to continue as far as Refuge de Larribet, but that would be rather a case of squeezing the day dry, while Arrémoulit's position offers a relaxing location for the remainder of the day. It will have taken between five and six hours from Pombie, so most people will have a clear conscience by the time they slip their rucksacks from their shoulders.

The next day brings a journey up over scree and rock and old slips of winter's snow to Col du Palas and a brief passage across Spanish territory to Port du Lavedan. From the first pass one gains a clear view of Balaïtous (3146m/10,322ft) rising to the east above a splay of ridges.

Between the col and the mountain a deep stony bowl contains the Lacs d'Arriel, and for those who would prefer the alternative journey south of Balaïtous to the Marcadau Valley, there is a route leading down there. From the lakes a path of sorts wanders through a rough landscape of claustrophobic little cirques and eventually escapes to a broader valley with the Respumaso lake dominating a somewhat desolate countryside. Up, then, to Ibon de Campo Plano, and three kilometres and five hundred metres or so above that (1640ft) you reach Col de la Fache, a welcome pass in the north ridge of the Grande Fache. It is all downhill from then on, in France once more, to the flower-speckled luxury of the Marcadau's pasturelands.

This alternative is no soft option. Although it avoids the scramble to Port du Lavedan and the subsequent steep descent to Refuge de Larribet, it is still a long (8 hours) trek over a wild terrain. It does, however, save a whole day's walking, but that day will doubtless be spent resting on the Marcadau's spongy turf before tackling the next stage to the Vignemale.

The main route, however, traverses from Col du Palas round the head of the Arriel cirque across the southern face of Pic Palas on broken rocks and scree, then up a projecting snout of rock to find Port du Lavedan, a narrow split in the wall linking Balaïtous with Pic Palas. It is a dramatic crossing, and steeply below to the north-east lies the forbidding gulf of Batcrabère. Sometimes snow and ice will be packed in the couloirs below Port du Lavedan late into the summer, in which event the descent will be precarious. This is only for experienced mountain trekkers.

Refuge de Larribet is found overlooking a handkerchief-sized marshy meadow to the north of Balaïtous. Above that meadow a complex of boulders leads to a high ridge that gives access to the Glacier de las Néous which, in turn, takes the climber onto the smooth granite walls that form the north face of this savage peak. The Larribet hut is therefore much-used by climbers, as well as by trekkers tackling the High Route. It is a small, simple shelter, but by virtue of its wild surroundings

and its isolation from the civilised world, there is often a delightful atmosphere invoked there. Day fades, the fire is lit, food served with smarting eyes as everyone clusters in the smoke-grey room, regardless of the weather outside, to eat together and to share the day's experiences. Somehow this shelter of humanity in the midst of an almost overpowering wasteland, in the midst of a stone desert, draws a warmth all of its own and a night there will be a night to remember.

Day 5: Refuge de Larribet to the Marcadau Valley

This stage takes you round the northern spur of Balaïtous, then south on an easy climbing path towards the Spanish frontier again. But

Above: **The Arratille Valley leads away from the Marcadau's pastures on a day's trekking that ends in full view of the North Face of the Vignemale.**

Above: **Having crossed the craggy ridge at Port du Lavedan, walkers must then tackle snowslopes and boulder slopes on the descent into the deep bowl of Batcrabère.**

just before reaching the border you must break away to locate Col de Cambales, the key to the Marcadau's green valley. The crossing of this pass is straightforward enough in clear conditions. However, snow lingers long in this high, north-facing mountain wedge, and even in midsummer difficulties may be encountered when the path lies completely hidden and total reliance is placed on a compass—especially when visibility is restricted by low cloud. My own first crossing was made in a fury of wind, mist and snow, and I recall now, many years later, the great sense of relief as we found our way onto the pass and a hint of the valley lay below.

It is a day of contrasts, fairly long (7 hours of walking, plus rests) but with mostly good PNP paths to follow. Dropping from the

Larribet hut you come to a narrow valley of shrubs, dwarf pines and streams, and this takes you into the valley of Arrens a little south of Lac de Suyen. Heading south the path leads into a long and rocky vale, the cold-looking Lacs de Remoulis below, steep crags rising above. Isard are often to be seen here.

A little short of the frontier pass of Port de la Peyre-St-Martin (a one-time smugglers' pass) you come to a few ruins which mark the spot where shepherds from both sides of the frontier traditionally met to settle disputes arising from 'cattle lifting'. Soon after these ruins are passed a path cuts away to the left, often under snow, climbing into a hidden land of cliffs and steeply plunging slopes.

In good weather conditions, Col de Cambales (2706m/8878ft) is a fine place to rest awhile. Gazing westward the ridges of Balaï-tous hold one's attention. It is indeed a wild and rugged mountain and it is entirely understandable that the first explorers of its inner recesses became so confused by the terrain that they made the ascent of Pic Palas, thinking as they did so that they were actually on the Balaïtous. Only when they reached the summit did they realise their mistake.

South of the col rises Pic de Cambales, from whose crown a wonderful panorama of immense depth is the reward for an ascent. (The route to it does not lead from the pass, however.) And eastward a string of tarns accompanies a delightful walk down to the splendour of the Vallée du Marcadau.

Days 6 to 8: Marcadau to Gavarnie

At the southern end of the Marcadau's valley, the Touring Club de France has a large rambling building, the Chalet-Refuge Wallon. Throughout the summer season this barn of a place is crowded with school parties, fishermen and general tourists, while next door and also owned by the TCF, is a rough-and-ready *petit refuge* that is kept for the less discerning mountain enthusiasts.

Opposite the Wallon hut stretches the Arratille Valley, and at its head Col d'Arratille (2528m/8294ft) overlooks the Spanish enclave of the Ara Valley. The walk to it makes for a very pleasant morning, wandering beside a clear stream, past shrubs and among flowers to Lac d'Arratille. After this tarn you lose grass and in its place look to a treadmill of screes and boulders until you come to a remote bowl of circling crags that trap yet another tarn with the col a few paces above it.

Across the head of the Ara Valley rises the Vignemale, highest frontier summit at 3298 metres (10,820ft). The route will pass below its great north face, then climb beyond it on the way to Gavarnie. First though, you must descend to the Ara, traverse round its head, and make your way to the Col des Mulets (2591m/8501ft) which is reached in about an hour or so from Col d'Arratille. On this pass you return to France after a very brief sojourn in Spain, and then wander down a broad gully littered with scree and the rocks from the walling mountains, with a view towards the glacial plain spread in front of the Vignemale's north face, and beyond the slab of Petit Vignemale to Hourquette d'Ossoue, the next pass to be crossed.

Refuge des Oulettes de Gaube overlooks the glacial plain and has a superb grandstand view of the three main north faces that form a cirque at the head of the valley. With sufficient days in hand I would advocate spending a night here rather than continuing over Hourquette d'Ossoue to the Baysellance hut, another couple of hours away. (Refuge Baysellance is in a fine position, and is an interesting hut in its own right, being the highest Pyrénéan *refuge* with a guardian. But it does not have the majesty of these north faces to study.)

On Hourquette d'Ossoue there is the temptation to leave rucksacks for the ascent of Petit Vignemale, seen to the right. It is a steep stroll of about an hour along an easy ridge, but it is worth the effort, given sufficient time and good visibility. Refuge Bayssellance squats below, and beyond this you wander past two of the grottoes carved out a century ago by that great eccentric lover of the Vignemale, Henry Russell. From these caves there is a fine view of the snout of the Ossoue Glacier which flows down the eastern flanks of the Vignemale and along which the standard ascent route is taken.

Below stretches the narrow Ossoue Valley with a good clear path leading through it. Follow this as far as a small dammed lake, then veer away from the Gavarnie road and head up towards the frontier ridge on slopes of grass. The ridge is followed as far as the termination of a toll road at the Port de Gavarnie. (The road has come from Gavarnie.) A broad and well-trodden path leads from the col in a south-easterly direction towards the Cirque de Gavarnie, passing directly below the Taillon and courting a little danger from falling stones and shortly after, crosses patches of snow. It leads directly to the Brèche de Roland hut, otherwise known as Refuge des Sarradets (2587m/8488ft).

Immediately above the hut yawns the great gash of the Brèche de Roland, seen at the head of a small, but steeply sloping glacier. But the eye is held by the sweeping walls of the cirque that plunge away to unseen depths. Pic du Marboré rises opposite, and from its slopes spurts the *Grande Cascade* which is seen in all its glory on the next day's descent to the floor of the cirque. The route down demands caution. It is always interesting, and quite a spectacular section of the walk, but once the floor of the cirque is reached, the crowds emerge once more, and the stroll down-valley as far as the village will invariably be accompanied by hordes of trippers riding donkeys or ponies in that timeless pilgrimage that helps make Gavarnie what it is.

WALK 5: The Tour of Pic du Midi d'Ossau

Above: **Refuge d'Ayous (1982m), the National Park hut which overlooks the Lacs d'Ayous and Pic du Midi.**

Location: Between the Col du Somport and Col du Pourtalet, France. The route lies entirely within the Parc National des Pyrénées.
Distance: 20kms (12¹/₂ miles).
Time Required: 2 days.
Type of Walk: A varied circuit with three true passes to cross on mostly good paths. Some rough sections.
Base: Laruns.
Start: Refuge de Pombie (2031m/6663ft).
Accommodation: Mountain huts (CAF and PNP owned).
Map: IGN Carte de Randonnées No. 3: *Béarn* 1:50,000.
Guidebooks: *Walks and Climbs in the Pyrénées* by Kev Reynolds (Cicerone Press). *Vallée d'Ossau* by Gérard Caubet (Randonnées Pyrénéennes).

By Col and Valley Round the Symbol of the Pyrénées

Of all the mountains of the Pyrénées Pic du Midi d'Ossau is the most easily recognised, the most distinctive and certainly one of the most satisfying; a mountain '. . . whose roots are in the vast forests of Ossau and whose crest is in the sky' (J.B. Morton). It stands alone, an abrupt rocky tower rising from green pastures unchallenged by neighbouring peaks and with such a unique profile that it is every bit as conspicuous when seen from the terraces of Pau, as from the summit of many another peak to either east or west.

It is certainly not altitude that is responsible for its individuality, for by no means does it claim to be among the highest of the range—its main summit reaches to only 2885 metres (9465 feet). It boasts neither glacier nor permanent field of snow, yet such is its character that Pic du Midi—or Jean-Pierre, as

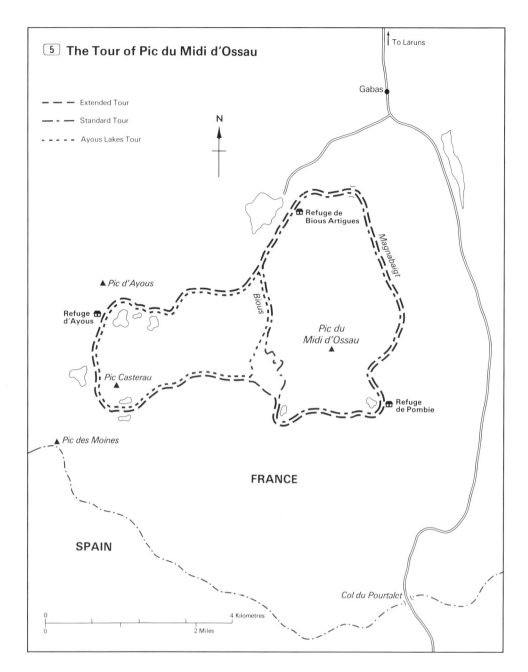

5 **The Tour of Pic du Midi d'Ossau**

— — — Extended Tour
—·—· Standard Tour
····· Ayous Lakes Tour

N

To Laruns

Gabas

Refuge de
Bious Artigues

Magnabaigt

Pic d'Ayous ▲

Refuge
d'Ayous

Bious

Pic du
Midi d'Ossau ▲

Pic Casterau ▲

Refuge
de Pombie

Pic des Moines ▲

FRANCE

SPAIN

Col du Pourtalet

0   4 Kilometres
0   2 Miles

it is affectionately known by those who live virtually in its shadow, or who are drawn regularly to climb upon its walls—has become the very symbol of the Pyrénées.

Somewhat reminiscent of Mount Kenya when seen in profile from the west, it is a great rust-coloured mountain with two main summits—the Grand Pic and the Petit Pic—separated by the deep cleft of La Fourche. Two further summits—Pointe d'Aragon and Pointe Jean Santé—overlook the bowl of the South Cirque, but these are not noticeable except from limited viewpoints. In addition, there are

lofty buttresses and walls scarred by gullies on which numerous routes have been developed over a very long period of sustained activity. So much so that it would be true to say there are more rock climbs on Pic du Midi than on any other Pyrénéan peak.

By virtue of its dominant position and enticing faces of rock it is hardly surprising that the mountain should attract the attention of climbers today. What is surprising, however, is that it should have been among the very first in the range to be tackled. More than three hundred years ago, Francois de Foix, the

Above: **Having crossed Col de Peyreget the route descends steeply past several pools with long views eastward to the Balaïtous.**

Count de Candale and Bishop of Aire, organised an expedition to attempt Pic du Midi with the principal aim of determining its height. In the spring of 1552 the fifty year old Count made his attempt in the company of several 'gentlemen and other young persons' equipped with ladders, grapnels, climbing irons and 'certain hooked sticks'. By four o'clock in the afternoon they were high enough to see clouds beneath them, but then 'the cold and rarefied air which surrounded them caused sensations of giddiness which made them fall down in their weakness' (Monsieur de Thou).

The attempt failed.

In 1787, or possibly the year before, the geographers Reboul and Vidal from the Academy of Toulouse, encouraged an unnamed shepherd from the Aspe Valley to climb the mountain and erect a cairn on its summit. Nine years later it received a second ascent, again by a shepherd—this one named as Mathieu who accompanied Guillaume Delfau.

At every stage of climbing development in the Pyrénées since then, Pic du Midi has been

at the forefront. It has become something of a testing ground and the routes which adorn practically every individual cliff, pillar, face and couloir reveal that fact, while the *voie normale* itself provides an interesting scramble on notoriously loose rock.

The first time I saw Pic du Midi I fell under its spell. Since then I've returned time and again to wander its valleys and to climb its unstable rocks. I have enjoyed the flowers at its ankles, watched groups of vultures picking at the carcass of a dead sheep on the edge of its screes, seen herds of isard grazing in the wilderness of a boulderslope below the Embarradère Pillar, photographed it at dawn, grown fearful as lightning dashed against its ragged crest, seen it bathed in subtle moonlight, watched it drown in mist. I have lazed by the side of its tarns and let the weariness of a day's activity drain away. And I have been taunted by nightmares after witnessing a climber killed by stonefall on one of its desperate walls. Jean-Pierre is always memorable—almost always rewarding. And so often when I've walked and climbed in other

Pyrénéan regions, it has been Pic du Midi's unmistakable signature that has beckoned from a far horizon.

From the summit there is a grand panorama of far-off mountains and distant plains, nearby cliffs and deep green valleys, rolling hillsides and tarns. Plenty of tarns. Jewel-like, they sparkle as diamonds in the soft turf, medallions to complement Jean-Pierre's crown. On the shores of two or three of these tarns lie mountain huts: Refuge d'Ayous, Refuge de Bious Artigue (sometimes known as Refuge Pyrénéa Sports) and the ever-popular climbers' hut, Refuge de Pombie. By linking these huts and the valleys they serve, one of the finest of all Pyrénéan walks becomes a practical reality—the Tour of Pic du Midi; the Circuit of Jean-Pierre.

It is a walk I've personally enjoyed on several occasions, tackling it clockwise and anti-clockwise, in part and as a whole. It is indeed a lovely walk, crossing as it does rough cols and boulder slopes, traversing valleys lush and green, delving into forests, over streams and beside tiny lakes, around lone peaks, across pastures pitted with deep *gouffres,* and always with splendid views. Pic du Midi dominates almost every view. Each of its faces is different, yet every one manages to impress itself upon the scene.

The Route

The standard tour of the mountain, linking the valleys of Magnabaigt and Bious with the rough combes of Peyreget and Pombie, gives a splendid day out of about six hours' walking. This is the walk that is tackled most frequently. Yet there is another tour, a longer route which strays westward above and beyond Bious to explore a loop of tarns with one of the finest views in all the Pyrénées as its reward, and this is the walk suggested here. It would be feasible to achieve this particular tour within a long day (actual walking time would be 8-9 hours), but I believe in making good things last as long as possible, so would advocate taking two leisurely days over it. By breaking this route with a night spent at the National Park Authority's Refuge d'Ayous one has the chance of catching the memorable sight of sunrise over Pic du Midi's shoulder.

As a circular route it may be started from any one of several accessible points, the more popular being the road-head at the dammed Lac de Bious-Artigues, which is reached by way of a narrow climbing access road that cuts away from the main Col du Pourtalet road at Gabas, a few kilometres south of Laruns. At the end of the road there's a car park and a National Park information board, and nearby will be found the Refuge de Bious Artigue, owned by the Club Pyrénéa Sport of Pau.

But my preference is to begin at Refuge de Pombie in full view of the soaring walls of Pic du Midi's South Face, and to work around the mountain in an anti-clockwise direction. To reach Pombie calls for a steep approach walk of two hours from Caillou de Soques in the deep Ossau Valley to the east or, rather less energetically, by a stroll of an hour or so over a very Welsh-like hillside from the Anéou pastures just short of the Pourtalet saddle. On this approach the summit crags of Jean-Pierre grow out of a hollow bowl as one gains the easy saddle a little west of Soum de Pombie, and the stroll down to the Pombie hut, across the folding green rucks of a one-time moraine, reveals the full extent of Pic du Midi's sombre South Face. Climbers are seen there daily—mere specks of colour against a vast bronze wall.

Refuge de Pombie, owned by the CAF, is one of the most popular of all Pyrénéan huts on account of its accessibility, its idyllic position as a base for rock climbers, and the fact that it sits fairly and squarely on both the routes of the HRP (Pyrénéan High Level Route) and that of a GR10 *variante*. For all that, it is a great place on its own account, overlooking as it does the little lake of the same name with the massive rock walls rising above, and a long view eastward to the wilderness country dominated by the Balaïtous, first of the 3000 metre peaks (9843ft).

Day 1: Refuge de Pombie to Refuge d'Ayous

The Pombie hut occupies a ledge of grass above its tarn. Often one can sit there of a summer evening and watch isard nosing beyond the tarn, or maybe picking a route across the great jumble of screes known as the Grande Raillere that comes sweeping from the South Cirque. There will undoubtedly be finches darting to and fro, and alpine choughs circling among the crags. Beside the path there are irises to brighten the way.

To the north of the hut a green projection links Pic du Midi with a significant lump of rock: Pic Saoubiste. Between the two lies the dip of Col de Suzon (2127m/6978ft) and the circuit of Jean-Pierre begins by crossing this. Walking to it is always interesting, for on the left is a desolate landscape of boulders, screes

Above: **Pic du Midi d'Ossau (2884m) is very much the symbol of the Pyrénées and is seen here from one of the Lacs d'Ayous.**

mountain is almost unrecognisable. On that North Face the pioneering team of Henri Brulle and René d'Astorg developed the first route in 1896 with Célestin Passet and François Salles as guides, and Douglas Busk and Caleb Gates made the first winter ascent—by mistake—in 1928. It's an interesting, rambling yet spectacular, line, but there are several others on the face that attack specific features of it. This face is seen in rather more detail later, from Bious Artigues.

The Magnabaigt Valley falls away steeply, never very broad, but with pleasures all the way. The easy path is often busy with walkers coming in the opposite direction; sometimes you may be lucky to catch sight of marmots. At first the valley's stream is barely noticed off to the left, but then it foams in a cascade with the path crossing nearby and then descends to woodlands—all shade and fragrance and bird-song. The route swings leftwards into the narrow marshy levels of the so-called Col Long de Magnabaigt, which is more of a woodland glade than a mountain pass and a stepping stone from one valley to the next.

Downhill again, steeply among trees with roots projecting to catch the unwary. Jean-Pierre is temporarily lost by a canopy of foliage, but then the path emerges at the unmade car park by the green dammed Lac de Bious-Artigues, and there it is, appearing out of the treetops, a surprise view of Pic du Midi towering overhead, its North Face black with shadow.

This is the lowest part of the circuit (1422m/4665ft). All the world, it seems, comes to Bious-Artigues. It's so accessible. Some of the crowd spill over into the woods and lush pastures of the Bious Valley ahead; some set out on the Tour of Pic du Midi too and may be met at some stage along the walk. But many, thankfully, go no further than the lakeside. There they will picnic, take their photographs and depart, leaving plenty of glorious mountain country ahead in which the walker may regain peace and tranquillity.

A broad trail heads south now into woodland shade once more. There comes a warm feeling of anticipation, as though one can sense something rather special ahead. I felt it on my first visit, and it is a feeling that has come every time since; an anticipation that has never yet resulted in disappointment.

Through the woods at first the river flows deeply below, but then a bridge leads the path onto the far bank and draws level with it as you come out of shade and into the full

and towering walls of rock on which climbers swarm like insects, the sound of piton hammers and falling stones mingling with the incomprehensible babble of distant voices. To the right a poor grassy hillside plunges away into a dark valley of pasture and forest, while far-off rise the big granite peaks of Balaïtous.

The pass itself is a joy too, for gone are the screes as one gazes down into the hummock-contortions of the Magnabaigt Valley, a green stepped vale embraced by the outstretched arms of low easy ridges that have individual peaklets jutting from them, and on a clear day you see beyond the immediate wall of mountains, beyond the foothills to the low plains of south-west France; a long view rich with contrast. Left of the pass a vague footpath leads to the start of the *voie normale* on Pic du Midi, but you ignore this to drop over Col de Suzon and down into the Magnabaigt Valley.

As you descend into the valley there is a tendency to keep looking back, and the reward for this interruption is a strangely distorted view of Pic du Midi's North Face. For once the sun-kissed splendour of the Bious Valley. It is a truly delightful place. A valley of lush green pastureland spattered with an extravagant flora in spring and early summer, smooth as a Surrey lawn with the river snaking through in great shallow ox-bows, clear and chuckling over its stony bed with the silver flash of trout, and frogs at its edges.

Above to the left soars Pic du Midi d'Ossau, majestic, impressive as ever, seen here with a greater revelation of height than from any other view. Ahead to the right the eye is drawn to the curious formations of the smooth-slabbed Pic Casterau behind which tomorrow's walk will pass. Directly ahead there's a pleasant, undulating ridge of easy peaks, and leading down from it a wrinkled meadowland of soft green baize. It's a lovely place for a picnic.

It is at this point that the circuit divides. For the standard, single-day tour, one heads up-valley through the pastures along the eastern bank of the river, then up steeply on a stiff woodland climb that leads to a superb belvedere of hillside enjoying magnificent views all around. From here the route swings south-eastward across Jean-Pierre's rough ankles where it is rejoined by the extended tour, before tackling the wild, steep valley of rocks to Col de Peyreget, beyond which lies a descent to the Pombie hut.

The alternative route, the extended circuit, skirts the Bious Valley by climbing in more woodland on a clear path up the right-hand hillside, eventually to explore a stepped terrace of little lakes trapped in rolling country high above the valley. This is one of those especially charming places where dreams and memories merge; a place of quiet beauty and colour and dramatic panoramas.

In a horseshoe scoop of mountains moulded by ice, then dressed in green, the Lacs d'Ayous allow no hasty goodbye. Above the largest of the three, Lac Gentau, the steep-pitched Refuge d'Ayous offers an ideal excuse and opportunity to stay awhile.

The hut was provided by the National Park Authority and it looks across the lake to a hint of the valley's depths far below. But more importantly, more impressively, there rises from the valley the wonderful shapely mass of Pic du Midi d'Ossau. Seen in all its glory, all its splendour—both right-side up and standing on its double-topped head in the water—Jean-Pierre shows itself to be what it is; the very symbol of the Pyrénées. No range of mountains could be better represented. It is indeed a classic view of a classic mountain; a sight to remember.

Day 2: Refuge d'Ayous to Refuge de Pombie

While strong walkers may not baulk at prospects of continuing the circuit without an overnight stop here, to do so would be to deny oneself the possibility of one of the special scenic pleasures of these mountains—catching sunrise over Jean-Pierre's shoulder. Since the hut practically faces due east with nothing to obstruct the view, it will be evident that given the right weather conditions sunrise will make a most dramatic spectacle. It is certainly worth waiting for.

The circuit continues, heading south now along the rising path of the High Route, over a rough slope, alongside a string of pools and up to yet another tarn, Lac Bersau. Peaks looming to the west long ago tossed down their excess boulders, and as the path heads among these moss-and-lichen-softened obstacles, so it delves into a narrow alley squeezed by the crags of Pic Casterau to the east, which effectively blocks Pic du Midi from view.

On reaching a nameless minor pass the path then begins to lose height round the southern slopes of Pic Casterau, swinging through a grassy scoop of rough, pock-marked pasture with yet another small tarn lying in it—and new views of Pic du Midi appearing ahead. Coming down here once, veils of mist played on Jean-Pierre with a tease of hide-and-seek as the wind billowed the vapour from the valley of Bious, sometimes allowing a peek of slab or buttress, now and then a summit and a wall, then nothing at all. Echoes of choughs crying unseen overhead were thrown back by the smooth features of Pic Casterau, turning the slope of rock and grass into a region haunted by the unknown.

Down and down goes the path, sometimes steeply, at other times less so. The shepherds' huts known as the Cabanes de la Hosse are passed off to the right, then the infant Bious stream is joined and accompanied for a short stretch along a soft levelling of turf. But as the stream veers northward to pour down towards the lovely valley of pastures and ox bows, you break away and scramble up a steep grassy slope to a tree-topped dome from whose summit another impressive shot of Pic du Midi looming over all is another good excuse for a rest. It is from here that the mountain begins to take on that Mount Kenya appearance.

The path bypasses another shepherd's hut,

Above: **Towards the end of September peasant farmers send their sheep down to the lower valleys for the winter, then vacate the little** *cabanes* **they've occupied all summer. Mules carry their few belongings.**

Above right: **Pic Casterau gazes down on the gentle Bious pastures.**

Cabane de Peyreget, and shortly after rejoins the standard Tour of Pic du Midi on a broad clear path. From here one gains a somewhat distorted view of the mountain, with the Petit Pic appearing almost as an aiguille, much higher even than the Grand Pic. All that remains now is a heart-pounding section beyond one more tarn, up and over a boulder-field with blocks as big as garages, little cairn towers directing the non-existent path over and round them to find a trail again that climbs steeply to the highest point of the whole walk, Col de Peyreget (2322m/7618ft).

Suddenly a new world is revealed. Off to the left there is a fine landscape of craggy ridges and towers and hollow cirques as you peer into the secret inner sanctum of Pic du Midi. Ahead, facing east, an enticing vision that consists of a sea of peaks dusted with snow, with shadowed valleys trapped within; an enchanted land to be explored on other days. And below, the mountainside plunges to yet more tarns and, unseen but suspected, the blue jewel of Lac de Pombie with its hut just beyond, representing the completion of the Tour of Pic du Midi; the Circuit of Jean-Pierre.

There is another classic day's walk based on a section of the Tour of Pic du Midi. This is the Ayous Lakes' Circuit; a five-hour ramble worth considering if you have a spare day in the neighbourhood. If you are one of those with a preference for returning to base each evening, it would be an idea to walk the standard shortened Pic du Midi outing one day, and this Lakes' Circuit the next.

For this walk, start at the Lac de Bious-Artigues and follow the path to Refuge d'Ayous. Continue on the tour described above along the edge of Lac Bersau and down beside Pic Casterau to pass the Cabanes de la Hosse. Then follow the stream as it flows into the Bious pastures on a clear path all the way to the dammed lake. It is a truly grand walk.

WALK 6: Gourette to Tech—and Back

Location: South of the Col d'Aubisque, mid-way between the Vallée d'Ossau and the Gave de Pau.
Distance: 27kms (16¹/₂ miles).
Time Required: 2 days.
Type of Walk: Fairly strenuous and with three passes to cross. Mostly on good paths, but sections of the descent into the valley of Labas are without evidence of a trail, although the course of the route should be obvious.
Base: Gourette.
Accommodation: Campsite at Lac du Tech. *Gite d'étape* and hotels at Arrens-Marsous.
Map: IGN Carte de Randonnées No.3: *Béarn* 1:50,000.

High Passes and Deep Valleys—A Two-Day Tour

Let me come clean. When we set out from Gourette on this walk it was to make a very different tour to the one described here. But halfway through our first day we changed our plans and crossed a neighbouring pass to that which we'd originally had in mind. I'm glad we

did, for what we discovered was a splendid series of landscapes full of variety and interest, and the circuit we eventually achieved was one that I'm more than happy to recommend. It has so much in its favour.

Gourette, I suspect, will not be most people's idea of a quaint mountain village. Situated a little below the Col d'Aubisque, it has been developed as a winter ski resort. Its buildings are shapeless and architecturally banal, and constructed with no concession to traditional form or pitch at the height (or depth!) of that period of insensitivity when a rash of purpose-built resorts were commissioned in the Pyrénées—and in the Alps—especially with the winter ski trade in view. It remains, in company with La Mongie and others, like a concrete wart on the face of the mountains.

Immediately to the south of Gourette the hillsides have been strung about with cable cars, chair lifts and ski tows. Skeleton frames march in long, disciplined lines toward the

Above: **Walkers high in the valley of Gave de Labas, on the descent from Col d'Uzious to the Vallée d'Arrens.**

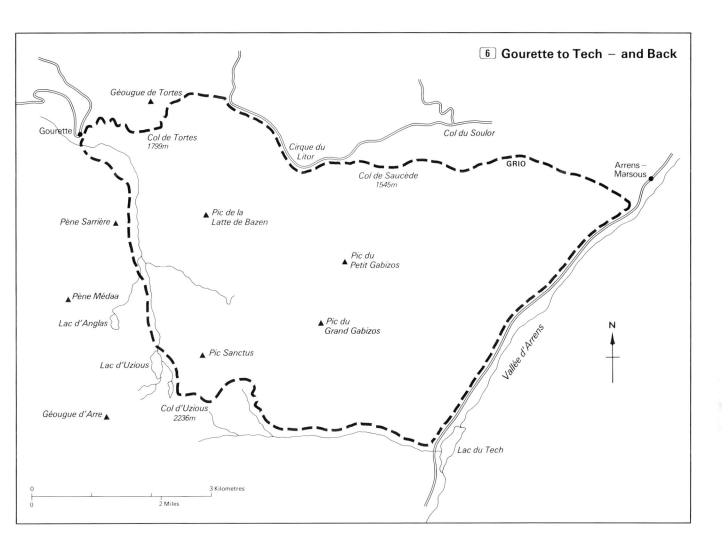

Géougue de Tortes

Gourette

Col de Tortes
1799m

Cirque du
Litor

Col du Soulor

Col de Saucède
1545m

GRIO

Arrens –
Marsous

Pène Sarrière

Pic de la
Latte de Bazen

Pic du
Petit Gabizos

Pène Médaa

Lac d'Anglas

Pic du
Grand Gabizos

Vallée d'Arrens

Lac d'Uzious

Pic Sanctus

N

Géougue d'Arre

Col d'Uzious
2236m

Lac du Tech

0 — 3 Kilometres
0 — 2 Miles

summits. The slopes are scarred in summer with broad, bare pistes, eroded by bulldozers and ten thousand pairs of skis. Hardly the place from which to begin a delightful walk, you might think. But you would be wrong.

It doesn't take more than a few minutes to leave all this behind, and soon there are other mountains, other hillsides, other valleys to gaze on and to be refreshed by. Landscapes of splendour become the norm, and before long you're among streams and tarns and lovely glacial cirques, and you can forget all about the machinery cluttering the hills, and instead concentrate on the wilderness aspect of the walk. There's a lot of it to absorb.

It hardly seems possible that within so short a space of time and distance from Gourette and the Aubisque road, you can be amidst such wild and seemingly remote landscapes. Certainly there are popular paths, but these do not stray too far along our route. The Uzious

tarns may well have one or two picnic parties along their shores, but beyond them there is so much 'empty' country. On our walk we discovered a number of griffon vultures feeding on the carcass of a cow that had recently died from what appeared to be a broken neck. We saw marmots—and heard many more. There were isard, too. And lizards, of course, and butterflies, and frogs in wayside pools, as well as thousands upon thousands of crickets leaping and chirruping in the grass. At times it was almost as though the grass itself had legs.

There were fresh and surprising vistas; huge views from Col d'Uzious, the welcome sight of Balaïtous from the Vallée d'Arrens, long and lush panoramas from the route to the Col de Saucède. Variety was very much the spice of this walk; its essence and its reward.

The Route

Initially heading south-east from Gourette

take a path signposted to Lac d'Anglas but break away from it after about 2.5 kilometres (1¹/₂ miles) onto a minor path that climbs to Lac d'Uzious. Beyond the lake cross Col d'Uzious and descend the steep valley of Labas to Lac du Tech in the Vallée d'Arrens. There is an official campsite at the southern end of the lake, the only other possibility for an overnight stay being down-valley at Arrens-Marsous.

The second stage of the walk goes north along a narrow road for six kilometres almost as far as Arrens-Marsous, then branches to the left to take the path of GR10 uphill to the neat dip of Col de Saucède. Over this, wander round the Cirque du Litor, then head southwest and climb the hillside to reach Col de Tortes. A short, steep descent from this pass leads directly into Gourette.

Day 1: Gourette to Tech

The path begins steeply, with no gentle lead-in. It climbs beneath a chair lift just behind Gourette, and by the time you reach the top of this initial slope, panting heavily, you'll be wondering if you might have overpacked your rucksack! But the gradient eases as you come round a slight curve and into the narrow Valentin valley to skirt the lower slopes of Pène Sarrière, a grey peak of modest height, but with a superb East Face that rises in great slabs above the path. On this challenging wall are a number of short, but difficult rock routes, and it is quite possible that you'll see climbers in action here as you pass below.

The path is invariably busy in summer, for the route to Lac d'Anglas is one of the most popular of all excursions from Gourette. Our route, however, leaves it shortly after passing a rough shepherd's *cabane* seen on the opposite bank of the Valentin stream, and at the point where the main path begins to zig-zag westward. At this junction a small cairn indicates a lesser path which breaks away and continues to head up-valley, but losing a little height to bring you to a rough bowl of pasture, heavily punctuated with boulders and the remains of an old *cabane*.

Now begins the real climb to a saddle beyond which lies Lac d'Uzious. A cairned path winds up a jumbled slope of scree and broken rock littered here and there with strips of rusting metal long discarded from mine workings near the saddle. Then you come to a pipe alongside which the path continues to climb, in places with the aid of steps cut into the rock, and a few have even been concreted—presumably as an aid to engineers working up here.

As we topped the slope and came onto the false saddle, we turned to gaze out at a froth of cloud-sea hiding all but the highest of peaks and swamping the distant lowlands. We were in full sunshine, but out there, no doubt, rain was falling.

On coming to Lac d'Uzious wander along the eastern shore and then take the narrow path that heads up the slope to find a second tarn, Lac du Lavedan, ten minutes or so beyond the first. This is a little smaller than Lac d'Uzious, but most attractive in its setting of green pasture with the mountains rising in a natural bowl around it. They are not forbidding mountains; steep maybe, but friendly and with sheep grazing on unbelievably exposed ledges. (When we made a short detour round the head of the valley, we had to dodge a number of falling stones that came hurtling towards us, disturbed by those sheep, and I considered the irony of possible injury caused by animal-tossed rocks! How d'you explain that on an insurance claim? I wondered.)

Above, and to the east of the second tarn, there is an obvious col. The path leads up to it without difficulty, and on arrival there you are presented with a glorious sight, for you gaze over a very deep valley to a collection of fine mountains built into a long wall on the far side of the unseen but clearly detected Vallée d'Arrens. Beyond them eyes look far off to the east where distant peaks and ridges are no more than images of blue fading against the sky. Nearer to hand, peering south, the high wall banking the valley of Labas seems impenetrable; a vast upsweep of rock flooded with sunlight.

Standing on the grassy saddle of Col d'Uzious (2236m/7336ft) in the early afternoon, I was totally captured by those stunning views. And what made them even better for me was the drapery of cloud spread midway across some of the peaks, and the shafts of light pouring into the valley off to our right. It was a scene of untold magic, and it added a tremendous boost to our day.

Turning steeply downwards you work a route on a narrow path that fades in places, but keeps faithfully to the left-hand side of the valley. (A few minutes below the pass we came across those vultures. Feeding, they appeared the size of overweight turkeys, but they took off after a short hop down the slope and rose effortlessly on huge outstretched wings. They have a wingspan of some 2.5 metres/9ft, and we watched as they rose in long and lazy spirals

Right: **On the long descent from Col d'Uzious to Tech, the route goes over grassy bluffs and round a shallow cirque. The author's wife plots the onward route.**

Right: **Above Arrens the hillsides are green and pastoral, dotted here and there with haybarns.**

high above our heads, waiting for our safe departure before they could resume their lunch.) There are plunging slopes of grass, and deep gullies. There are promontories bright with alpenroses and aromatic plants from which more stupendous views are offered. And there's a high, but shallow amphitheatre which the path circles before resuming its downward route.

A delicate cascade pours through a gully near the point where the path crosses a side stream, and below this the path leads steeply down to the valley floor which it reaches near a rather basic *cabane*. In emergency this would provide a rough shelter. There's a fireplace and sufficient space on a sleeping platform for about half a dozen people, but it would need to be a very bad storm to make it a willing choice for overnight accommodation.

Follow the main stream down-valley for a while, then, where it cuts through a deep bed, leave it and follow a faint continuing path that traverses the left-hand slope again. At the point where a small concrete dam crosses the stream you have a choice of routes. The main path crosses here and joins a track to wind down the right-hand side of the valley. Continuing on the left bank a smaller path eventually leads into a tangled woodland and brings you at last to the Vallée d'Arrens by the Lac du Tech, a short distance from the alternative track.

Once in the valley bear right and a few minutes later you will reach the campsite at the end of the lake.

Day 2: Tech to Gourette

A narrow road leads through the Vallée d'Arrens from the village of Arrens-Marsous at the mouth of it in the north, to a point nearly four kilometres south of Lac du Tech where there is a *Maison du Parc* and a small area for car parking at the entrance to the National Park. From this point a path leads into some lovely wild country at the foot of the Balaïtous massif, one of the more forbidding and barren regions of these mountains, and in direct contrast to the thick foliage of the lower valley.

In the valley itself the dammed Lac du Tech, like so many other accessible lakes of the Pyrénées, is very popular with anglers. Most days in summer will see Frenchmen standing quietly on the banks gazing at their lines waiting for a bite. Horses and cattle graze the surrounding pastures and by midday families will be gathering on its margins to picnic. But if you leave the campsite fairly early, the walk down-valley to Arrens-Marsous will be quiet enough. It's a walk along the roadside all the way (about 6km/3½ miles in all), but it is not without interest, and there will be very little traffic. There are haybarns and a few isolated houses beside the road, and on the far side of the valley as you near Arrens, steep pastures with attractive, if modest, mountains rising from them.

It is unnecessary to walk right into the village, unless you need supplies, as on the very outskirts, near a sanatorium converted from a former hospice, you break away to the left on a track that is waymarked with the GR10 sign. This leads north-westward among trees and hedges steadily rising along the hillside, with an occasional brief glimpse allowed down to a delightful landscape of meadows and barns, with villages spreading off to the north-east.

The track leads to a narrow lane, still among trees, and this lane is followed for a short distance until you leave it by a lone farmhouse and take to a farm track beyond. By now you begin to lose the shade of trees as the way takes you through sloping pastures and beside more haybarns, the views opening and becoming yet more pastoral. It is a lush green countryside. A countryside that is tended and grazed. It is neat and tidy. Hay is cut and stooked in orderly piles, the few scattered buildings appear weather-proof and sturdy. It is all so well-managed after yesterday's taste of wilderness.

On the far hillside the route to Col du Soulor twists its way steadily upward, but the sound of traffic negotiating its hairpin bends is rarely heard in the breeze and bears no unwelcome intrusion.

The last haybarns are passed and the path becomes very narrow, following for a brief spell a lively little stream before straining up a steepening grass-covered spur. In turn this leads to broader hillside pastures open fully to the sun and with a magnificent panorama to enjoy behind when you pause for a breather. Horses graze up here. Cattle and sheep too. And off to the left a ribbon of a waterfall sprays out of a cliff face. It really is a lovely, colourful area.

Col de Saucède announces its presence some way before you actually reach it. It is very much a gateway through an extended ridge thrown out by Pic du Petit Gabizos, and when seen from the GR10 path, it is immediately recognisable. At the northern extent of this spur, before it sweeps up to the next minor peak, lies the Col du Soulor, one of the gentlest

Right: **Looking north to a cloud-sea swamping the foothills, from the minor col below Lac d'Uzious near Gourette.**

and more picturesque of the road passes across the Pyrénées which, with Col d'Aubisque further west, links Argelès-Gazost and the valley of the Gave de Pau, with Laruns in the Vallée d'Ossau.

Crossing through Col de Saucède another fine view opens ahead, this time across the Cirque du Litor where the road winds from Col du Soulor to find the Aubisque. Waymarks lead the path down a rough gully and onto the road. There you bear left and walk alongside it for about three kilometres—passing through two unlit tunnels—before branching off to the left and heading up a steep hillside towards the final col.

The map shows three paths heading up the hillside west of the road, but we only found two. One branches off right to cross Col d'Arbaze before descending to the Aubisque. Our route heads for Col de Tortes, a little south-west of the point where you leave the road, and it makes a steady ascent of the hillside combe among shrubs and boulders, with sheep grazing all around.

All morning we had walked in bright sunshine, but as we worked our way towards the col, mist came tumbling from the heights to obscure our vision, hiding, until the very last moment, any hint of a pass. Sheep appeared and as suddenly disappeared once more in the mist. As did the path. But there are waymarks now and again on the rocks, and the occasional cairn acts as a guide, so even in poor visibility there should be no real difficulty in finding the way.

Col de Tortes (1799m/5902ft) is a grand little crossing. On either side ridges rise abruptly; to the north to Géougue de Tortes, and south to Pic de la Latte de Bazan. There's a grass-covered cone leading onto the col, and this we found to be a veritable flower garden, highly fragrant and extremely colourful.

The descent to Gourette is a devious twist and turn among boulders, dwarf pine, juniper and alpenrose and countless alpine flowers growing among the rocks and in the sheep-cropped grass. It's a fairly steep path too, for about 450 metres (1476ft) of height is lost in a short distance, although there's nothing remotely difficult about it. The only sadness comes from an inevitable reluctance to trade the wild mountain scenery for the drab clutter of the ski resort where even the drinks are over-priced. But if nothing else, Gourette will elevate in memory those fine untamed acres of the high mountains and empty valleys, and help put the walk into its true perspective.

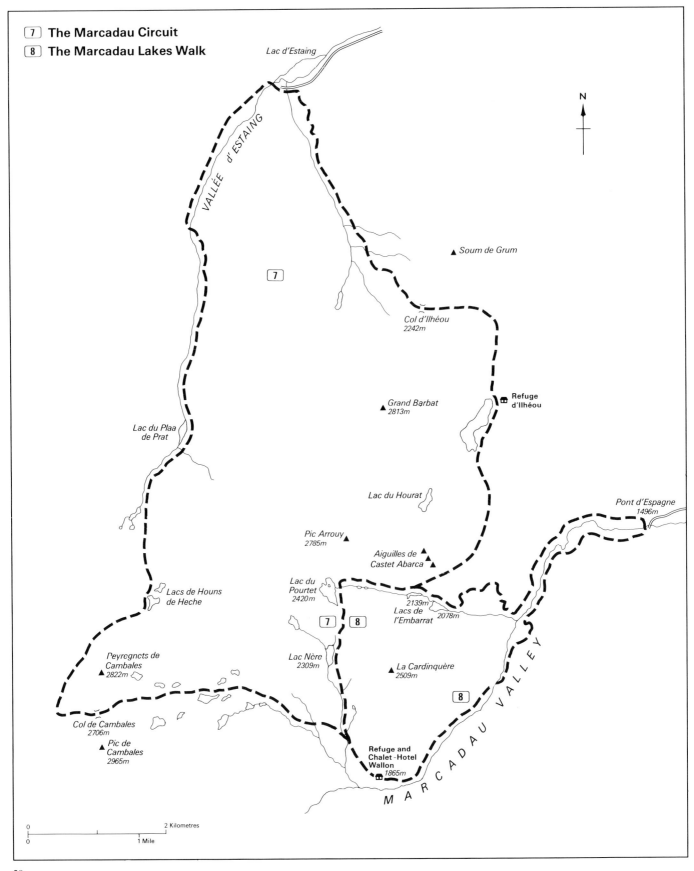

7 **The Marcadau Circuit**
8 **The Marcadau Lakes Walk**

Lac d'Estaing

VALLÉE   d' ESTAING

7

▲ *Soum de Grum*

Col d'Ilhéou
2242m

▲ *Grand Barbat*
2813m

🏠 **Refuge
d'Ilhéou**

*Lac du Plaa
de Prat*

Lac du Hourat

Pont d'Espagne
1496m

Pic Arrouy
2785m ▲

Aiguilles de ▲
Castet Abarca ▲

*Lac du
Pourtet*
2420m

*Lacs de Houns
de Heche*

2139m
7   8   *Lacs de
l'Embarrat*   *2078m*

*Peyregnets de
Cambales*
▲ *2822m*

Lac Nère
2309m

▲ *La Cardinquère*
2509m

8

M   A   R   C   A   D   A   U   V   A   L   L   E   Y

Col de Cambales
2706m

▲ *Pic de
Cambales*
2965m

**Refuge and
Chalet-Hotel
Wallon**
🏠 *1865m*

N

0   2 Kilometres
0   1 Mile

WALK 7: The Marcadau Circuit

Above: **Teasing above an easy saddle, the Barbat peaks hint that they would repay the attention of a rock climber. Only the cattle show no interest at all.**

Location: South of Lourdes. Approached by road via Argelès–Gazost along D103 to Lac d'Estaing. The actual circuit is contained within a wedge of country bordered on the north and west by the Vallée d'Estaing and to the south and east by the Marcadau Valley, which is reached from Cauterets via Pont d'Espagne.
Distance: 29kms (18 miles).
Time Required: 2-3 days.
Type of Walk: Strenuous and with some difficult sections without paths, especially on the approach to Col de Cambales. Not to be tackled in inclement weather, or by inexperienced mountain walkers.
Starting Point: Lac d'Estaing.
Accommodation: Mountain hut, or Chalet-Hotel (small dormitory-style rooms) in the Marcadau; mountain hut at Lac d'Ilhéou. Campsite at Lac d'Estaing. Meals are available in the Chalet-Hotel Wallon and Refuge d'Ilhéou during the main season when they both have a guardian in residence.
Maps: IGN Carte de Randonnées No.3: *Béarn* 1:50,000.

Tarns and Passes in the National Park

I have a particular penchant for the Marcadau Valley that neither time nor familiarity have even begun to subdue. It has an aura about it that is hard to define, yet much of its atmosphere is clearly due to the peculiar liquidity of its light. As southerly mountains the Pyrénées all bask in a purity of light, but in the Marcadau it is even more intense, more iridescent; its brilliance seems to be reflected by the numerous streams, pools and tarns that dazzle among the pastures and act as so many mirrors of reflection. The Marcadau is, indeed, an oasis of light.

It is a soft green valley too. A feminine valley wedged between the raw landscapes of the Balaïtous to the west and the harsh form of the Vignemale to the east. At its head individual peaklets like Grande Fache and Pic Falisse show no sense of austerity, for they gaze down into the valley from their perch on the borders of Spain with an air of benevolence, and even where vegetation almost runs out near Col de Cambales, still the countryside beams a smile that can be trusted.

Immediately to the north rises a knot of mountains scooped with hanging valleys. Some of these mountains are adorned with crocodiles' teeth of rocky *gendarmes*. The Aiguilles de Piarrouy (or du Pic Arrouy) above Lac du Pourtet are a first-rate example, while to the north of these a splay of shapely crags, largely unknown, would make superb individual features to adorn any mountain region. These are the Barbat peaks that form rocky fence posts in a back-country wonderland on the very edge of the National Park.

Below the Barbat peaks to the north there runs another fine valley contouring a similar swathe to that of the Marcadau. This valley, the Vallée d'Estaing, unlike the Marcadau, is inhabited lower down with a few small villages, while in its upper reaches spreads a shallow lake, almost the width of the valley, that draws countless visitors throughout the summer. Lac d'Estaing is reached by road and makes a delightful picnic site, but south of the lake the road ends and only keen walkers venture deeper into the tight cleft that pokes south towards a wedge of mountains topped by Peyregnets de Cambales.

Linking the valleys of Marcadau and d'Estaing at their broadest point are two minor valleys joined by the grassy Col d'Ilhéou (2242m/7356ft), and an easy, if steep, path crosses the col to enable a pear-shaped circuit to be made of this ever-interesting region. This circuit is justifiably included as one of the classic walks of these lovely mountains.

The Route

Starting at Lac d'Estaing where there is a campsite, restaurant and ample room to park cars, the route heads south to the very head of the valley, then climbs rough hillsides to find Col de Cambales. Over this a path descends eastward into the Marcadau where accommodation is to be found either at the Chalet-Hotel Wallon, owned by the Touring Club de France, or in the spartan *refuge* next door.

From Wallon the previous day's route is retraced a short distance before veering north on another good path among a series of lakes. Above the first of the Lacs de l'Embarrat the path forks and you continue on the upper route to cross Col de Haugade, and then drop down towards the northern end of Lac

d'Ilhéou where a fine modern *refuge* stands overlooking the lake.

The third stage of the walk takes you from Refuge d'Ilhéou on a steeply climbing path heading north, then west, to cross Col d'Ilhéou, followed by a long and steep descent through a bare valley and, in its lower reaches, through forest to the shores of Lac d'Estaing.

Day 1: Lac d'Estaing to Refuge Wallon

All the world comes to Lac d'Estaing when the sun is shining. With easy road access, a restaurant when you arrive and fine mountain scenery, it is not hard to understand why. However, it's simple enough to lose the crowds when you've a rucksack on your back and a plan to delve deeply into the high mountain recesses. Just wander south along the track that leads towards the head of the valley, and gradually you lose all sense of company.

The track is bordered by shrubs and trees; dark woods clothe the lower slopes of the mountains ahead, while the silver dash of streams glisten above. The track swings left to cross the Gave de Labat de Bun and a stony path then leads on, climbing up into the shade of woods. When you emerge from them you wander through a narrow shaft of valley, rough underfoot and with boulders scattered across the floor. But after a while you come to a broader plain where the mountains are set back in a horseshoe, and in the horseshoe lies a green reedy tarn, Lac du Plaa de Prat. The stream that flows into it is clear and cool and so refreshing on a hot day.

The path continues across this undulating grassy plain and begins to wind up rough slopes broken with alpenroses, bilberry bushes and juniper trees. Boulders distort the hillside, and coming over a shelf you find another tarn, this one black and unwelcoming, trapped amidst a wild and lonely cirque. The remains of old stone walls criss-cross the cirque, as though shepherds came here at one time to pen their sheep—though what those sheep would have grazed on is beyond me.

Now the climb to Col de Cambales begins in earnest. It slants in zig-zags up the left-hand mountainside to pass the Lacs de Houns de Hèche and into a wild upper sanctuary. Peaks and ridges close in on three sides with barely a break between them, but you climb up and over the western ridge, and then skirt stony slopes above the narrow upper slice of the valley of Arrens. There you find cairns and other signs of a crossing route. Branching off

Above: **Refuge d'Ilhéou (1988m) is a National Park hut in an idyllic situation overlooking the lake of the same name.**

to the left, work along those cairns and emerge finally, and rather thankfully, at the col. Here a splendid view shows the bulk of Balaïtous to the west, all ridge and glacier-drape and bold domed summit. But our route leads east, down into a very different world to that of the Balaïtous wilderness, and you turn your back on the harsh crags and aim instead for greenery and the fragrance of flowers.

The descent, which is rather steep at first, soon eases to pass a string of tarns trapped in a granite upland. Below them beams the pasture-land of the Marcadau; streams, cascades, stunted pine trees, flowers and shrubs and more tarns. And as you wander down the well-cairned path, so the view ahead unfolds and you gaze off to the Vignemale rising above intermediate ridges.

Treading soft turf you bear round a bluff and there stands the barn-like Chalet-Hotel Wallon, with the rough little climbers' hut beside it and a chapel a few paces away.

Days 2-3: Refuge Wallon to Lac d'Estaing

It would be possible to return to Lac d'Estaing in one day from the Marcadau, but if you've time to spare, I would urge you to make a two-day journey of it. The Marcadau will, after all, make demands on your time. There is so much to gaze on, to explore, to enjoy. And the route to Refuge d'Ilhéou has so much variety that it would be a crime to scurry along without doing it justice. Step gently and draw out the full impact of the day.

Return up-valley on the path towards Col de

Cambales then, where a stream comes dancing from the right, break away on another path heading uphill to the north. This leads into a secretive hollow where Lac Nère appears like a fjord, trapped as it is by the steep and rocky walls of surrounding mountains. The path continues above its eastern shore and crosses to the north among boulders and grassy patches bright with flowers early in the summer. Lac du Pourtet is next, the Aiguilles de Piarrouy (or du Pic Arrouy) snarling at its far end.

Now you rise up to a false col and look down onto a falling hillside with more tarns sparkling below, and beyond them over intervening ridges and mountain spurs towards the foothills far off. It is a lovely view, and one that is a delight to walk into.

The descending path will tighten the muscles over your knees, but just above the first of the Lacs de l'Embarrat an alternative path strikes away from the main route and traverses steep slopes below the Aiguilles de Castet Abarca, before climbing to Col de la Haugade (2311m/7582ft). Below lies Lac d'Ilhéou (otherwise descriptively known as Lac Bleu). Towering over it are raw, scraggy peaks. Grand Barbat (2813m/9229ft) rises on the far side, but at the north-east opening of this deep scoop the world presents a different face and you gaze out towards green hills fading to blue in the distance.

From the col cut down over rocks and scree on the path which leads to the steep-pitched Refuge d'Ilhéou another of those fine *refuges* provided by the National Park Authority. Here, in as fine a mountain setting as you could wish, you will find all the excuses you might need to spend the remainder of the day in relaxation, with the prospect of little more than a morning's walk to complete the circuit over Col d'Ilhéou to Lac d'Estaing the next day.

Should you have no need to return to Lac d'Estaing, however, an alternative route follows the path of GR10 to Cauterets. This is a broad, much-trodden trail that first goes down to Lac Noir, a small tarn lying below the hut to the north-east, and from there along the obvious valley curving to the right. It is an easy, often crowded walk, especially at weekends, for halfway along the valley there is a car park and a road leading up to it from the town.

The route to Col d'Ilhéou, on the other hand, is less likely to be busy. It is a steep path in places, but always clear and without difficulty. It leads north from the *refuge* and goes through a tranquil little meadowland combe before beginning the real climb to the pass. Initially you gaze out towards the foothills, but soon the long green wall of the Crête du Lis blocks all views as it closes in on you. On the far side of this *crête* is Cauteret's main winter ski area with all the mechanical impedimenta associated with it lacing the slopes of the Cirque du Lis. But the pastoral valley through which our route climbs is in marked contrast to this. Cattle graze the steep slopes, and just below the pass there's a small *cabane* seemingly lost to the world.

Col d'Ilhéou is a grassy undulating saddle on one of the ridges dipping from Grand Barbat. Above to the north rises the Crête de Mourtara which leads to the easy summit of Soum de Grum. It all seems so gentle, so friendly and benevolent, but as you wander down the steeply winding path from the col, you catch a glimpse of those Barbat peaks rising off to your left above a bowl of pasture. These are fine indeed and enticing to climbers, yet hidden away from the more obvious, more accessible climbers' peaks found elsewhere in the Pyrénées, they will only attract the more adventurous of scramblers who are not averse to a long walk-in.

Wandering down the path from the col one sun-bright afternoon I stopped to speak with a lone French walker out on a long circuit from Cauterets. A professional artist, he was making notes and sketches for a commissioned mural. We discussed the mountains and the valleys, gave each other advice on various routes, traded 'secret' corners and special viewpoints. I mentioned the jagged Barbat peaks and he opened his rucksack and produced a large chunk of rock absolutely glistening with crystals. 'That is where I found this,' he said, delighted with his find. It was certainly the most crystal-encrusted rock I'd ever seen, and I made a mental note to go searching too, one of these days. (One of these days . . . Are there sufficient days in just one lifetime to do all the things one plans? I doubt it.)

Horses, cattle and sheep graze these steep hillsides. There is another rough *cabane* on the left bank of this narrow valley with a tarn hidden above it, and streams come flowing from many directions to unite in one dashing force (much-diminished late in the summer) well below the path. You wander down, always down and often steeply, on the right bank. Then the slope eases in a broad meadowland at

the mouth of the valley on a green sill. Below lies a dense covering of forest. But first a patch of shrubbery and another *cabane*, that of Arriousec, on the very edge of the forest.

The route continues to descend, now in tree shade and still steeply, until at last you break out of the trees and drop down the final slope to the road that runs alongside Lac d'Estaing.

At such times civilisation, in the form of a restaurant, is extremely welcome.

Above: **The Gave de Labat de Bun pours from the woods in a series of minor cascades. The path crosses below these, loses the stream in the woods, but then regains it later in a rocky little valley.**

WALK 8: The Marcadau Lakes Walk

Above: **The walk to the Wallon Hut from Pont d'Espagne keeps company with the river for most of the way and crosses it once or twice on sturdy wooden bridges.**

Location: South of Lourdes, and reached by way of Cauterets from where there are occasional buses (or taxis) to Pont d'Espagne along the Val de Jéret. Plenty of parking space for private vehicles at the end of the N.21c road, just beyond Pont d'Espagne.

Distance: 16 kms (10 miles).

Time Required: 6-7 hours.

Type of Walk: Fairly strenuous, but visually spectacular and constantly varied. The paths are good throughout, although the terrain is somewhat rough in places. There should be no route-finding difficulties.

Base: Cauterets.

Start/Finish: Pont d'Espagne.

Refreshments: At Chalet-Hotel Wallon, a little under half-way along the walk.

Maps: IGN Carte de Randonnées No.3: *Béarn* 1:50,000.

Guidebooks: *Walks and Climbs in the Pyrénées* by Kev Reynolds (Cicerone Press).
100 Randonnées dans les Pyrénées Occidentales by Georges Véron (Randonnées Pyrénéennes).

Green Valleys and Rock-Girt Tarns—A One-Day Outing

The Marcadau Circuit (Walk 7) involved some very rough walking and the crossing of a high, remote and somewhat difficult pass. As such it would necessarily exclude a number of readers from tackling it. This is a pity, the more so because the Vallée du Marcadau is an utterly charming area with numerous possibilities for exploratory outings that would be well within the capabilities of most hill walkers. Using the Chalet-Hotel, or Refuge Wallon as a base, several days of a walking holiday could be spent there quite happily. There are easy peaks to wander up. There are passes to visit, side valleys to explore, collections of tarns to dream beside. With more space at my disposal, I would undoubtedly include other Marcadau outings as 'Classics' in their own right. But the Marcadau Lakes Walk stands out in a class of its own, and a small section of it was included in the previous chapter. As a single day's outing from the little resort town of Cauterets, this walk is a must.

It has everything: a tranquil valley, green, flower-strewn and with a clear stream flowing through it. There are cascades and shallow pools, deep tarns trapped in high rocky basins. There are fine mountains to gaze upon; the chance to watch isard chasing across the hillsides. There are marmots in secluded corners; far views and intimate scenarios; steady ascents and steep descents; the opportunity for refreshment part-way round the walk and countless idyllic spots in which to laze and soak the country's splendour.

The Marcadau is a valley of dreams. It is also a valley in which to make those dreams come true.

The Route

Either take a bus or taxi from Cauterets, or drive through the narrow, wooded Val de Jéret as far as Pont d'Espagne where there is a large car park. The Vallée du Marcadau continues to the west, then curves to the south-west. Walk through this as far as the Chalet-Hotel Wallon, then head north on a climbing path to link a series of tarns, before descending past yet more on a continuing path that leads into the valley again at Pont du Cayan. Once in the valley bear left and walk down to Pont d'Espagne.

The Walk

There are two large parking areas at Pont d'Espagne. The first serves those bound for Lac de Gaube—either on foot or by *téléférique*—while the second is more useful for Marcadau-bound walkers. From here one can either enter the Marcadau by taking the path on the northern side of the river, or the broad track on the left. My preference is to take the footpath for journeying into the valley, and save the track for the outward walk.

Almost immediately after leaving the roadhead the path rises over an undulating meadow, curves round a bluff and shows a glimpse of the valley's true worth. Ahead, beyond a foreground of winding streams, clumps of pine and alpenroses, the mountains beckon. At this point there are no peaks of character to be seen, but as a background the converging ridges are inspiring enough, and I have never failed to be moved by this initial view, whether I've been laden with climbing equipment or simply out for a day or two's walking.

The faint path leads easily across soft-turf grasslands, and now and again you have to leap meandering side streams that cut down from the hillsides on their way to the main Gave du Marcadau. In that main river, trout flicker darkly in the shallows. Frogs and salamanders inhabit the margins and are visible on the path as well. (These salamanders are colourful creatures with livid gold and black markings over their backs. They waddle on what appear to be very sore webbed feet, but spend much of their time among the rocks near water. They are more often found on the Spanish side of the Pyrénées, near the centre of the range.)

Soon after entering a lightly wooded area you come to a bridge crossing the main river. This is the Pont du Cayan, and off to the right a path can be seen climbing among trees and shrubs. This path leads to the Lacs de l'Embarrat, and will be the one from which you descend later.

Cross the bridge and continue up-valley on a broad stony track that soon narrows to a good mule path. It climbs through woods and then levels along a fine stretch where you cross the stream on another sturdy bridge. This is a very good place for alpine flowers, especially in June when the snows are still receding up the hillside—although June is not normally a good month for tackling this circuit, on account of avalanche danger.

The way continues, climbing once more over rocky knolls, then winding beside shallow pools with views opening ahead and the trio of peaks that head the valley rising out of the pastures: Pointe de la Muga, Pic Falisse and Grande Fache, with Port du Marcadau and Col de la Fache offering easy passages into Spain. The path comes round a bluff and there ahead stands the Wallon chalet-hotel, accompanied by the squat *refuge* and an attractive white-walled chapel in an idyllic site.

Staying here once with my family early in the summer we rose early and watched as isard came down from the snows to drink at the nearby stream. Other times I've camped not far away, listening of an evening to marmots whistling among the boulders, watching birds and butterflies, photographing the flowers, planning new routes on neighbouring peaks, absorbing the very special atmosphere that emanates from this sunlit sanctuary. But I've also been trapped here by bad weather, spending long, frustrating hours inside the dining room of the Wallon chalet-hotel as a storm boomed outside and the room filled with steam from damp clothes hanging over a glowing wood-burning stove. When that storm

Above: **Pic Falisse and Grande Fache seen from the path below Refuge Wallon in the Marcadau valley.**

finally blew itself out there was fresh snow on the mountains and a taste of winter before its time.

Always, though, the Marcadau responds with its own brand of enchantment. Beyond the Wallon hut the valley spreads itself to the north-west. A path heads up towards the unseen Col de Cambales among gnarled pine trees and masses of alpenrose and juniper. Above the trees the path forks and you head off to the right, climbing more energetically now to gain a high scoop of mountainside in which you will find Lac Nère trapped by the steep mountain walls. The path takes you onto a sloping shelf above the lake's eastern bank to emerge into another level, a secret little valley of grass and rough boulders with the next tarn, Lac du Pourtet, lying at its head. On the far side of this tarn screes come sweeping down from the jagged teeth of the Aiguilles de Piarrouy, and there is an interesting, but demanding, traverse to be made by crossing a narrow col among these Aiguilles and descending on the far side to Lac du Plaa de Prat and the Vallée d'Estaing. Our route, however, has other plans, and heads up to the right to cross a false col, a stony saddle which looks down a steeply plunging slope to the Lacs de l'Embarrat, three hundred metres or so below.

The path takes you down to them. And all the way are splendid long views out towards the foothills. The closer Aiguilles de Castet Abarca also catch your attention, while the empty gulf of the Marcadau draws you with its promise of more fine things to come.

The Lacs de l'Embarrat are lovely tarns. The first has a splay of level turf around it. The second, and larger tarn is partially enclosed by low cliffs, but at its eastern outlet there is a picturesque spot in which to spread yourself in the sun to rest while you enjoy the views, undisturbed by any sound other than the splash of a frog leaping into the water, or a marmot calling nearby. I've seen many isard on the neighbouring slopes as well.

The severity of the path barely eases on the continuing descent. From the tarns the way is initially still mostly rough and stony, but with shrubs growing among the rocks. Then you enter woodland shade with vagrant streams running across the path, and there are wild raspberries on which to gorge yourself as you near Pont de Cayan and the floor of the Marcadau again. Once down, cross the bridge, bear left and follow the track all the way to Pont d'Espagne.

But as you come to the end of this walk, it is my bet that you'll have seen enough of the Marcadau for its magic to have had some effect, and you will no doubt soon be planning a return to make more discoveries of your own. However, you will not be the first to come under its spell nor, no doubt, will you be the last.

WALK 9: The Two Parks Walk

Location: France and Spain; Cauterets, Ordesa and Gavarnie regions.
Distance: 49kms (30 miles).
Time Required: 3-4 days.
Type of Walk: A mixture of valley and mountain walking over rough ground with some exposure, on paths and tracks. Two high passes to cross, one small glacier (without crevasses).
Start: Refuge des Oulettes de Gaube (2151m/7057ft).
Finish: Gavarnie.
Accommodation: Mountain huts, and hotel in Torla. (Camping allows greater flexibility, but note that camping is forbidden in the Ordesa Park).
Maps: IGN Carte de Randonnées No. 4: *Bigorre* 1:50,000. Editorial Alpina: *Ordesa* 1:40,000 but note that much of the Ara Valley is not covered by either of these maps.
Guidebook: *Walks and Climbs in the Pyrénées* by Kev Reynolds (Cicerone Press).

From France to Spain and Back Again

With two Pyrénéan National Parks backing against each another—one in France, the other in Spain—it will become evident that a considerable area of interesting and scenically spectacular country exists on both sides of the watershed. A roughly horseshoe-shaped trip gives the opportunity to make a tour through some of the best of both.

On the northern slopes this walk takes you through two valleys of the *Parc National des Pyrénées Occidentales* (PNP); one to begin the trek, the other to complete it, and between the two, on the Spanish side, you explore the marvellous canyon scenery of the *Parque Nacional del Valle de Ordesa*. In addition there is a descent through the lonely Ara Valley, and a return to France by way of that classic high

Above: Emerging from the Brèche de Roland onto French slopes again, you gaze across the Cirque de Gavarnie to Pic du Marboré.

Right: **Huge stemless thistles, the size of dinner plates, adorn the dry grass and warn you to look first before sitting down.**

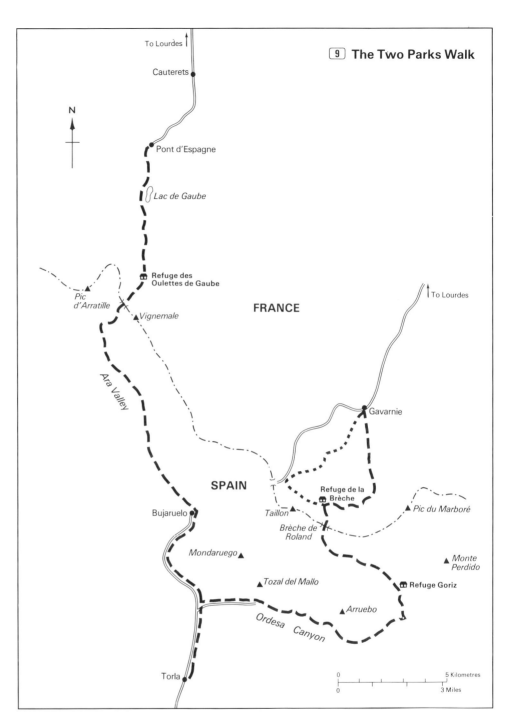

N

Cauterets

To Lourdes ↑

9 The Two Parks Walk

Pont d'Espagne

Lac de Gaube

Refuge des
Oulettes de Gaube

Pic
d'Arratille

▲Vignemale

FRANCE

Ara Valley

To Lourdes ↑

Gavarnie

SPAIN

Refuge de la
Brèche

Bujaruelo

Taillon ▲

▲ Pic du Marboré

Brèche de
Roland

Mondaruego ▲

▲ Monte
Perdido

▲ Tozal del Mallo

Refuge Goriz

▲ Arruebo

Ordesa Canyon

Torla

0   5 Kilometres

0   3 Miles

pass sliced in the crest of the Cirque de Gavarnie, the Brèche de Roland. It is a walk which displays well the scenic, vegetation and cultural differences between one side of the watershed and the other, and offers a constantly varied experience.

Cauterets is the most convenient centre from which to set out on this trip, while Gavarnie marks the finish. Both have public transport connections with Lourdes. Cauterets is set on the very edge of the National Park and makes the most of its position. From this busy little spa town numerous excursions are made possible, both within the Park and outside its boundaries. There are cableways that open up some high wild country on the fringes of the Park, and a winding road that heads through the Val de Jéret among forest and beside numerous cascades—Tennyson's 'stream that flashest white'—as far as Pont d'Espagne. Pont d'Espagne is very much a gateway to the wonderland of the Marcadau Valley and the valley of Oulettes de Gaube, and as a consequence is invariably busy during the summer months, although there's not much there, other than an hotel, a large car park, the swirl of glacier-born streams and the promise of fine country all around.

The real start to this walk lies at the head of the valley of the Oulettes stream, at the foot of the North Face of the Vignemale (3298m/ 10,820ft), highest mountain on the Franco/ Spanish frontier. It is reached by a pleasant approach walk from Pont d'Espagne on a clear path that takes you first to the justifiably popular Lac de Gaube, whose *hôtellerie* is usually the limit of exploration for most tourists. From here one gains a first sighting of the Vignemale to the south.

The head of the valley is blocked by a tight amphitheatre of high peaks dominated by the Vignemale's magnificent North Face. But next to that is the triangular wedge of Piton Carre, then Pointe Chausenque and finally, Petit Vignemale. Each summit is well over the 3000 metre mark (9843ft). Each mountain boasts great slabs of wall that set a climber's fingers itching, and between Piton Carre and the main Vignemale peak (Pique Longue) there runs the deep 600 metre (1968ft) ice-choked seam of the Couloir de Gaube, first climbed in 1889, but not repeated for forty-four years! The Vignemale's massive North Face rises for about 800 metres (2625ft) out of the remnants of its glacier, and below that spreads a little glacial plain, marshy in places, rock-strewn in others, with streams meandering through. On a rocky knoll at the northern end of this plain sits the CAF's Refuge des Oulettes de Gaube.

Day 1: Refuge des Oulettes de Gaube to Torla

This is a long day's walk. In many respects it is too long, because the valley through which it leads is far too good to hurry; one should wander slowly with eyes, ears and nostrils alert to the myriad sensations that fill the scene. It is a valley that deserves to be experienced at leisure, not with one eye on the hands of your watch. Backpackers then, will win the day, for they can pitch their tent where they will—as I have done—and actually turn this stage into a two-day delight. But for those intent on a bed for the night, a long push will be necessary. The choice is yours.

From the terrace in front of the *refuge* is a splendid view of the Vignemale's cirque. Gazing at the main peak you see a bold ridge slanting down to the right (north-west) and overhanging in places. This is the Arête de Gaube along which runs the Spanish frontier. The ridge sweeps down to an obvious col, then rises again to Pic des Oulettes, now part of the valley's western wall. The col is the key to our crossing into Spain, and it lies some 455 metres (1493ft) above the hut. It is reached by a vague path aided by occasional cairns, first along the edge of screes, then over grass and rocks beside a stream with interesting views to the Vignemale, now seen in profile, and to the Arête de Gaube which is accessible from the col. As you struggle up the final slopes to the pass you look onto the north-western side of the mountain, to the Clot de la Hount Face which is so different from that of the great north wall.

Once on the pass a new world is revealed. Spain lies below, but at this point it is merely an enclave for across the Ara Valley to the west the mountains are French mountains, and beyond them lies the Marcadau Valley. But the Ara soon leaves all trace of France behind, for it plunges southward into a land of baked sierras on its way to the Ebro, and via that thirsty river to the Mediterranean. On the pass you stand at a watershed in every sense. Behind, in France, you leave gaunt faces of rock and glacial scarves. Ahead, Spain offers rolling hills and aromatic plants that seethe with insect activity.

There is no real path from the col down to the valley bed, but a gully with a stream flowing through it allows a descent to be made without too many difficulties, although in places it is rather steep. At the foot of the gully veer left over rock and grass to traverse steadily towards the infant Ara stream, with a vision ahead to the south of a seemingly untracked valley awaiting exploration.

This upper part of the valley is somewhat barren and dry. At its head a craggy ridge is spiked with the Aiguilles du Chabarrou. West of these runs the Arratille ridge, and to the south-east the ridge that leads to Pic des Oulettes. Screes fan down into a horseshoe scoop in which, somehow, the Ara is born. Lower, screes, boulders and rocks give way to a poor covering of grass, but as the valley falls away and the stream grows in confidence, so the vegetation becomes more lush, and there are flowers and low-growing shrubs and charming natural hanging rock gardens that exploit the spray of intimate cascades and

Above: **Petit Vignemale, seen ahead, is an easy summit reached from Hourquette d'Ossoue. This photograph was taken on Pic des Oulettes after a 3-day snowstorm.**

tumbling streams.

The route leads for several hours along the left bank of the stream. Above, to the east, the Spanish slopes of the Vignemale hold little appeal, but the valley's western wall has plenty of promise for the inquisitive hill walker, with hanging valleys and unknown cols leading to unknown valleys. Through the Ara Valley the walk takes you along sloping hillsides, across level pastures and grassy bluffs. I have seen large herds of isard grazing here, and marmots too. I've watched buzzards and vultures high above, and crickets and salamanders around my boots. And the deeper one goes, the more pungent the fragrance of countless plants wafting in the breeze.

At one point you traverse the steep edge of a minor gorge, and soon after this come to the treeline. There are dappled woods, and in their clearings pleasant-scented clumps of box, so that as you brush past the fragrance is disturbed and it rises to settle upon you as you continue down-valley. Then you come to a dusty track that leads beside the river for a couple of kilometres to the ancient hamlet of Bujaruelo, San Nicolas de Bujaruelo, a huddle of semi-abandoned buildings and a hump-backed bridge, where you can buy refreshments. More often than not there are members of the Guardia Civil here for there is an ancient and still-used mule track that goes up to the Port de Gavarnie, the crossing of which is a more popular (though far less interesting) route than ours. On occasion trekkers may be asked to show their passports—one of the few places in these mountains where such a demand is not infrequently made.

The walk from Bujaruelo to the mouth of

the valley a little north of Torla is all along a rough dirt road that leads through the Ara's gorge. (Halfway between Bujaruelo and the end of the valley, you pass a terraced campsite with a clean and modern restaurant attached.) Shortly after leaving the hamlet the valley is squeezed by towering cliffs, and shadows draw a welcome coolness after the open sun-drenched pastures of the upper reaches. Swifts race screeching among the cliffs. Gorse splashes gold on either side of the river, and trees rustle their leaves about you, but the romance of this gorge is spoiled somewhat by the occasional passing car.

The gorge ends and in its place there comes a sudden flood of light as the Ara opens to join the flow of the Rio Arazas. The track leads to a bridge with the grandiose title of the *Puente de los Navarros*—the Bridge of the Men of Navarre. Ahead the river flows on, now through a much broader, more dazzling stretch of valley. To the left reaches another valley, the valley through which you will walk the following day; Ordesa. But ahead, a little farther along the Ara's valley and standing on a bluff overlooking the river, can be seen the buildings of Torla, a village with a medieval charm about its narrow alleys and dark crowded doorways.

Day 2: Torla to Refugio de Goriz

Torla has its eyes both up and down the valley. Down-valley distant views are bothered with haze. Mountains on either side fold into a blurr of heat and even the river seems sluggish in its stony bed. But up-valley—now that is something else! A great wall of mountain advertises the entrance to the National Park of Ordesa. This is Mondarruego (2848m/9344ft), a broad multi-hued mountain face appearing even higher than it really is, for the village squats no less than 1800 metres below it (5906ft) and one gazes up from the cobbled streets with a sense of wonder at the contrast between the low patchwork valley and the towering brazen cliff. Between valley and mountain wall there is a dense apron of forest, but the rock openly displays itself, revealing its primeval submarine formation in striped bands, and makes a fine sentry to the valley that stretches away to the east of it.

Retracing the route back to the Puente de los Navarros, Ordesa gradually imposes its personality. The way swings to the right away from the Ara's gorge and you peer into the canyon, here seen as an immense shaft of rock with a silver spray of water bursting through. Few mountain regions in Europe can match the wild romantic scenery of Ordesa. It is one of the dramatic highlights of the Pyrénées with its lavishly coloured castellated rocks, its lone pinnacles and forests of pine, silver fir and beech; its dark ravines with pouring cascades, where swifts, rock doves and hoopoes dart to and fro. That great pioneer Ramond de Carbonnières first remarked on the wonders of the canyon in 1802; then came Charles Packe who rediscovered it in the early 1860s. Not a man to allow extravagant phrases to slip easily into his writings, he was clearly impressed by what he found, and more than twenty years later he made a nostalgic return. Steadily you draw nearer until '. . . the fantastic walls and pinnacles, which are the reverse side of the Cirque de Gavarnie, begin to tower over you all glowing red'.

After Mondarruego the eye is held by the slender, surrealistic, almost-completely-detached slab flake of Tozal del Mallo, whose South Face rises almost vertically for 400 metres (1312ft) out of the forests. Then comes the knuckle indent of the Circo de Salarons, and beyond this rise the cliffs of Punta Gallinero.

There is a large car park and a restaurant at the roadhead below Punta Gallinero. This is invariably crowded, but the path that leads on soon loses all but the keenest of walkers. There are neat lawn-like meadows speckled with clumps of box and you pass the entrance to the Circo de Cotatuero whose guardian cliffs are as colourful as any yet seen. There is a novel scrambling route through this cirque leading to the Brèche de Roland, with an ascent of Cotatuero's left-hand wall fascilitated by a number of iron pegs placed by E.N. Buxton, a British ibex hunter, in the 1880s. His book *Short Stalks* gives an evocative picture of the area a hundred years ago, with some charming illustrations by Whymper.

Beyond the mouth of the Cotatuero cirque the path begins to climb among woods with the boom of waterfalls sounding off to the right. On reaching the top of a particularly steep section there is a view onto the Cascada Frachinal, a burst of water, a cloud of spray and a long vista across the woods to the canyon walls stretching away to the west.

Once out of the forest a soft pastureland opens in natural terraces. On either side the canyon walls have lost their towering majesty for you have gained plenty of height, but at the head of the valley the limestone cup of the

Circo de Soaso is topped way above by the South Face of Monte Perdido, third highest Pyrénéan mountain at 3355 metres (11,007ft). From this angle the 'lost mountain' appears rather graceless and certainly much less attractive or formidable than from the north, where it shows a series of glacial tiers undercut by banks of séracs hanging motionless on the face. From these upper meadows of Ordesa, Perdido appears to be little more than a gigantic lump of chalky limestone wearing a few tatters of last winter's snow.

Of more interest is the valley bed across which the route leads. There is a rocky section where the Arazas stream floods down in a series of cascades over one broad step after another. This is Las Grados, as delightful and tranquil a scene as any on this walk. The stream is bordered by spongy cushions of moss and dwarf pines and rock plants resplendent with jewelled goblets of spray. The path picks a way up the rocks to the side of them.

Steep zig-zags ease the ascent of the terraced wall of the Soaso cirque, then the way swings to the north-west, wanders over rough outcrops of rock towards a dry, thirsty landscape and comes to the Refugio de Goriz, base for climbs on all but the North Face of Perdido. After the lush glories of Ordesa the country

Above: **Wandering down the Ara's valley you catch the full glory of Spain's warmth. In the breeze drifts a fragrance unique to these southern valleys in the heart of the Pyrénées. All and everything makes a dramatic contrast to the French side of the mountains.**

around the Goriz hut appears incredibly desolate, empty, savage even.

There has been a hut here for a very long time. In the first edition of his *Guide to the Pyrénées,* published in 1862, Charles Packe wrote of one of the earliest of these huts: 'The *cabane* is one of the usual dirty little stone boxes, just capable of holding four packed side by side.' Later he was even more scathing when he described it as 'a nest of filth'. Today's *refugio,* built in 1963 by the *Federación Española de Montañismo* (FEM), is a considerable improvement!

Day 3: Refugio de Goriz to Gavarnie

The route to the Brèche de Roland leads through a barren stony desert, a landscape littered with the skeletons of dying mountains. There is very little vegetation, hardly any water. There are no trees, no meadows, no glaciers or fields of snow in summer. A parched, lifeless wilderness. But there are long and interesting views. Long views out to the haze of distant Spain; interesting views over the head of the Cotatuero cirque, or up to the frontier ridge where the rocky architecture is curious, to say the least. And then, as you emerge through the large U-shaped gap of the Brèche, a remarkably different view appears. It is one of the wonders of this stage of the walk; the dissimilarity of one side of the watershed from the other. There are few other places in these mountains where such contrasts are so dramatically shown.

Leaving the Goriz hut a path takes the walker bound for the Brèche de Roland across Nature's demolition site, a battleground of rock and scree and huge boulders. It is a peaceful, almost silent land where no birds sing and few streams gurgle. Paint splashes on rocks and a few small cairns direct the way where no path is evident on the ground. You cross a Death Valley-like region, over the limestone desert of the Plan de San Ferlus with a hint of the depths of Cotatuero off to the left, and then quite steeply ascend up to the Collardo de Descargot where one gains the initial sight of the frontier ridge—first with the slender breach of the so-called False Brèche, then the Brèche de Roland itself.

A short distance to the north-west of the Descargot col lies the entrance to the ice cavern of the Grotte Casteret, one of the natural wonders of the Pyrénées discovered by the great French speleologist Norbert Casteret in 1926 and described so graphically in his classic book, *Ten Years Under the Earth.* To explore this cave properly requires head torches, ropes and crampons.

Going up to the Brèche the way leads tightly against the right-hand wall of the Casque du Marboré and is aided by a length of steel cable. A few moments later you stand on the borders of France and Spain astride sunshine and shadow. The world takes on an entirely new aspect.

To the left of the Brèche de Roland, about an hour or so away, rises the Taillon (3144m/10,315ft). Despite being the easiest three thousand metre summit in these mountains, it offers a wonderful panorama and is highly recommended for those with time and energy to tackle it. There are no technical difficulties at all; it is simply a steep walk on a clear trail all the way from the Brèche.

The descent into France heads down a short, easy glacier devoid of crevasses. To the right the great walls of the Cirque de Gavarnie curve round in a dramatic horseshoe. Across the far side the feathery waterfall of the *Grande Cascade* pours from a lip below the summit cliffs of Pic du Marboré, but one can only guess at its landing place for it falls way out of sight.

At the foot of the glacier stands the ever-busy Refuge des Sarradets, otherwise known as the Brèche de Roland hut. It occupies an airy position with fine views across the cirque, and from here you are faced with a choice of routes down to Gavarnie. The easiest way heads westward along a clear PNP footpath to the Port de Gavarnie, then down via the gentle Vallée de Pouey Aspé. An alternative route into the Pouey Aspé cuts away from the Port de Gavarnie path a little beyond the Taillon Glacier, and drops very steeply over rough ground to the green swathe of valley below. But the finest descent route of all plunges from the hut to the east down the steep cliffs of the cirque into the stony bed far below. There are smooth worn steps of rock to descend at the *Echelle des Sarradets,* and extra caution is advised before tackling it. The views on this descent are quite magnificent, but the route is tricky in mist and could be dangerous in wet weather.

If you descend via the Vallée de Pouey Aspé an easy green terrace of hillside leads safely down to Gavarnie, but if tackling the cirque route, the final valley plod to Gavarnie will be alongside strings of tourist-laden donkeys and ponies. The solitude of the higher mountains is all too quickly lost.

WALK 10: Through the Valleys of Lutour and Gaube

Location: South of Lourdes and accessible from Cauterets.
Distance: 27kms (16¹/2 miles).
Time Required: 2 days.
Type of Walk: Fairly energetic, but mostly on good paths. Some steep rough sections, especially in the crossing of Col d'Arraillé. A mixture of woodland, valley and mountain to give a constant variety of scenery.
Base: Cauterets.
Accommodation: Refuge d'Estom (1804m/5919ft), also Refuge des Oulettes de Gaube (2151m/7057ft)
Map: IGN Carte de Randonnées No.3: *Béarn* 1:50,000.

Trout Streams and Tumbling Cascades—A Two-Day Tour

Overnight snow turned to rain as we descended to Gavarnie. Clouds hung low on the cirque face to obscure any view and little streams ran through the deserted, manure-littered street. There were no coachloads of tourists, no donkeys or ponies waiting to be ridden to the Hotel du Cirque. All the postcard stands were covered in polythene and dragged indoors out of the rain. There was an air of sullen dejection about the place as a cold wind gusted along the valley and Alan Payne and I, splashing our way to a steamed-up bar, reckoned that summer had played itself out. There was no point in considering what might have been; our gamble with late September had not paid off.

Over large warming cups of coffee we discussed strategy. To return home now, when there were still a few days left, was to admit too readily to defeat. Yet the forecast was far from promising and there was little to be achieved by sitting out the remainder of the holiday in the bars of Gavarnie. That was not what either of us had gone to the Pyrénées for.

Above: **Lac de Gaube**—a popular site for more than a century—on the way from Pont d'Espagne to the Vignemale.

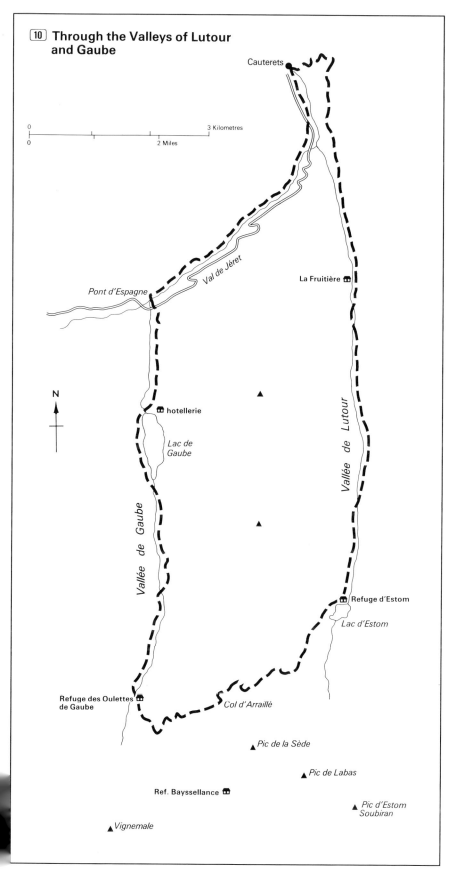

10 Through the Valleys of Lutour and Gaube

Cauterets

0   3 Kilometres
0   2 Miles

Val de Jéret

La Fruitière

Pont d'Espagne

N

hotellerie

Lac de Gaube

Vallée de Lutour

Vallée de Gaube

Refuge d'Estom

Lac d'Estom

Refuge des Oulettes de Gaube

Col d'Arraillé

Pic de la Sède

Pic de Labas

Ref. Bayssellance

Pic d'Estom Soubiran

Vignemale

Out of dejection came inspiration. Alan's eyes suddenly gleamed. 'If we have to spend the rest of the trip getting cold and wet, let's go to you-know-where,' he suggested.

Of course; the Vallée de Lutour! It was not so far away, and we'd used it as a bolt-hole before. A lovely valley, long and narrow and with a fine stream gambolling through it. At its head a secretive little amphitheatre cradled the tarns of Estom Soubiran. Below them, another tarn with a *refuge* beside it. In the middle reaches of the valley a series of cascades conjured their own rainbows. Isard were often seen on the rocky lower slopes of the walling mountains and the woods were busy with red squirrels. At the end of the short approach track stands a small *hôtellerie* with a café-bar where you can sit on a wet morning and watch the clouds tumble. Come rain or shine the *patron* would invariably be found thigh-deep in the stream fishing for the trout that would find their way onto the evening menu, while his wife and daughter ran the bar in his absence. (When age has worked its mischief and I can no longer walk and climb, I've promised myself that I'll take a rod and line—without hook attached— and spend my time gazing vacantly into the Gave de Lutour.)

It was still raining as we reached Cauterets, and raining even harder in the Vallée de Lutour. There was no respite, the mountains were running with streams and the valley growing more soggy by the hour. That night I was woken by the thunder of a rockfall caused by the incessant downpour, and I lay in a state of unease wondering by what touch of madness we had been driven here.

But morning dawned with a kiss of magic. The rain had ceased, clouds were lifting, and as they did, so they revealed a white coating of snow that glistened in the early strain of sunlight. All the peaks at the head of our valley had grown overnight. In their new livery they had attained the stature of proud giants. Presented with such a surprise gift, Alan and I were anxious to get out there among them.

There are many delightful valleys in the Pyrénées—far more than the mere handful mentioned within the pages of this book. There are others with steeper, higher, more challenging and memorable mountains than those of Lutour. There are richer collections of tarns, better pastures, bigger rivers, more dramatic waterfalls than will be found here. Yet there is something undeniably attractive about the Vallée de Lutour that makes it rather special, and days spent within it have been, without exception, days to remember.

West of Lutour, and running parallel with it, is the valley of Oulettes de Gaube. This too, is a magnificient valley, but far better known than its neighbour, for there is easy access to it by way of *télésiege* from Pont d'Espagne. During high season scores of tourists make a daily excursion as far as Lac de Gaube, where they bask in the sun, picnic by the lake and cool themselves with drinks from the *hôtellerie* that overlooks it from the northern shore. At the head of the valley stands the magnificent, yet gaunt, North Face of the Vignemale.

By linking the two valleys with a crossing of a 2500 metre (8200ft) pass, a fine two-day loop trip can be achieved. Yet although only two days will be required to walk the circuit—to and from Cauterets—they will be quite hard days, and indeed the valleys themselves hold so much of interest that given sufficient time, two whole days could easily be spent exploring each one of them.

The Route

In Cauterets take the GR10 footpath as it winds steeply among woods up the eastern hillside behind the Thermes de César, and continue to climb after the path forks, at which point GR10 branches left. Soon after this, the path veers off to the right (south) and traverses the heavily wooded hillside, rises gently above the lower reaches of Val de Jéret, and enters the Vallée de Lutour. Follow the path through the valley, keeping on the eastern bank of the stream most of the way, until shortly before reaching Refuge d'Estom, a small mountain hut with room for twenty. Meals are available here between mid June and mid October when the guardian is in residence.

From the *refuge* take the higher of the two paths above the left bank of Lac d'Estom, and follow it towards the hanging valley of Arraillé, seen off to the south-west. The path works a tiring route through this somewhat wild hanging valley, reaches Col d'Arraillé (2583m/8474ft), then descends to Refuge des Oulettes de Gaube below the North Face of the Vignemale.

Continue past the *refuge* on a clear path that takes you down-valley, past the Lac de Gaube and through woods to the Cauterets road a short distance below Pont d'Espagne in the Val de Jéret. Bear left to the bridge, cross over and then head downstream on a GR10 *variante* all the way to La Raillère, and from there along the road to Cauterets.

Day 1: Cauterets to Lac d'Estom

With its eleven natural springs, Cauterets grew rapidly as a spa town, and it ranks today as one of the most important of many such thermal resorts in the Pyrénées. However, for our purposes it has two factors that put it high on the list of mountain centres; the first is that it is accessible by public transport, being linked conveniently with Lourdes by bus, and the second is that it is a particularly good town in which to stock up with provisions for a few days' trekking. There is an undercover market, several supermarkets, bakeries, mountain equipment shops, and bookshops selling IGN maps and guidebooks (in French) for a host of walks and climbs in the neighbouring area. For the motorised walker it makes a worthy base, too, for there are plenty of accessible valleys nearby in which a wide variety of outings are possible. It also boasts a guides' bureau in the main street, and is a major ski resort in winter.

Heading up through the woods on the initial climb out of Cauterets, the beginning is harsh, but as the town lies in a steep bowl of mountains there are few alternatives, other than the easy option of taking a taxi to the mouth of the Vallé de Lutour. But having gained the first hundred metres or so the path eases and you make a steady rising traverse, heading south in woodland shade for some time, emerging only after you've entered the valley proper above the splendid Cascade de Lutour. A broad track leads as far as La Fruitière, the little *hôtellerie*, and a clear path continues beyond it.

The mountains at the head of the valley now begin to present their credentials, but of more immediate impact is the glorious cascade which comes dancing over a short terrace of rock bordered with pine trees and a lush undergrowth of shrubbery. Beyond this white foaming extravaganza there are rough pasture-lands with woods on the left and stony slopes on the right. Wandering up here on two separate occasions I've watched herds of isard scrabbling among the boulders on the far side of the stream; the stream which here marks one of the boundaries of the National Park.

The way leads past an unusual little hut tucked among rocks and trees, and soon after this a minor path cuts away to the left. This offers an interesting route via Col de Culaus across the eastern wall of the valley and down to the village of Gèdre below Gavarnie; another of the many options available for energetic excursions round here. On the way to the col, this path visits Refuge Russell, a small,

Right: **Above Lac de Gaube a sturdy footbridge takes the path over the stream as it emerges from a narrow, rocky cleft.**

unmanned hut owned by the Touring Club de France and named after Count Henry Russell, the great eccentric of Vignemale fame. Unfortunately the hut has been subjected to mindless vandalism and was last reported to be in a very sorry condition. Considering the effort required to reach it, one questions the mental stability of those responsible for mistreating such a potentially important shelter.

In true Pyrénées style, the Vallée de Lutour rises in steps, dividing small grassy plains known as *jasses*. Between several of these steps more waterfalls come crashing through dark chasms that they've cut for themselves over thousands of years of industry. In the spring thaw, and especially after heavy rain, the booming of these waterfalls is clearly heard as you approach, and the spray thrown by them catches individual haloes of colour to pattern the smooth rocks behind.

Above one such waterfall you come to the final 'step' of the valley and there, overlooking a most attractive tarn, squats Refuge d'Estom. Views from it are delightful, for a short distance away to the south Pic de la Sède, Pic de Labas, Pouey-Mourou, Soum d'Aspé and Malh Arrouy cluster together to form the ragged horseshoe of Estom Soubiran and the headwall of the Lutour. Given time to spare, a day based around this hut will allow an exploration of that cirque. A path leads up into it on a journey of discovery among half a dozen tarns of varying size, and from them the possibility of a rather difficult continuing route over Col des Gentianes (2729m/8953ft) to the Refuge Bayssellance—base for climbs on the Vignemale. (Experienced trekkers attracted to such an outing could extend it as a circuit by crossing Hourquette d'Ossoue above the Bayssellance hut, descending part-way into the valley of Oulettes de Gaube, then crossing Col d'Araillé back into the Vallée de Lutour.)

Day 2: Lac d'Estom to Cauterets

An early start is advised for the long walk back to Cauterets. To begin with there will be nearly 800 metres (2625ft) of height to gain before the pass is topped, followed by a good many kilometres of valley to descend. In addition there will be no shortage of distractions en route to delay you.

The path climbs steeply in places on the rising traverse from the hut to the entrance to Araillés hanging valley, but all the way to it you are presented with the pleasing spectacle of Lutour's shapely headwall, and when you

pause for a moment to look back, Lac d'Estom shimmers in the morning light while all the length of the valley beams its farewell. The hanging valley is, by comparison, a stone desert, rough underfoot and with barely a scrap of vegetation to relieve its savage countenance. Yet up here we saw two or three isard, and marmots sent their shrill whistle into orgasms of echo among the crags.

Descending on the western side of the pass you first look across the Gaube valley to Pic des Oulettes, on whose two shoulders dip easy saddles that lead into Spain. Then off to your left you suddenly find yourself peering at a huge grey slab of a wall, almost pear-shaped and tapering to a fine-looking summit. Slicing it to the east is a deep cleft, choked with snow and ice, and to the side of this another smooth slab. Only when you're down in the valley near the Oulettes de Gaube hut is it possible to view properly the quartet of peaks that make up the north-facing cirque which blocks this new valley: Petit Vignemale, Pointe Chausenque, Piton Carré and finally, Pique Longue—the Vignemale itself. It is without question one of the most remarkable mountain sights in all the Pyrénéan range.

It is tempting to rest at the hut, to buy a drink from the guardian and sit outside, back against the wall, and simply gaze at the Vignemale. It rises in a stupendous shaft of smooth grey stone out of a brief ruck of glacier. Below that dying icefield spreads a smooth flood-plain, streams meandering across it to unite not far from the hut. It is certainly a view that I will never tire of. I've seen it curtained between layers of mist. I've gazed on it plastered in snow. I've seen it bathed in cloudless sunshine and lit by the silver beams of the moon. I've stood beneath that face and peered up at it, and I've dangled my legs from the summit and gone dizzy with the horror of exposure beneath my feet. The Vignemale and its near neighbours simply dominate the scene and impress themselves indelibly upon your memory.

Tearing yourself away, cross the footbridge below the hut and follow the clear path heading northwards down-valley. It takes you over rough pitted meadows, through boulder fields and gravelly plains. Then, crossing the stream again, this time to the right bank, the path makes a steady descent to a new level, and having lost some height you look back to see a long spout of a cascade pouring from the upper sill of the valley in an arc of spray to the snaking pastures below.

Above: **Midway along the Vallée de Lutour this ancient** *cabane* **offers primitive emergency shelter.**

A little later you cross another footbridge beside a smaller cascade that comes booming from a tight rocky cleft, descend to a marshy plain studded with clumps of pine, and come to the shores of Lac de Gaube.

Along with the Cirque de Gavarnie this is one of the 'sights of the Pyrénées', known and fêted for well over a hundred and fifty years. Early visitors to Cauterets would invariably take a donkey or horseback ride through the Val de Jéret to Pont d'Espagne, and from there on a winding mule-track to the lake. This journey was often the limit of mountain adventure for the majority of tourists—as indeed it is today, although today's visitor will invariably drive as far as Pont d'Espagne and then take the *télésiege* in order to minimise physical effort!

In 1832 William and Sarah Pattison, a young British couple on their honeymoon, met with tragedy when boating on the lake. He fell overboard and she, attempting to save him, was pulled into the water and they drowned together. Or so the story goes. The death of the couple, so soon after marriage, was suitably captured in melodramatic Victorian verse by Richard Monckton Milnes, which no doubt helped to vest the site with an additional morbid interest, though it is doubtful whether

many of the holiday makers who gather round its shores today know much about it.

Two paths lead north from the end of the lake. The left-hand route takes you to the *télésiege*, while the right-hand path, almost paved in its lower reaches, goes down through the woods to the Val de Jéret near Pont d'Espagne. Once on the road bear left for a short distance and cross the wild foaming cataracts of the river over the Pont d'Espagne itself, then break away on the route of the GR10 *variante* which leads down-valley beside the river and along the edge of steep forested slopes.

The river, born in the Marcadau and strengthened first by the Gaube torrent and then by that from the Vallée de Lutour, is a thunderous wash of powerful cascades and bullying currents. Tennyson wrote of it:

'All along the valley, stream that flashest white,
Deepening thy voice with the deepening of the night.'

One waterfall after another comes roaring beside you as you slog down towards Cauterets. A furious companion it is, but one whose spirit is the very spirit of the hills, and one that will be sorely missed when at last you come off the path at la Raillère and face the final stretch of tarmac that leads into town.

WALK 11: The Spanish Canyons Tour

Location: Entirely in Spain, south of the Cirque de Gavarnie. By road the easiest approach to Ordesa is from the Col du Pourtalet, south to Biescas, then east to Torla. Alternatively, through the Bielsa Tunnel, south to Ainsa, then north-west to Boltaña and Torla. The majority of this walk lies in the *Parque Nacional del Valle de Ordesa*.

Distance: 44kms (27 miles).

Time Required: 3 days.

Type of Walk: Very varied. There is much height to gain and lose and, although the paths are mostly good, the terrain can be extremely rough, with some dramatically steep descents. There are stretches without any paths at all, and on the final day a total absence even of guiding cairns. It is a walk only to be attempted in good conditions.

Start/Finish: Ordesa car park.

Accommodation: Mountain hut (Refugio de Goriz), and private accommodation in Nerín.

Maps: Editorial Alpina: *Parque Nacional del Valle de Ordesa* 1:40,000.

IGN Carte de Randonnées No. 4: *Bigorre* 1:50,000.

A Three-Day Exploration of the Ordesa and Anisclo Canyons

Huge cliffs, multi-coloured and awe-inspiring . . . deep shadowed canyons full of mystery and wonder . . . waterfalls pouring in ribbons of spray . . . jade-green pools dappling their light onto water-smoothed rocks . . . dense forests and gentle, broadleaved woodlands . . . a high limestone wilderness, barren and apparently lifeless . . . 'lost' villages by-passed by the modern world.

This walk has them all, and much more besides.

Monte Perdido (to the French, Mont Perdu—the Lost Mountain) rises as a great limestone hub with spectacular valleys radiating from it. To the north, in France, the valleys are cut by the Gaves de Pau and Estaubé, each one flowing from dramatic cirques. In Spain to the south-east runs the lovely Pineta, its broad stream bordered by a lush shrubbery and delicate birches, with

Above: **The final stage of the tour of the Spanish canyons involves the dramatic descent of Ordesa's great south wall.**

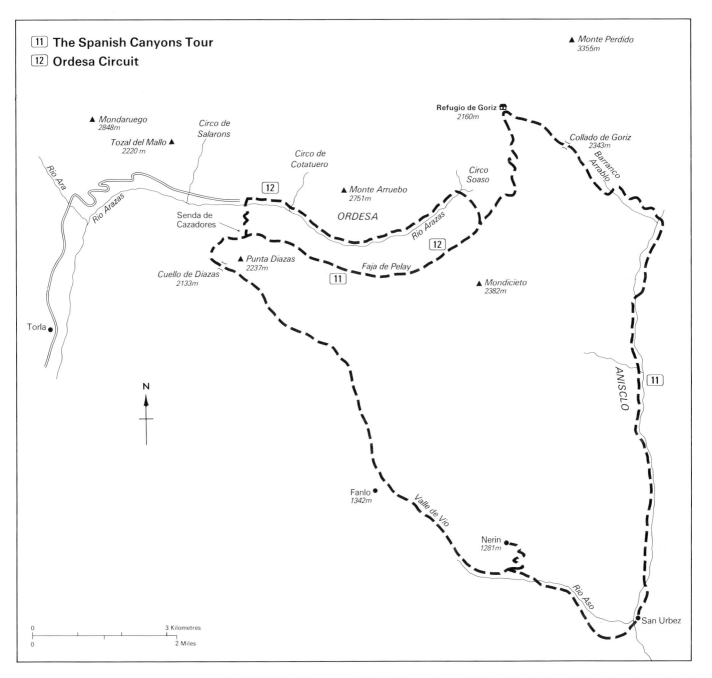

splendid high ridges to wall it. Almost due south of Perdido a great bleached plateau has been sliced as if by a twisted knife blade: that slice is Anisclo. And to the south-west falls the magnificent canyon of Ordesa.

Gazing from the summit of Perdido (3355m/ 11,007ft) the eye is inevitably drawn to the deep shafting Spanish valleys. Belloc called them *'clefts* sunk deep into the stuff of the world and bounded by precipices upon either side'. From each one there emanates a sense of compelling mystery—those yawning gulfs,

filled with shadow. What lies down there? What wonders are there to be revealed?

The *Parque Nacional del Valle de Ordesa* is visited elsewhere in this book, and is traversed on the Two Parks Walk. But our route through it on this circuit is a different one. Different, but no less interesting or spectacular, while Anisclo—the Vallée de Niscle—is treated to an exploration as delightful and rewarding as it is challenging. It is not a walk to be attempted by those without a steady head for heights. Nor is it a walk for the unfit, nor one that should be attempted in unsettled conditions. Heat and accompanying thirst can cause problems. Go prepared for both, but do not be daunted by either. Careful preparation can lessen their impact, but keep on the alert for potential difficulties.

The Route

The walk may be started either in the delightful medieval village of Torla just south of the entrance to the National Park, where hotel accommodation is available and there are two campsites nearby or, for those with their own transport, in Ordesa itself. Motorists are warned, though, that overnight parking is forbidden in the official Ordesa car park. Those intending to head off into the wilderness for two or three days should leave their vehicles alongside the road that leads into the National Park.

While the Two Parks Walk heads directly up-valley through the Ordesa Canyon, this route climbs steeply up its south wall to gain a high terrace path known as the Faja de Pelay. This takes you eastwards to the head of the valley, and from there to the Goriz hut on the barren flanks of Monte Perdido. Although it is a reasonably short day's journey, it is a somewhat arduous one.

Day Two leads from Goriz to the crossing of a minor col, and from there on an airy descent into the head of the Anisclo Canyon. And what a joy this is! Waterfalls and tumbling streams and the beckoning unknown of the lower valley. The walk south through the canyon is full of interest every step of the way, and when at last you emerge where the Rio Aso flows in from the north-west, so the scenery makes another dramatic change. The route now heads up the Valle de Vió on a road above the Aso stream, then a side turning winds up to the little village of Nerín for overnight accommodation. (Camping is very difficult in this valley because of the lack of water.)

The final leg of the walk takes you to the head of the valley; a dry, seemingly forgotten land littered here and there with low walls of one-time farmsteads and corrals, now deserted and left to the crickets and lizards. Crossing the Cuello de Diazas, you make for the lip of the Ordesa Canyon and plunge down on a spectacular path hewn in the great southern wall. It is a most dramatic way to end an unforgettable three-day walk.

Although it would be possible to tackle this walk as a backpacking exercise, as has already been noted, camping is difficult in the Valle de Vió. There is a water source in the valley, but it may not be permanent. Better to travel light, spend a night at the Goriz hut and another in Nerín. Meals are available in both places.

Day 1: Ordesa to Refugio de Goriz

In summer Ordesa seems to draw heat from the lowlands. That heat is then trapped by the soaring canyon walls that reflect and magnify it. Barely a breeze finds its way in, and midday out of shade can be torture for those with a fair skin. Yet once out of the constrictions of the valley bed the temperature is much more favourable and the walker steps from one island of shade to another catching whatever air is moving. This walk, happily, makes most of its height-gain in the shadow of forest, on the cooler side of the valley.

There is a bridge leading over the Rio Arazas from the end of the road, and a path which takes you straight away into a pleasant woodland glade, fragrant with pine and box trees, and then begins to work a way up the steepening hillside. This path is the Senda de Cazadores, a well-made, alpine-like trail gaining height in nicely graded zig-zags, all the while among trees and only occasionally allowing a sudden brief glimpse out to the vast line of cliffs on the far side of the valley. For maybe an hour you wander steadily upwards, then come onto the traversing Faja de Pelay and bear left.

Within ten minutes you come to a shelter with a spectacular viewpoint overlooking the canyon. Almost directly opposite there is the deep indent of the Circo de Cotatuero with a milky-white cascade breaking the shadows. To one side of it stands the fabulous multi-coloured Fraucata wall of Monte Arruebo; on the other, Punta Gallinero and beyond that, the broad flake of Tozal del Mallo. Above them all you can make out the curious shapes of mountains that form the frontier ridge, and it is hard to believe that those ghostly formations actually drop northward into the Cirque de Gavarnie with terraces of snow and ice and huge fantail cascades damping their cliffs. From the Faja de Pelay you gaze upon an almost unreal landscape; a vertical landscape erected above a mattress of green. There is so much of it—a photograph cannot do it justice.

The Faja de Pelay is a belvedere of delight. It takes you on a fairly level course way above the valley, sometimes among trees, sometimes

Above: **Aniclo's Canyon is
much narrower than that of
Ordesa, and the descent
through it leads among
fragrant shrubberies of box.**

which you now find yourself.

In its apparently lifeless state of limbo, there's an air of fascination about this bleached wilderness of stone that is difficult to comprehend. It can be an eerie place, but at night, if you're lucky enough to have a clear sky and a rising moon, the whole place glows in the silver lunar beams, and the silence of a hot afternoon is replaced by the sound of gushing water over cooling rock from the hut's nearby spring.

Day 2: Refugio de Goriz to Nerín

An early start is recommended, not simply because of the distance to be covered, nor indeed on account of the terrain (which is demanding enough to warrant it), but in order to give you time to stop here and there to absorb the glories of Anisclo. There will be plenty of individual features crying out for close examination. There will be tempting places to sit by the river and dream. Or to leap in for a swim on a hot afternoon. There will be flowers and insects to gaze at; cliff faces for rock climbers to plan future routes on; woodlands to get lost in. Oh, Anisclo is a magical place! It's far too good to hurry through.

With good visibility the route to the Collado de Goriz should cause no problems, but with swirling mists difficulties are sure to arise. This is in any case, a day worth setting aside for fine weather. Fortunately, in summer the weather in the Pyrénées is often brilliantly clear for weeks on end.

It is not far from the Goriz hut to the col, and with a little under 200 metres of height to gain, half an hour should see you there. The col is a broad saddle slung between the southern slopes of Sum de Ramond and the steeper rise of Punta Custodia, and it looks over a surprisingly soft bowl of pasture with the hint of Anisclo beyond.

Going down into that bowl is a welcome change, for you leave behind the bleak acres of bare stone and replace it with soft grass and a lovely clear stream that pours into a great cleft; the Barranco Arrablo and its ravine. This ravine, dramatic though it certainly is, is merely a leader for the Anisclo Canyon—an introduction and an access route. But as you come to the lip of the gorge it seems impossible that a route could exist down the excessively steep terraces, other than by abseiling. Then you find a line of cairns that lead to the key passage which takes you down the first band of

on open, almost pastoral sections; sometimes broad and gentle, sometimes narrow and with a little exposure. But it's an easy path all the way, and the only difficulties arise from the constant urge to stop and simply gaze at the unfolding panorama.

Eventually the lower forests give way to valley pastures closed at their head by a grey cliff face rising in terraces to bleak slopes, devoid of vegetation, and with the big bald dome of Monte Perdido looming over all. The path of the Faja de Pelay forks. One branch drops into the Soaso meadows, the other climbs among rocks to work round the terraces of the amphitheatre, now full in the sun and with the heat of day reflected from the limestone. The path continues to gain altitude, rising from one terrace to the next, and then heading up to the empty wilderness where the Refugio de Goriz provides almost the only water supply for a very long way. Although the walk has occupied little more than half a day, you'll no doubt be quite content to stop, and to laze away the remaining hours in quiet contemplation of the unique landscape in cliffs, then along a level grassy terrace starred with edelweiss. (If you miss the initial cairn, it is quite likely that you'll not find the route down. On no account should you attempt to descend the cliffs other than on the marked route.)

Dropping from terrace to terrace the route becomes surprisingly easy. It brings you to the stream which you cross on water-smoothed slabs, and then descends slopes of grit and scree relieved by cushions of a very spiky plant, coming soon to the first clumps of pine and alpenrose, with views opening into the main canyon that runs at right angles ahead. Then suddenly the magnificent Fon Blanca waterfall is seen pouring in a great burst of spray from a rock face nearby. It is a splendid sight, and one that will have keen photographers reaching for their cameras. But be sparing with your film as there is plenty more to photograph later.

The final descent out of the Arrablo ravine and into the main valley, is among tangles of shrubbery and half-hidden boulders. Fighting these you soon come to the graduated steps of the Anisclo stream, seen cascading in a series of minor falls. This idyllic place demands another rest, for by now the splendours of the canyon will have captured your imagination, and it will be a long time before the magic fades.

A hundred years ago it was Franz Schrader, the great French Pyrénéan explorer, who made the first detailed study of Anisclo during the late 1870s. Charles Packe also descended the valley on two or three occasions and wrote in rapturous tones about it. Yet somehow it has remained generally unsung, while neighbouring Ordesa has been proclaimed far and wide. There was even a plan in comparatively recent years to dam the lower canyon, which would have resulted in part of its splendour being flooded. Now, however, Anisclo has been incorporated into the Ordesa National Park and we may hope for a complete protection of this unique region.

There is a path leading down-valley beside the stream. At first on grass, then among shrubs and low-growing trees, climbing here and there with the river soon carving a deeper trench way below. Then the path eases to traverse the monstrous cliffs that rise on the left bank—there is another path lower, on the right bank, and the two converge later when the left-hand trail drops in zig-zags to a footbridge and crosses over. The canyon is extremely narrow in places, the cliffs looming high overhead—even overhanging in places—

displaying a wonderful palette of colours, with individual pines growing on impossible ledges way above.

Following the path above the right bank of the river you are soon among woodlands; beech, pine and yew, soft underfoot with deep carpets of dried leaves, while the beech trunks are furry with moss or draped with straggly beards of lichen. These woods conceal the river for much of the way, but here and there you gaze down into beautiful tempting pools, or at waterfalls pouring foam into hidden gulfs, or

Above: **Jade green pools dapple the light deep in Anisclo's Canyon and make inviting picnic sites for passing trekkers.**

wander beside a calm region where the river runs easily along horizontal channels of smooth rock. Seldom are you out of range of its song. Often the path leads through natural avenues of box. Wild strawberries are there for the picking beside the trail and in open sunny glades. Every step of the way is a step of enchantment.

After several hours the path is returned to the left bank. The canyon begins to swing south-eastward and opens to accommodate the entrance of the Valle de Vió. You wander past the little shrine of San Urbez (or San Urbano), cross the river once more on a modern bridge built above a splendid medieval hump-backed affair, and join the road going up into the Valle de Vió.

The descent of the Anisclo Canyon now complete, the 6 kilometre (3¹/₂ mile) walk to Nerín comes as something of an anti-climax. Not that the Valle de Vió is uninteresting, it is heavily wooded, but occasional views lead the eye once more into Anisclo, or across to tiny hamlets on the far hillside, and as you gain height, so a view opens behind to reveal the lovely shape of Peña Montanesa. Anisclo was special, very special, and the hours of walking through it will have brought on a weariness that is inevitably aggravated by the steady incline of the road.

Nerín reclines on a grassy knoll high above the valley, with terraced pastures below and bare hillsides above. (A track leads over the upper hillside and makes a shadeless return to the Goriz hut for those with plans other than ours.) The village is almost archaic in appearance. In the square, facing the water supply, there is a house advertising *refugio*, but the better plan for overnight accommodation here is to enquire at the single restaurant; a simple but friendly plàce.

Day 3: Nerín to the Ordesa Canyon

Since the majority of this stage of the walk is across open countryside without any shade, it is advisable to set out very early—certainly before dawn and with water bottles filled. You begin by returning downhill to the valley road and then walk up-valley almost as far as Fanlo, a romantic-looking village perched on a commanding hilltop, with access to the 'outside world' by way of another valley that cuts away south-westward behind it.

Shortly before Fanlo a track breaks off to the right and almost at once it is possible to see the pass you are making for. Way ahead, on the ridge of hills blocking the valley, Punta Diazas is a prominent conical peak with an obvious saddle to the left of it. (The French map does not recognise Punta Diazas, but calls it Punta Acuta). The pass itself, Cuello de Diazas, lies at an altitude of 2133 metres (6998ft), and will take about three hours to reach from Fanlo.

The track is clear for much of the way, winding with determination into a big landscape of scrub-covered hills with natural forests taking over a large portion in the west. Once these hills were fertile. There would have been pastures here grazed by sheep or cattle, but there has been a drift away from the mountains and the land is now largely deserted. There are low walls that represent one-time settlements or field boundaries. Box trees now grow from them and the hills are a mass of aromatic plants and spiky cushions and thistles.

When the track gives out you make your way as best you can across this strangled land, keeping the pass in sight and working up towards it. The final haul is a steep, shadeless, tiring stretch, and when at last you reach the Cuello de Diazas, it is with no small sense of relief. But then you find an unsurfaced road along which Land-Rover taxis bring tourists from Torla to see this inner wilderness without the effort that you have just made. It's a cruel contrast.

Not far to the north of the pass you will find a path leading to the very lip of Ordesa's canyon. What a dramatic sight unfurls before you, with the canyon wall plunging more than 1000 metres (3281ft) to the valley floor. Yet somehow a path has been created down this wall, and you wander down and down, over rock and scree and grass, in among trees and out over ribs of limestone, with the most incredible views challenging your attention— which should be fully occupied with the demands of the descent.

This path is an extension of the Senda de Cazadores which began the walk, so you will come to recognise features from the outward route. Crossing the Faja de Pelay, make the final descent to the valley through familiar forest, the temperature rising as you lose height, until the forest ends and you cross the bridge over the Arazas without shade, and feel the enervating strength of the Spanish sun as never before.

Fortunately at the restaurant near the car park they keep their drinks in the refrigerator. You'll have earned one.

WALK 12: Ordesa Circuit

Location: South of the Cirque de Gavarnie, and entirely in Spain. The nearest centre is Torla, reached from France by road over the Col de Pourtalet, then south to Biescas and east from there to Torla and the Ordesa National Park.

Distance: 12kms (7¹/₂ miles).

Time Required: 1 day.

Type of Walk: Scenically spectacular, on clear paths through forest and over pasture, but also along a high terrace with some exposure. A short section of steep ascent, and a steep descent at the end of the walk. It is, however, one of the easiest walks in the book.

Start/Finish: Ordesa car park, at the end of the canyon's approach road.

Map: Editorial Alpina: *Parque Nacional del Valle de Ordesa*. 1:40,000.

Guidebook: *Walks and Climbs in the Pyrénées* by Kev Reynolds (Cicerone Press).

A Single-Day's Tour of the Ordesa Canyon

Two walks have already been given through the Ordesa Canyon, but these are routes of passage and Ordesa is such a magnificent valley, and it attracts so many walkers, that it seems advisable to offer a day's outing to give newcomers to the region the opportunity to explore some of the best areas it has on offer. This walk, which combines sections of two previously described outings, is no less a classic for being only a day's length. That day will be quite long enough for most hill walkers.

When you first enter Ordesa from the south it is the towering cliffs forming the northern wall that make the greatest impression. They rise in great coloured bands of limestone out of

Above: **Torla, a lovely medieval village, makes a perfect base for exploring the Ordesa Canyon.**

the mixed forests—some with fantastic shapes to them, like Tozal del Mallo, 'the ruddy pinnacles and bastions towering above the trees for a thousand metres' (Charles Packe). These are mountain walls to lure top-grade climbers with their vertical pitches and nightmarish levels of exposure. But between them are cut narrow cirques, suggestive of dimpled knuckles—enormous knuckles, too! These cirques, of Salarons and Cotatuero, also have amazing routes down them, leading adventurous walkers and climbers to or from the Brèche de Roland—routes made a very long time ago by ibex hunters.

But as you wander up-valley beyond the entrance to the Cotatuero cirque, it is the great waterfalls that dominate the scene. If you go early in the summer, in June for example, there is the constant boom of cascades showering through the shadows as one waterfall after another attempts to outplay its neighbour in volume. It is the power of the Arazas river, after all, that is responsible for Ordesa's deep cleft, though later in the year the river's strength is considerably weakened now that the snow-and-ice fields of Monte Perdido at its head have mostly disappeared from the southern slopes.

Above the forests a high mountain pastureland changes the whole nature of Ordesa. It is soft and gentle, and the walls on either side seem much less severe than before, though the whole scene is overpowered by the bulk of Monte Perdido looming from a brash limestone wilderness ahead.

This part of the walk opens the visitor's eyes to several aspects of the canyon, while the return by way of the high traversing path of the Faja de Pelay will draw out its full drama and illustrate beyond doubt why this National Park should have such magnetic appeal.

The Route

From the large unsurfaced car park at the end of Ordesa's approach road, take the continuing path heading up-valley across open lawn-like meadows dotted here and there with fragrant box trees. The path soon enters forest and begins to climb through dense woods above the river which is now thundering off to the right. The falls are mostly unseen, but on reaching the head of a particularly steep section there is a good view onto Cascada Frachinal. The path climbs on, leaves the forest behind and crosses the pastures leading to the Circo de Soaso.

Near the head of the pastures, cross the stream and take a rising path heading southwest. This is the Faja de Pelay, and it leads as a steadily rising traverse along the steep southern slopes of the valley. With its gentle height-gain and the plunging valley floor, the Faja de Pelay is soon a considerable distance above the valley. It takes you along a panoramic terrace for about 6 kilometres (3½ miles) before making a sudden descent by way of the Senda de Cazadores, bringing you back to the car park once more.

The Walk

The first time I walked through Ordesa I was heavily laden with a fortnight's climbing and camping equipment. Three days previously I had been knee-deep in fresh snow and seriously worried by the threat of avalanche, but Ordesa had been unbelievably hot, with cloudless blue skies and practically no air at all. And certainly no snow anywhere. My partner, Keith Sweeting, and I had spent a long time sitting in the shade at the restaurant until the worst of the day's heat was over, before setting out to walk to the Goriz hut. Even so, the heavy sacks and the energy-sapping afternoon temperature threatened to turn the walk into a misery of suffering.

None of it!

We were so taken with the beauties of the canyon, its coloured rocks and dappled forests, its tempting cirques and thundering cascades, its flashing birds and noisy crickets, its lizards and flowers and intoxicating fragrance, that we forgot the discomfort and walked as in a dream. And so it has been on every subsequent visit.

There will always be crowds of visitors within a short distance of the car park, but the further you walk from it, the fewer people you'll find. The soft meadows, neat and trim and bright with *daphne mezereum* or the purple-pink flowers of the autumn crocus, are soft as a Surrey lawn, incongruous here in Spain with high mountains all around. Then comes the forest walk; all shade, fragrance and birdsong.

Climbing higher I longed to catch a glimpse of the falls that could be heard so clearly crashing through a dark defile off to our right. Then came the point where we could look down onto the great Cascada Frachinal which now showed as a huge spout of foam dropping among rainbows of spray with forest on either side. And the view looking back the way we had come was quite magnificent, for it displayed the great line of cliffs in profile—

Tozal del Mallo in particular standing out like a misplaced Dolomite aiguille.

I remember the surprise as we left the forest behind and wandered easily into that upper region of pasture, stream and lower cliff. The idyllic steps of the Las Grados cascades, bordered by lush greenery, contrasted with the savagery of the limestone wilderness dominated by Monte Perdido ahead. Early evening had drawn a grey scum of cloud from nowhere, and Perdido scowled. But on other visits blue skies have been the norm, and the cascades have dazzled in the sunshine.

Returning along the Faja de Pelay is one of those memorable walks that are instantly recalled years later whenever certain scents come unbidden. Walked on a bright afternoon, the light shining into the canyon ahead is almost liquid-blue. You are drawn along that pathway, over grass slopes and among dwarf pine, juniper and alpenrose, with vistas of wonder growing out of a close horizon. Distance has no meaning. It is the great walls

opposite that hold your attention, and though the path only rises gently, the valley falls away so suddenly that it creates the impression that you've completed a stark ascent.

This dramatic stroll, without difficulty or any real danger, unfolds a world of height and depth as remarkable as any to be found elsewhere in these mountains, and with an ease unmatched by any other area I know. It is a pathway of romance, set out in artistic proportions. None could be disappointed by it.

When at last you come to a small shelter with a projecting walled bay overlooking the depths of the valley, you will know that the descent is about to begin. Soon after leaving it the path forks at a signpost, and you head downhill into the forest once more on the Senda de Cazadores. By this time your legs will be feeling the strain and your knees will soon be like rubber. But what a walk, and what memories to take away with you!

This is, indeed, one of *the* classic walks of the Pyrénées.

Above: **The huge south-facing walls of Ordesa's Canyon are seen clearly on the approach from Torla.**

WALK 13: Gavarnie to Luchon

Above: **With the big West Face of Pico de Posets luring him on, Alan Payne heads down to the valley of the Cinqueta de la Pez through acres of alpenroses now, alas, out of bloom.**

Location: Central Pyrénées, France and Spain, along the frontier ridge.
Distance: 102kms (63 miles).
Time Required: 7 days.
Type of Walk: Fairly demanding with a considerable amount of height gain and loss. Some exposed ridge walking, a little scrambling in one or two places, often without paths and sometimes with no waymarking.
Start: Gavarnie.
Finish: Bagnères de Luchon.
Accommodation: Mountain huts, *pension* or hay barns. One night without accommodation, in which case bivouacking or camping will be necessary.
Maps: IGN Cartes de Randonées No. 4: *Bigorre* & No. 5: *Luchon* 1:50,000. Editorial Alpina *Posets* and *Maladeta-Aneto* 1:25,000.
Guidebooks: *Walks and Climbs in the Pyrénées* by Kev Reynolds (Cicerone Press). *Pyrénées High Level Route* by Georges Véron (Gastons-West Col).

Ridge Walks and Spanish Valleys

By adapting part of the middle section of that great Pyrénéan traverse, the High Level route, an exhilarating walk of about seven days can be achieved. It is a demanding route in places, calling for experience and commitment on one particular stage where bad weather or even a slight accident could have serious consequences. Daily there are high passes to cross. There are stretches of exposed ridge walking with barely an escape route. There are remote valleys to pass through, dramatic cirques, a romantic summer grazing hamlet, big mountains looming overhead—the biggest of all the mountains in the Pyrénées. At the end of most days there will be overnight shelter available, either in mountain huts, *pensions* or haybarns, but the walker must be prepared either to camp or bivouac on at least one occasion, carrying food supplies for a couple of days or so, as well as emergency rations.

The walk begins in France and looks at four cirques in succession—Gavarnie, Estaubé, Troumouse and Barroude—each one very different from the last. It then follows along the frontier ridge, drops into Spain for an introduction to the range's two highest massifs and returns to France again on the final leg through the historic pass of the Port de Venasque. Since at least two of the stages should only be attempted in settled weather, allowances must be made for the possibility of sitting out bad-weather days when planning the walk. But as there are plenty of options available for exploring specific regions along the way—particularly in the Gavarnie, Barroude, Viadós, Estós and Esera districts—a fortnight's holiday could be well spent along this route using up any spare time getting to know more intimately some of the more remote inner valleys.

The walk is ideally suited for those travelling to the Pyrénées by public transport—by rail or by air. Gavarnie is reached by bus from Lourdes, while Luchon (or Bagnéres de Lu-chon, to give the town its full title) has a rail link with Toulouse and/or Tarbes via Mon-trejeau. Food supplies must be carried from the start, for between Gavarnie and Luchon the route visits only one permanent commu-nity, Héas, and that is no more than a sparse hamlet without a single shop, although just two days from the end of the walk you pass within a few kilometres of Benasque, a sizeable village with food and equipment stores, as well as a Post Office and public telephone if required.

Day 1: Gavarnie to Héas

Discounting Lourdes, which is really in the foothills, Gavarnie is without doubt the most visited place in all the Pyrénées; the Cirque de Gavarnie being the best-known feature. Day in and day out through the long weeks of summer streams of cars and motor coaches grind up the long winding road from Lourdes to spill their passengers into the single street of this sin-gularly unattractive little village, which is reminiscent of a wild west township at carnival time. Horses, ponies and donkeys stand teth-ered everywhere. Manure litters the street which is lined with souvenir shops and postcard stands. There is a constant babble of laughter. Crowds stray to and fro, caught in the holiday atmosphere. The bars are crowded, ice cream stalls do a steady trade.

At the head of the valley, four kilometres ($2^1/_2$ miles) from the village, rise the great curving tiers of rock and snow that create the walls of the Cirque de Gavarnie. For something like 1400 metres (4590ft) these walls tower above the valley to a cornice-rimmed crown, the highest point being Pic du Marboré (3248m/10,656ft), the lowest being the base of the Brèche de Roland (2807m/9209ft). The cirque makes an impressive sight, especially in spring when the walls are pouring with feathery cascades. 'It's both a mountain and a wall,' exclaimed Victor Hugo. 'It's the most mysterious of buildings, by the most myster-ious of architects; it's Nature's Coliseum; it's Gavarnie!'

For more than a century there has been a pageant played out in Gavarnie; a pageant and a pilgrimage. Tourists by the score hire donkeys, ponies or horses to take them up-valley as far as the Hôtel du Cirque for a closer view of the cirque and the *Grand Cascade,* an impressive but slender waterfall which sprays from a ledge below Marboré. On arrival at the hotel everyone dismounts stiffly for a quick drink before being carted rather inelegantly back to Gavarnie and the coach ride home.

Then, and only then, do the mountains draw unto themselves the peace and solitude that is their due.

Our route does not necessitate a visit to the cirque however, but instead climbs out of the village and up the eastern hillside over grassy slopes with lovely views to the open book-like faces of the two Pics d'Astazou. On the way to the first col of the trek, which is found a little north of the Pics d'Astazou, the trail wanders past Refuge des Espuguettes. This hut, pro-vided by the PNP authorities in 1973, occupies a splendid position overlooking the unseen valley of the Gave de Pau, with the snowy mass of the Vignemale off to the west and a clear view of the Cirque de Gavarnie to the south. Above the hut, in the ridge that sweeps from the easy Pimené to Pic Rouge de Pailla, an obvious trail crosses through a craggy nick of a pass, the Hourquette d'Alans (2430m/7972ft). It is a fine pass, narrow, rocky, wind-blown, and it takes you out of Gavarnie's clutches and into the valley of Estaubé, at the head of which is another cirque, much smaller and less grand than Gavarnie's, but with a charm of its own. Over the top of the Cirque d'Estaubé you may just catch sight of the summit dome of Monte Perdido standing in Spain.

On the eastern side of the pass the descent

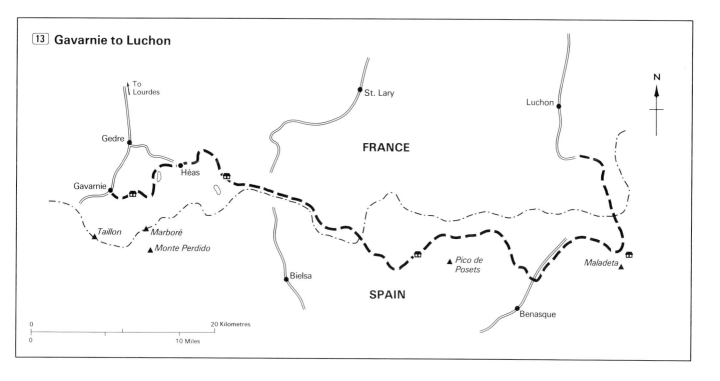

from wind-swept crags to the green pastures below is achieved by numerous zig-zags. Then follows a leisurely valley stroll northwards with a stream for company and cattle grazing on both sides of it. At the northern end of the valley the Gloriettes dam holds back a rock-girt lake, and a service road leads from it down to the valley of the Gave de Troumouse. Once in the valley you are forced to tread tarmac for a further two kilometres as far as the little hamlet of Héas. But once you leave Héas there will be no more road under foot until two days from the end of the walk.

Day 2: Héas to Barroude

Héas is a scattered community consisting of a few houses and barns, a café or two and an historic chapel, and it spreads itself in a rather disorderly fashion among rough pastures below the largest of the amphitheatres in this corner of the mountains, the Cirque de Troumouse. This is a lovely cirque, making even more of a horseshoe than the cirque of Gavarnie, and with several summits along its crest topping the 3000 metre mark, thus maintaining a similar altitude to that of its more illustrious neighbour. From its snowcaps and tiny hidden tarns comes leaping a bois-terous stream to join that of the Gave de Pau in the village of Gèdre below Gavarnie. Sheep and cattle graze on the pasturelands embraced by this great bowl of mountains, and beyond it

on its eastern side lies the Cirque de Barroude, which is Day Two's destination.

Out of Héas the road—and the Cirque de Troumouse—are soon left behind by a steeply climbing path that leads into a high scoop of pasture. This grassland valley seems locked away from the world of cars and tourists. It is a landscape that belongs to a former age, where shepherds keep lonely vigil and only birds and marsh-loving frogs break the peace. There are steep walls rising to the north and east, and it is difficult to work out exactly where a weakness lies to allow escape. But having crossed one or two streams and a marshy area, the path continues on and begins to toil up the hillside towards the Crête des Aguillous. High up, the path has been cut as a ledge which leads to the surprise col of Hourquette de Héas (2608m/ 8556ft), a gain of around 1100 metres (3609ft) since leaving the hamlet of Héas more than three hours before. (Early in the season this pass could well be snow covered, in which case difficulties may be encountered by the inexper-ienced trekker.)

As with the crossing of Hourquette d'Alans above Gavarnie (*hourquette* being the Pyrénean term for a steep pass), this col is also a rocky niche that suddenly reveals a new valley system. To the north a confusion of peaks and ridges represent the outliers of the Néouvielle massif, a nature reserve of much wild charm. But nearer to hand, jagged crests

81

offer a promise of entertaining scrambles for other days, while deep below, on the very edge of the National Park, there gleams the little Lac de Badet.

Down, then, to the head of the valley, followed by a rising traverse to gain the next pass, Hourquette de Chermentas, with yet another fresh valley system opening below. To the right, above grey screes and snow-trapped gullies, a long wall of mountain stretches south-eastwards. It is impossible to guess it at this point, but this great slab is the start of the impressive Barroude Wall. Soon it begins to show itself properly. A rock climber's dream of a wall, rearing steeply for something like 500 metres (1640ft) out of the screes that bank the waters of Lac de Barroude, and stretching for about 3 kilometres from Pic des Aguillous in the north, to Pic de Troumouse on the Spanish border. On the eastern side of the lake a green bluff contains a second, much smaller tarn, and between the two sits the idyllic little Refuge de Barroude.

Days 3 and 4: Barroude to Viadós

The Cirque de Barroude is so peaceful and isolated that it is tempting to succumb to its charms and spend a day or two relaxing here, simply gazing from the green belvedere at the limestone wall opposite, or out to the north-east where distant hills fold into the gulping hint of the Vallée d'Aure. The frontier ridge stands off to the south. From the hut it seems to be blocked by a mound of shale, but a stroll up there gives an astonishing view down into the Spanish Cirque de Barrosa, with a trace of path leading to the valley far below. To one side, gazing from the crest, steep plunging crags topple into mysterious ravines, while across wild ridges to the east a view shows Pico de Posets beckoning. In two days' time you will be in its shadow.

The stage which leads from Barroude to Rioumajou is a demanding one. It follows the frontier crest for several hours, exposed, dry, shadeless. There is only one remote possibility of finding water along the ridge. There is barely one escape route should the weather turn, and when the time comes for the descent to be made to Rioumajou's pastureland, even this is somewhat taxing. But for all that, it's a fine day's trekking. Study the weather, fill water bottles before leaving the hut, and if all is clear, make an early start and go for it.

At first the ridge is a steep whale-back

rolling far off, with poor grass to its very summit. There is no real path and the grass slopes can be treacherous after rain or even a heavy dew. Take care. After a couple of hours or so you reach the little rocky nick of the Port de Bielsa, about the only practical escape route along this stage of the walk. It's an ancient crossing from France into Spain, 'so often traversed by the restless lords of the valley of Aure' (Ramond de Carbonnières), but its use has now been superseded by a road tunnel far below.

Grass-thatched ridges give way to tilted rocks, and peaks rise along the watershed to create obstacles. Some are traversed on their Spanish slopes, some on their French side, others are tackled over their very summits on a delightful scrambling course. Views are always extensive. From some vantage points it is possible to look back and see Monte Perdido gleaming white like a cloud-bank on the horizon. Mostly one peers into lush green valleys; Pinara and Tringoniero to the south, Moudang to the north. Traversing Pic de Marty Caberrou above the Moudang Valley there's a tiny spring of clear water bubbling from the turf of a projecting bluff a few metres below the route. Beyond that, nothing until Rioumajou.

Continue again on the crest, on windblown shale with ridges converging ahead and huge views to north and south, and then, beside Pic de Lia, prepare for the descent. First down clattering schist, then over broken rocks and ankle-twisting scree, round stony bluffs and onto a never-ending slope of grass and shrubbery, over streams and marshy patches with cotton grass like downy feathers. Down to dwarf pine then woodland trees and finally a levelling of meadowland through which a lovely stream tumbles. Rioumajou.

The Hospice de Rioumajou is an ancient, historic shelter. Until recently it was the last remaining example of the primitive inns for which the Pyrénées were notorious. Henry Russell called here a hundred years ago and wrote of the milk soup offered to him. He had to sleep in the hay, for there were no beds, and even a few years ago there were only a few crude mattresses for those who would brave a night here. But then the hospice was forced to close for safety reasons, although a considerable amount of rebuilding work has now taken place. In the summer of 1988 the money to pay for this work had run out, but it is hoped that in the near future the Hospice de Rioumajou will again be open for business. Though no

Right: **The climb out of Rioumajou involves an extremely steep slog to reach Port de Caouerère on the way to Viadós.**

Far right: **On the outskirts of Gavarnie stands a statue of Count Henry Russell, the great mountaineering eccentric of the nineteenth century whose great love was the Vignemale. Here his eyes gaze longingly towards it.**

doubt standards of accommodation and hygiene will be rather more in tune with our times than those of Henry Russell and his fellow pioneers.

The valley of Rioumajou makes a soft contrast to the exposed ridge leading from Barroude. There are clear streams, fragrant shrubs, pines and ancient barns, and the horseshoe of peaks that cup the valley head seem to stand back a little shyly, as if determined not to impose their personality on the valley itself. But in the morning, when you must face the task of crossing those mountains, it soon becomes evident that they are much higher than first they appeared.

There are several high passes in the horseshoe crest that gives access to Spain. However, not all are of use for this traverse, and the pass to look for is Port de Caouarére. It's an arduous, very steep haul out of the Rioumajou to reach it; a difference in altitude of 966 metres (3169ft), which is quite enough to tackle straight after breakfast, especially as the final long slope consists of appalling, steeply angled, schistose scree. But the pass is eventually reached in about three hours and Spain lies before you. It's an empty Spain. Empty of habitation and roads and all the trappings of man; but across the deep hint of attractive valleys the eye is drawn by the imposing mass of Pico de Posets.

Port de Caouarére itself is not particularly memorable, yet it leads to a wonderland. For down below, across open slopes and huge hillside banks of alpenroses, through pine woods and sunny glades, you come to the valley of the Rio Cinqueta de la Pez, a valley with all the warmth and romance so typical of

these Spanish valleys of the central Pyrénées. There lingers a special fragrance that tells of aromatic plants and sun-dried grass, of dust and pine and spray-damp moss. There are insects in full high-pitched debate among the flowers and shrubs and grasses. Crickets leap away in their thousands from the threat of your boots as you follow the stream down-valley, while buzzards and vultures hang in the sky.

The Cinqueta de la Pez is squeezed by converging hillsides as it flows into the Cinqueta de Añes-Cruces where wild raspberries grow beside the path. Here you turn up-valley on a broad dusty track and come to the granges of Viadós.

Days 5 and 6: Viadós to Refugio de la Renclusa

Viadós has an enchanting setting. On a steep slope of terraced grassland above the right bank of the Cinqueta de Añes-Cruces, it gazes across to the lovely Valle de Millares reaching away to the east, and up at the big West Face of the Pico de Posets (3375m/11,073ft). The head of the Añes-Cruces valley is lost behind successive projecting spurs of the walling mountains, and even the river itself is lost from view, although minor streams streak the hillsides and in places have been disciplined through irrigation ditches to water the meadows.

There is a simple, private *refuge* here, standing on a bluff overlooking the row of thick stone-walled barns that comprise the hamlet of Viadós. It makes an unpretentious overnight resting place, much-used by both mountain trekkers and climbers bound for the Posets, and also acts as a meeting place for shepherds and peasant farmers.

The onward path leads up-valley with the river far below to the right, contrary to what is shown on the Editorial Alpina map! Mostly the route is straightforward and safe, but there is one small section where care should be exercised, with a long drop to the river should you slip. Then, in a bowl of mountain near the head of the valley, you must cross the stream and work a route on the far side, climbing into a rough stony vale formed by the lower, broadening slopes of the northern ridges of Posets. At the top of this, a new panorama opens as the Col (or Puerto) de Gistain is reached at 2572 metres (8438ft) and ahead the country falls away into the Estós Valley. Far off rises the great mass of the Maladeta with its little glaciers and snowfields draped below an

otherwise bare crest. To the left every mountain reaches up to the frontier ridge. To the right a desert of rocks hides the topmost crags and dying glaciers of Posets.

It is always a great pleasure for me to tread the pastures of the Estós Valley. The stream is clear and sparkling. Pines and shrubs give off a heady fragrance. The light is Mediterranean pure as it floods through the trees and reflects from the streams. There are herds of isard to spy on, and always delightful views to capture on film. The recently rebuilt hut there allows numerous excursions to be made into secluded hanging valleys, as well as providing a base for all the popular climbs on the Posets and its many satellite peaklets.

An easy stroll takes you down towards the valley of the Esera. It's not a walk to hurry for there are too many good things to study on the way, but all too soon the Estós stream drops out of its valley to join with that of the Esera about 3.5 kilometres (2 miles) north-east of Benasque. If it is your intention to spend extra time in the upper reaches of the Esera Valley, this would be a good opportunity to wander down to the village to stock up with food or films.

The walk through the long valley of the Esera is a taste of purgatory after all the days of remote mountain and lost valley trekking,

Above: **Cloud-magic around the Cirque de Gavarnie, seen from the Refuge des Espuguettes built by the National Park authorities.**

Above: **The Cirque de Barroude**.

tone seam to become the Garonne, that great river of South-West France which waters the vineyards of Bordeaux.) There are outings of great charm to be undertaken here, or climbs of almost every standard of difficulty for those adequately equipped. Time spent here will seldom be time wasted.

But the final stage of the walk leads away from the Maladeta and back to France.

Day 7: Renclusa to Luchon

The northern wall of the Esera contains the international frontier. Almost due north of the Renclusa hut stands Pic de la Mine and to the west, the dome of Pic de Sauvegarde, the easiest summit in this corner of the mountains, but with one of the best viewpoints. Between these two peaks the ridge dips and is cut by a slender nick. This little nick is the classic Port de Venasque (2448m/8031ft), an historic, chilly pass 'where waits neither father for son, nor son for father'. Through this pass, over several centuries, have travelled armies, merchants, explorers and climbers. Yet despite its regular use it has in no way lost its air of romance and mystery. Every crossing is a magical journey, made more so by the remarkable, contrasting views on either side of the pass.

There is an easy path leading to it. A hundred years ago a Spaniard was employed to guard the pass on the southern side and to extract a tax from all who passed through. Happily the taxman has long since deserted his post, although you can still see the rocky outline of the hut in which he sheltered.

Through the Port de Venasque steep slopes of scree and rocks lead to a collection of tarns and an unmanned *refuge,* and beyond, down endless zig-zags, to the Vallée de la Pique and the ancient Hospice de France. For centuries the Hospice was the traditional shelter for practically all those who set out to cross the Port de Venasque. (There was another in the Esera Valley, but that fell into disrepair a long time ago.) It features in many tales of adventure and exploration, but since the road linking the Hospice with Luchon was cut by a landslip in the 1970s, it has become an isolated, sorry place, now serving as a gathering place for shepherds.

A long walk through lush forests completes the journey from Gavarnie to Luchon, exchanging the solitude of mountain wilderness for wide, tourist-busy boulevardes and fashionable boutiques. Luchon, pleasant though it is, comes as something of a culture-shock after all the days of high adventuring.

for there is a major road (that goes nowhere!) heading up-valley too, and you are forced to wander along it for some time. Fortunately there is very little traffic to contend with, but it still makes a crude intrusion.

Once into the upper sanctuary of the Esera where the valley makes a sharp elbow-turn to the east, the surfaced road runs out and only a track continues as far as a meadow below the Renclusa path. (For many years there has been speculation that the road was intended to link with France by way of a tunnel, but so far, thankfully, the French authorities have shown no sign of building a corresponding road on the northern slopes.)

The upper reaches of the Esera form a lush pastureland moat to the Maladeta massif. All around rise big mountains, including Pico de Aneto (3404m/11,168ft) whose summit is the highest in the Pyrénées. This remains unseen from the Renclusa hut, the *refugio* from which the majority of ascents are made, but shows itself clearly above the level plain at the head of the valley.

There are many opportunities for easy and safe explorations of the northern slopes of the Maladeta with its hidden corries and gleaming tarns, its jutting peaks and glacier-spawned streams. With time to spare there's the fine, wild Valleta de la Escaleta to wander in, or the Plan de Aiguallut to visit, with its curious hollow, the Trou de Toro, into which Aneto's streams make their dramatic disappearance. (They reappear on the northern side of the mountains, having tunnelled through a limes-

WALK 14: Classic Crossings No. 1—Brèche de Tuquerouye

Location: East of Gavarnie and the Ordesa Canyon. Brèche de Tuquerouye is found in the headwall of the Cirque d'Estaubé and above the Cirque de Pineta. It links the French valley of Estaubé with the Spanish Valle de Pineta; the villages of Héas and Bielsa.

Distance: 27kms (16½ miles).

Height Gain: 1207 metres (3960ft).

Height Loss: 1560 metres (5118ft).

Time Required: 2 days.

Type of Walk: A mixed walk. It begins easily enough through the Estaubé glen, but the couloir leading to the brèche makes for a strenuous approach. (Ice axe and/or crampons recommended.) The descent of the Pineta cirque is also rather tiring, but is followed by a gentle valley stroll.

Start: Héas, above Gèdre.

Finish: Bielsa.

Accommodation: A few rooms available in Héas. Mountain hut in Brèche de Tuquerouye (unmanned, basic facilities—no water available so fill bottles before starting in the couloir). Hotel and rooms in Bielsa. Wild camping possible in Valle de Pineta.

Maps: IGN Carte de Randonnées No.4: *Bigorre* 1:50,000. Editorial Alpina: *Ordesa* 1:40,000.

From Héas to Bielsa

There are several high passes on the frontier ridge between France and Spain that could easily be awarded the status of classic crossings. The Brèche de Roland above Gavarnie (already described in the reverse direction on the Two Parks Walk) immediately springs to mind. Then there's the rock-guarded slice of the Port de Venasque opposite the Maladeta massif (included in the Four Passes Walk and

Above: **Having descended from the Brèche du Tuquerouye, Monte Perdido's ice cliffs appear to hang overhead as you work towards the Balcon de Pineta.**

Right: **The Pineta cirque blocks the head of its valley**

at the end of the route from Gavarnie to Luchon). There's also lofty Port d'Oô overlooking Pico de Posets in the heart of the range. And further west, giving a wonderful view of the North Face of Monte Perdido, the historic Brèche de Tuquerouye.

It was Ramond de Carbonnières who made the first recorded passage of Port d'Oô in 1787, and it was he who was also the first man to reach the Brèche de Tuquerouye ten years later when making an abortive attempt on Monte Perdido. (He made two attempts via the brèche in 1797, and finally achieved his ambition of climbing Perdido—third highest Pyrénéan summit—in 1802.)

Brèche de Tuquerouye is a nick in the headwall of the Cirque d'Estaubé east of Gavarnie. It lies at an altitude of 2660 metres (8727ft) and is approached by way of a steep and, at times, dangerous couloir choked with snow or ice. The use of crampons and/or an ice axe can often be a distinct advantage in scaling this couloir, depending on conditions, which may vary considerably throughout the season. Perched in the pass itself is the little Refuge de Tuquerouye, the first such hut to be built in the Pyrénées by the C.A.F.

When Ramond first climbed to the brèche he and his party spent two hours in the couloir, climbing the ice 'with cramping irons and hatchets'. But when he returned a month later he found the ice much harder than before, so hard in fact, that his alpenstock made little impression, and it took a full five hours to reach the top. Nowadays, normal summer conditions are much more favourable, but for most mountain walkers the couloir remains a serious obstacle that should not be taken lightly.

The crossing of the Brèche de Tuquerouye would alone be worth tackling for the sudden outstanding view it grants of Perdido's ice-clad North Face. But when included as the crux of a journey from Héas to Bielsa, its true value is drawn out to full extent.

Héas looks not to the Cirque d'Estaubé, but to the largest of the three neighbouring cirques, that of Troumouse. It is typical of the French Pyrénées; low, grey-roofed buildings, a little untidy but workable, streams dashing with unchecked enthusiasm through rough pastures, mountains crowding on three sides, snow lying in pockets through the summer months, clouds often hanging low.

Bielsa is so different. It's a bright little village built around a square on the right bank of the Rio Cinca at the mouth of the lovely

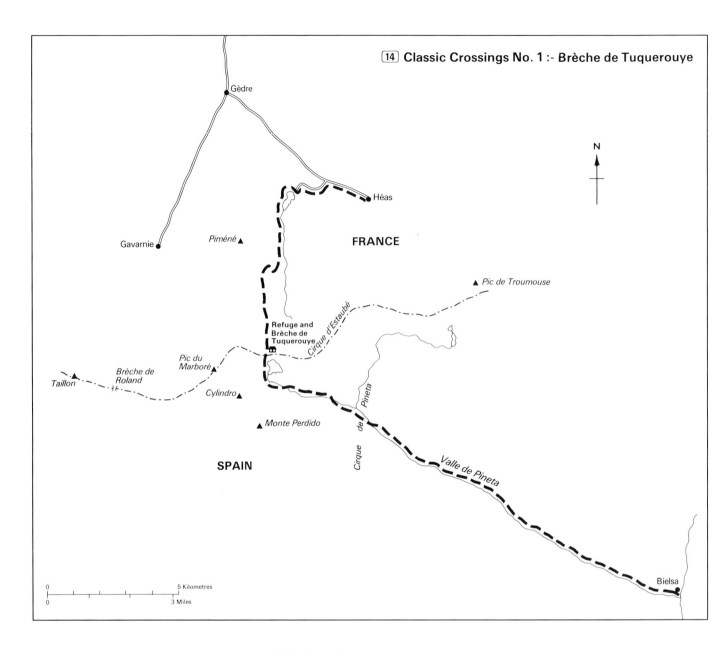

Pineta Valley. Taken there blindfolded, you would know the moment the covering was removed from your eyes that you were in Spain. It could be nowhere else. It's a light, sun-bleached place that attracts plenty of visitors from both sides of the border, since the opening of a tunnel through the mountains at the head of the Cinca provides easy access with France via the Vallée de la Neste d'Aure.

Between these two villages there lies a lot of interesting, often scenically spectacular country; two valleys, the Estaubé and Pineta, that are as different in character as are the villages they serve. There are memorable views at almost every turn.

The Route

From Héas walk down-valley towards Gèdre and then turn left up a side road to the Gloriettes dam which holds back the waters of a blue lake. Follow the path along the western shore and continue towards the head of the valley. The path climbs the western slopes to Hourquette d'Alans and Gavarnie, but forks halfway up. Take the left branch which leads to the obvious couloir at the top of which is the Brèche de Tuquerouye. Climb the couloir on its western edge.

From the brèche descend the southern slopes to a tarn, Lago Helado de Marboré (otherwise known as Lac Glacé, or Lago de

Above: **Farm and barn near Héas on the approach to the Cirque de Troumouse.**

Pineta), then follow a line of cairns leading south-east through a bare region of slabs and boulders to the Balcon de Pineta. A series of steep zig-zags takes a path down the face of the Pineta cirque and brings you to the Pineta valley. Walk down the valley on the left bank of the stream following a broad track that soon becomes a road. This leads directly to Bielsa.

The Walk

Héas is reached by road from Gèdre, a short distance down-valley from Gavarnie in the valley of the Gave de Pau. It's a very small village, no more than a hamlet really, with a chapel that is the site of an annual pilgrimage. It was here, in a barn, that Ramond spent the night prior to his first attempt on Monte Perdido in August 1797.

With the Cirque de Troumouse blocking the valley above the village, Héas is ideally situated as a base for a number of worthwhile walks and climbs. But the route to Bielsa via the Brèche de Tuquerouye heads in the opposite direction, away from Troumouse, and you wander down-valley for a little over a kilometre before striking off to the left on a service road which winds up to the Gloriettes dam. The dam looms threateningly overhead, but you cross to its northern side and take the path leading south above the lake and into the valley of the Gave d'Estaubé.

From this point the snowy summit of Perdido is clearly seen above the Brèche de Tuquerouye in the cirque ahead, and it is easy to understand how Ramond and his party were mistaken in their belief that the mountain was much nearer than it really is. 'I pointed it out to my young companions,' he wrote, 'who, seeing it so clearly, thought themselves already nearing the end of their journey.'

The path takes you deeper into the valley, always keeping to the right of the stream. Estaubé is a short, narrow glen; in places, a waste of rock and snow hemmed in on three sides by the dark rise of steep mountains. Cattle and sheep are grazed here in summer, and walkers on the High Route pass through it on their way from Gavarnie to Héas. Otherwise it's a quiet place without the obvious attractions of either Gavarnie or Troumouse. Only the croaking of choughs, the soft chortling of the stream or the clatter of stones disturbed by a high-grazing sheep break the silence.

Soon the path begins to rise up the western hillside. It steepens to gain height, and works its way towards the Hourquette d'Alans which leads over the ridge to Gavarnie. Then, about halfway to the pass, another trail branches off and heads towards the Cirque d'Estaubé on a steady traverse curving round the western edge of the cirque, and then along a line of cairns to climb above the Borne de Tuquerouye, a prominent lump of rock near the base of the Tuquerouye couloir.

It is interesting to speculate why Ramond chose this couloir, rather than taking the easier route to the Port de Pinède further east. After all, the Penède was even then reasonably well known, and said to be used frequently by smugglers. Indeed, shepherds he met at the head of the valley advised him to use it, rather than attempt a route to Tuquerouye. But Ramond was still under the impression that Perdido could be reached directly from the brèche, and stuck to his original plan.

It is steep work in the couloir, or gully, which is some 400 metres long (1312ft). Broad at its base, it grows narrower towards the top and you emerge from it at last with a sense of relief to be dazzled by the view before you. What a remarkable change from one side to the other! One moment you are hemmed in by tight walls, dark and constricting. Then, in one step, you seem to pass from darkness to light as you come out onto the very edge of a new country. For a moment the *refuge* is ignored as you gaze at the ice cascades which adorn the face of Monte Perdido across a shallow, barren valley, with a lake immediately below. One glacial tier rises above another, separated by bands of limestone, and with a broad summit dome crowned with snow. Ramond described it in these terms:

'A succession of steps sometimes draped in snow, sometimes covered with glaciers which at times overflow and pour themselves one over the other in large and motionless cascades, even to the borders of a lake . . . We were contemplating the most imposing and frightful scene in the Pyrénées. All and everything defied comparison.'

Refuge de Tuquerouye may not be the most comfortable place in which to spend the night, but it will certainly be unforgettable. Rarely will you be there without company, for it has a certain aura about it, based more on its position than on any particular facility on offer (although at the inauguration ceremony held there on 5 August 1890, no less than 843 kilos of food were carried up for a banquet!) The hut may indeed be basic but it is also historic (Russell gave it a limited lifespan) and with prospects of that magnificent ice face glowing in the light of a full moon, a night spent there will be an unforgettable Pyrénéan experience.

The descent to the lake is a short one, and once down you wander round its southern shore and follow a cairned trail across a bare region of boiler-plate rocks, former glacial moraine and daubs of old snow in a somewhat desolate hanging valley. There are one or two memorial plaques and crosses fixed to the rocks in honour of Spanish climbers who lost their lives on the neighbouring mountains, and these do little to alleviate an air of sorrow that hangs over this lifeless region. But this atmos-phere is instantly erased by turning your attention to the imposing view of Monte Perdido's great ice-draped face.

When you come to the edge of this hanging valley—the Balcon de Pineta—you see over the lip of a steep-walled cirque into the Pineta Valley that stretches far ahead towards the south-east. At first it seems doubtful whether a route could be found down the cirque walls, but a path does exist, and it leads easily, if steeply in places, on a series of zig-zags all the way to the valley. On the way down here one hot September afternoon, I caught sight of a small herd of isard on the steep cliffs bordering the path, and had to dodge the stones they sent down as they raced away.

The Pineta Valley is broad, flat-bottomed and smiling; a dramatic and not unwelcome contrast to the scene of desolation and decay left behind. It draws the sun and reflects its brilliance from a line of great limestone cliffs stretching south-eastward from Monte Perdido. Pine trees cling to those steep sun-washed walls, and in the valley itself there's a mixture of pine, box and birch growing in friendly rivalry. Luxurious shrubs adorn riverside meadows. Lazy waterfalls dangle like ribbons of silk against cliff faces. Butterflies drift from flower-head to flower-head; lizards make staccato movements over rocks that are hot to the touch.

To walk down the Valle de Pineta on a summer's afternoon is to experience all the rich, warm nature of the Spanish Pyrénées. There's a taste of freedom; the landscape is carefree and friendly, there's colour and fragrance. Everywhere flowers turn to the sun.

You have to cross the river and follow it downstream on the left bank. There's a Parador hotel near the head of the valley, and wild camping allowed on the right bank. The road is long and dusty, but you can stray down to (and into) the river to wash off the dust and cool down. And although when you look back there is little evidence of Perdido's ice face above the Pineta cirque, you do at least have that splendid long wall of mountains of the Sierra de las Tucas for company on the other side of the valley. Up there, undetected from the valley, lies a pass which will lead down into the Anisclo Canyon. (Ah, another glorious outing!). They are silent companions, but they lead you gently—as that is the only way to travel through the Pineta—to journey's end at Bielsa. And Bielsa is as charming a village as any you're likely to find in these parts. Even if you had the energy to go looking for others.

WALK 15: The Néouvielle Lakes Circuit

Above: Lac de Bastan lies trapped in a bowl bordered by rocky cliffs on one side and a pine-topped bluff on the other.

Location: Entirely in France, the Néouvielle massif is situated to the north-east of Gavarnie and south of the Col du Tourmalet road. The route described makes a tour of the *Réserve Naturelle de Néouvielle* on the edge of the National Park.

Distance: 30kms (18 1/2 miles).

Time Required: 2 days.

Type of Walk: A moderate mountain walk mostly on clear paths although there are some rough sections that require a little care. Diffi culties may be encountered in poor visibility, especially between Hourquette Nère and Refuge du Bastanet.

Base: Barèges.

Start/Finish: Pont de la Gaubie, 3.5kms (2 miles) east of Barèges.

Accommodation: Refuge du Bastanet.

Map: IGN Carte de Randonnées No. 4: *Bigorre* 1:50,000.

Guidebook: *Vallée d'Aure et Barronies* by Gilles Cappe (Randonnées Pyrénéennes), in the guidebook series *Au Pas de l'Homme.*

A Two-Day Tour of the Néouvielle Nature Reserve

The Néouvielle massif covers an extensive area. It is a high region of granite peaks, numerous lakes and tarns, of pine woods and hidden meadows with streams winding through. Only on its southern edge has there been any attempt to subdue the wilderness, and this has been achieved by engineers who have painstakingly forced a narrow, twisting road into it from Aragnouet-Fabian in the Vallée d'Aure. This road leads to the largest of the region's lakes, Lac de Cap de Long, with another spur forging northwards to the Lacs d'Aumer and Aubert. Some of these lakes have been harnessed by the Electricity Board for whom the road was built, but the road also provides access for the many fishermen attracted to the area—as well as the inquisitive car-bound tourist. However, as with almost every other corner of the Pyrénées, it is only by deserting the roads and heading into the heartland of the mountains that one can discover the true nature and beauty of them. This circuit does just that.

The *Réserve Naturelle de Néouvielle* lies at the north-eastern extremity of the *Parc National des Pyrénées*. In the west it is bordered by the valley of the Gave de Pau which flows out of Gavarnie; in the south by the National Park and the upper reaches of the Vallée d'Aure—which also forms the region's eastern limits—and in the north by the road that climbs over the Col du Tourmalet.

There are several multi-day circuits that could be created in this delightful region, but I have chosen this particular medium-grade tour for the great variety of scenery it portrays, and for the interest that never wanes. It makes a delightful two-day outing.

There are three main passes to cross, and a minor ridge which leads into one of the finest valley systems of the massif. Then there are the tarns. I gave up counting after more than a dozen were met on the first day, but the tour will be remembered for the almost constant dazzle of water—from tarns, streams or cascades. After the tarns come the mountains that cup them. The long, granite ridges that embrace the walk also have an attraction, while many individual peaks stir ambition amongst those who delight in scrambling to remote summits.

As with most circuits this walk could be started from any one of a number of places, but since the little village of Barèges makes the most convenient base from which to explore the area, in winter or in summer, our tour begins here.

The Route

The walk begins roughly halfway between Barèges and the Col du Tourmalet where a scoop of valley cuts away to the south. The valley curves to the east and opens at its head to a large bowl of pasture and tarn. There is an unmanned *refuge* here and a choice of four cols to cross. Our route tackles Hourquette Nère, then descends eastward, initially among a rough landscape that soon becomes more gentle and tarn-bright before climbing to a pine-topped ridge. This leads to a splendid hut, Refuge du Bastanet, overlooking Lac du Milieu.

Heading south the route takes you from tarn to tarn on a steady descent to the northern shore of the large Lac de l'Oule, then breaks away to the west among woods to a grassy col

which opens to views of the main Néouvielle summits and the dammed lakes below. In the distance, on the long northern ridge of Pic de Néouvielle, Hourquette d'Aubert is clearly seen. It's a long walk to reach it, but beyond there follows a clear path leading among yet more tarns, the last of which, Lac dets Coubous, gives way to a steep drop into the valley through which the circuit began.

As a two-day outing the circuit offers a modest challenge. Paths are mostly clear. There are some waymarks and a few cairns where the trail is a little thin, or when it crosses a boulder field. There should be no difficulty in finding drinkable water along the way, and as Refuge du Bastanet has a guardian in summer residence, meals should be available here, thereby enabling the tour to be made with reasonably light rucksacks and broken at a convenient halfway point.

Day 1: Pont de la Gaubie to Refuge du Bastanet

The Tourmalet road climbs out of Barèges along a pleasant valley walled in the north by a long mountain ridge which culminates in Pic du Midi de Bigorre (2872m/9423ft), whose summit is marked by a slender television relay mast and an observatory. About three kilometres (2 miles) along the valley the road makes a sudden hairpin bend at Pont de la Gaubie where there is a café invariably crowded with motorists, cyclists and coach parties. There is a rough, unmade car park here, and from it you can often watch brightly coloured parachutes descending from the mountains opposite as there is a *parapente* school based nearby.

That long distance Pyrénéan traverse, GR10, heads south from Pont de la Gaubie into a somewhat bare, narrow valley, and our route adopts the same path. Initially it's a broad track high above the Coubets stream, but that track runs out soon enough where the valley curves away towards the east and a second stream comes dashing from a stunted wall off to the right. A signpost indicates a choice of direction here, with one path climbing south and another heading deeper into the valley. Bear left, but note that the alternative path will be taken on the return journey as you descend from the Lacs dets Coubous, hidden beyond an obvious saddle from which the stream falls in a ribbon of spray.

After the eastward bend the valley narrows even more for a while. It is guarded by a jumble of rocks, but among these rocks wild

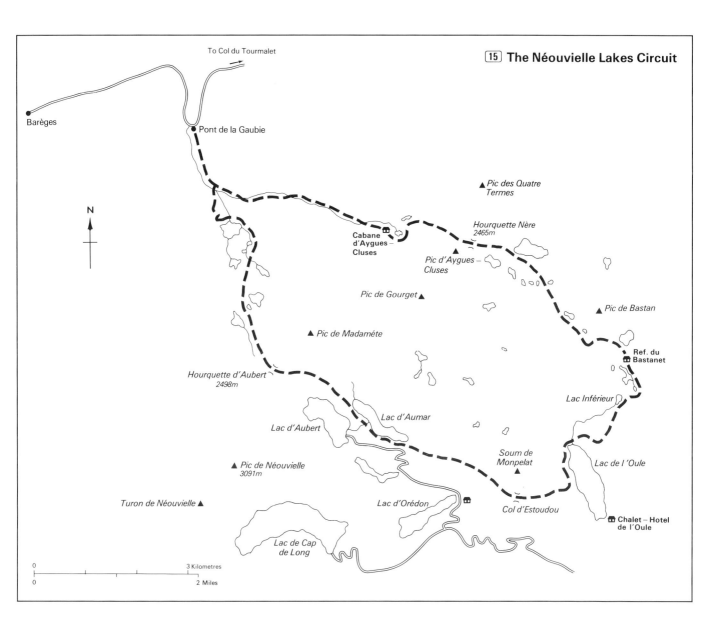

raspberries offer temptations in late summer, while in June and July it will be alpenroses that brighten the way. As the path leads deeper into the valley, so it becomes less desolate and there are small grassy levels through which the stream twists its way. Marmots may be heard whistling their shrill warning from the stony margins, and if you're observant you may well catch sight of these furry creatures bounding off to their burrows. It's a lively stretch of valley with little cascades and shallow pools among the streams where frogs spawn and small trout move darkly in the waters to capture your attention. The mountains play second fiddle until later in the day.

After about two hours of walking from Pont de la Gaubie you come to a large bowl of grassland spreading in an arc below a great semi-circle of mountain ridges. In it lies Lac de Coueyla-Gran, a picturesque tarn that makes an idyllic site for a midday picnic and the focus for a day's outing from Barèges. On bright summer days there will often be small groups of walkers sprawled out in the sunshine around its edges. Above the tarn stands Cabane d'Aygues Cluses, a small unmanned *refuge* with a fireplace and mattresses for six people, while opposite the hut rises a peak bearing the same name. On either side of Pic d'Aygues-Cluses lie accessible cols: to the north, Hourquette Nère; to the south, Col de Barèges. The easier of the two is Hourquette Nère

(2465m/8087ft).

To gain this saddle you wander over a richly vegetated bluff with small pines growing among the boulders, and beyond this to Lac d'Agalops where a clear path then works a way steadily up towards the pass, growing steeper towards the top. Once on the pass a new landscape, new valley systems, new tarns and ridges, and folding, distant hills unravel their mysteries before you. It's a fine place to spend half an hour in relaxation before tackling the descent.

Having dropped a short distance from the pass the path, now narrow but still clearly defined, heads off towards Lac de Port-Bielh. It is not necessary to go as far as this lake, however, and you can cut down the steepening slope to pass above a string of smaller tarns, then up a minor spur to the lovely Lac de Bastan whose northern shore is wild and rocky while to the south, green turf and a hillock of gnarled pine trees give the luxury of colour and fragrance; a delightful spot with yet another tarn not far off.

You then begin to climb towards the pine-topped ridge that will give access to Refuge du Bastanet. Grass slopes, steep yet easy, take you to the ridge which suddenly levels out to a mixture of grass and boulders with fine views back towards the west, to curving granite ridges and knobbly peaklets full of character. A short distance away to the north Col de Bastanet hides another region worth exploring, but below to the east the gleam of more lakes draws you down to find the steeply-pitched Refuge du Bastanet (2250m/7382ft).

This hut is owned by the sports club of the Toulouse PTT, but like those of the CAF and the National Park authorities, it is open to all-comers. It's a fine hut, situated amid good walking country and with lovely views over Lac du Milieu. In addition to the Néouvielle Lakes Circuit there are several other very fine long walks that use the hut as a staging post. There's GR10, a Néouvielle North-South Traverse and the multi-day Tour de la Vallée de Campan, so the *refuge* will often be busy with walkers in the main summer season. During this period there will be a guardian in occupation, but there is also a portion of the hut open during the winter for ski-touring parties.

Day 2: Refuge du Bastanet to Pont de la Gaubie

Leaving the hut you wander down-valley above the east bank of Lac du Milieu and a much smaller tarn below it, then swing westwards into a glorious view of crowding mountains topped way-off by Pic de Néouvielle. The path slopes downhill into a hidden bowl and brings you to Lac Inférieur, to my mind the loveliest of all the tarns on this circuit. I came to it late one bright afternoon and immediately fell under its spell. It's a magical place, and seen in those first-time conditions of dazzling light with far-off ridges softening into blue haze, it struck me as the epitome of a Pyrénéan landscape; a sheen of ripple-free water, a maze of craggy ridges, stunted pines on a grassy bluff; and that liquid purity of light. Lac Inférieur has it all.

The path descends to Lac de l'Oule by a succession of short, level, grassy steps interspersed with steep slopes. GR10 breaks away eastward to cross an easy saddle before tackling a ridge above the Vallée d'Aure, while our circuit rounds the head of the large lake (it is dammed at its southern end), wanders along its shore then begins the climb to Col d'Estoudou (2260m/7415ft). After a lengthy spell of downhill and level walking, the sudden upturn of the path comes as a shock. It winds up through fragrant pinewoods, red squirrels scampering overhead, jays giving loud warning of your approach, and over open glades that produce surprise views up-valley and onto yesterday's mountains.

Col d'Estoudou brings a fresh revelation. It is a wide cup of a saddle, often grazed by unattended horses wearing bells round their necks. From here you suddenly look onto a wild landscape which man has done his best to control. Off to the west you see the great barrage at the end of Lac de Cap de Long, and the spiral of road leading to it. Above rise grey, gaunt peaks, scowling at this intrusion. Pic de Néouvielle, the shapeliest summit in all your field of vision, stands aloof; untouched, unscarred. An easily recognisable peak, it sends out a long high ridge to the north-east, dipping here and there to obvious passes. Hourquette d'Aubert can be clearly seen. A path slants across the slopes of Pic de Madaméte to reach it, but although it is evident from this distance, it will take another 2-2^1/$_2$ hours to reach it.

From the col there is a choice of three different routes to take; one high, which leads over Soum de Monpelat and along a ridge to take in Pic d'Anglade before dropping to Lac d'Aumar; one low, descending to the *Refuge-Hôtel* at Lac d'Orédon and then taking

Above: **There are many superb wild camping spots in the Néouvielle massif. This Phoenix Phalcon is tucked away in a quiet corner.**

the road to Lac d'Aumar; and the third, recommended option which heads along a GR10 *variante* among pinewoods on a mid-level traverse heading north-west. This is a most enjoyable stretch for it leads in and out of the shade of trees, crosses small streams and comes onto a gentle crest with splendid views. Flowers adorn the grass of this crest, and in boggy sections cotton grass waves in the breeze. The crest takes you into an open moorland-like patch and this, in turn, leads to Lac d'Aumar with its highly photogenic vista of Pic de Néouvielle spun on its head in the water. Fishermen stand in quiet contentment around the shores of this lake, but the proximity of a road comes as something of a culture shock after the day and a half of wilderness, and it's likely that you'll scurry away with an eager eye on the Hourquette d'Aubert beckoning with its promise of new horizons and the peace of high mountain country once more.

That promise is fulfilled. The route to the pass is easy enough—a good path that tackles the slope with an engineer's eye for slackening the gradient where possible—and yet there is danger too. That danger comes from magnetic views that insist on drawing eyes away from the trail, and out to soaring rocks and craggy peaks, to snowfields lodged in shadowed gullies, to blue-washed mountains far-off, to lake and tarn and silver stream below. The pass is a relief. You can spread yourself against a boulder and commit eyes and mind to the country with no other cares.

It's a raw landscape that takes you down on the final leg of the circuit. More tarns lie on the route; more than half a dozen of them scattered among the granite boulders of nature in chaos. But among those boulders, amid that chaos, there are bilberries and wild raspberries again, and insistent shrubs like alpenrose and juniper. There are marmots too, and lizards flashing across the path, and hundreds of crickets leaping and buzzing in grassy islands marooned amid the stony desert.

Lac dets Coubous is the final lake, the last blue sheen on the tour of the Néouvielle lakes. From its northern shore the path falls away in a series of tight zig-zags to the Bassin du Bastan and the familiar track which began the walk. Down then, to Pont de la Gaubie, to the stream of traffic grinding along the Tourmalet road—and a welcome glass of something cool at the café conveniently placed at the end of the path.

After the wilderness, civilisation still has a few consolations.

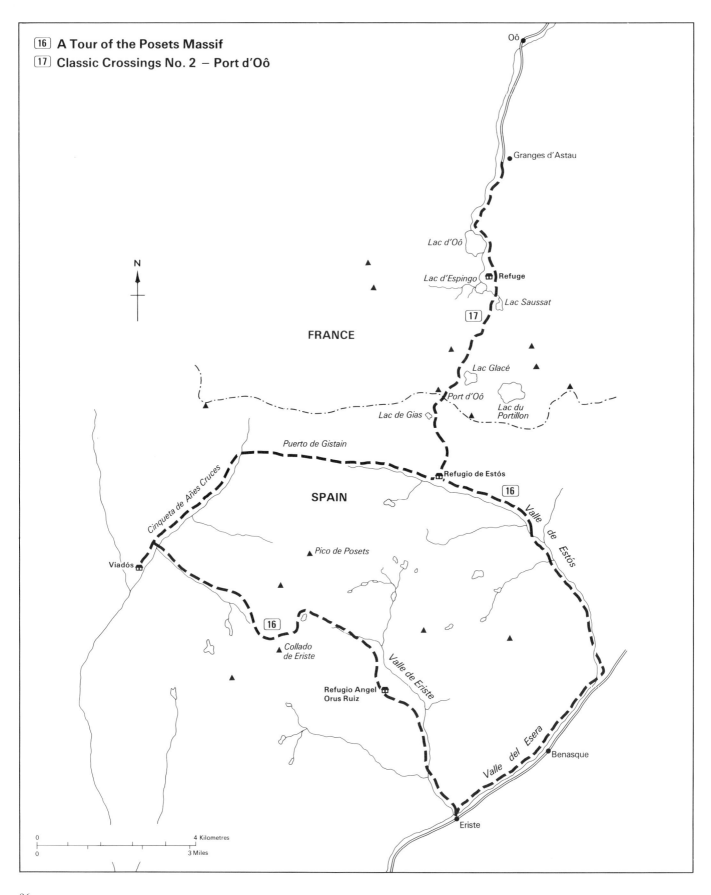

WALK 16: A Tour of the Posets Massif

Above: **Most Pyrénéan mountain huts are supplied by mules. The guardian of the Estós hut descends to Benasque to restock.**

Location: In the heart of the range, entirely in Spain. Near the head of the important Valle del Esera.

Distance: 44 kms (27 miles).

Time required: 3 days. (It would be possible to complete the circuit in just two days, but to do so would be to miss the opportunity to absorb the essential character of the region. Better really to stretch it to four days.)

Type of Walk: Basically a valley walk, linked by the crossing of two passes; one moderate, the other high, wild and a little demanding. Each valley is different. The Esera is broad and inhabited, and with a major road running through. The Estós is beautifully soft and pastoral—one of the loveliest in all the Pyrénées. The Cinqueta de Añes Cruces is somewhat bare in its narrow upper regions, but at Viadós is bountiful and tended in summer. The Millares valley offers soft pastures at its lower end, and raw screes and slabs near its head, while the Valle de Eriste goes from a gaunt wilderness to dense vege-

tation in striking contrast. In parts there are no paths and few, if any, cairns or waymarks. Mostly, though, the way is clear.

Base: Benasque.

Accommodation: Hotels, campsites in or near Benasque. Mountain huts in the Estós valley, at Viadós and in the Valle de Eriste.

Map: Editorial Alpina: *Posets* 1:25,000.

Three Days Round the Viceroy of the Pyrénées

At 3375 metres (11,073ft) Pico de Posets is the second highest mountain in the Pyrénées; a great swollen block of granite that culminates in crumbling schistose ridges. Yet despite its height and despite the ease with which its surrounding valleys may be reached, it is not a mountain that is often seen except from a distance. Even then one does not become immediately attracted by it, for apart from its

West Face, the peak itself is often belittled by satellite peaklets, or contorted by folds of strata. There are few glaciers left, and those that do remain are mere shadows of their former selves; insignificant scarves draped round a schistose neck.

When Charles Packe climbed Posets in 1861 (the third ascent on record) he found large glaciers flowing through now-stony corries, but these glaciers have since withdrawn in the consistent heat of one bright summer after another. It was Packe who gave Posets its reputation for providing the finest view from any Pyrénéan summit (a claim with which I rather tend to disagree, despite the vastness of the panorama). Yet four of the five valleys that surround it are unarguably among the loveliest of all those south of the frontier. These valleys: Estós, Cinqueta de Añes Cruces, Millares and Eriste are totally different from one another, yet each has a character of great charm and merits further exploration. Indeed when they are linked by two dissimilar passes that cross shoulders of Posets, they make a circuit of this lofty massif a magnificent outing.

The Route

Starting from Benasque in the Esera Valley, you wander up-stream for a little over 3 kilometres (2 miles) as far as the entrance to the Valle de Estós, then head up into this on a clear track all the way to the smart, newly rebuilt *refugio* which stands on a knoll way above the river. Next day, continue to the head of the valley to cross the Puerto de Gistain on the northern shoulder of Posets, and descend into the valley of the Cinqueta de Añes Cruces. This leads to the grazing hamlet of Viadós where accommodation is available at a privately owned *refuge*. The hut gazes into the Valle de Millares across the Cinqueta stream, with Pico de Posets rising steeply to the north-east.

From Viadós you cross the Cinqueta and work a route through the Millares woods and pastures, climbing steeply into a stone-cluttered hanging valley and up to the Collado de Eriste. The descent from this col is, for the first part, over very rough terrain, turning green and lush lower down beyond the fine new *refuge* named after a young Spanish climber who died in Chamonix in 1981, Angel Orus Ruiz. The Eriste Valley opens above the village of the same name down in the Esera, and you then walk along the Esera back to Benasque.

Three days should be ample for the completion of this circuit, although it is a route to savour at an easy pace. For those with sufficient time at their disposal, it would be worth taking four days over it, spending a last night at Refugio Angel Orus, in order to have the opportunity to explore further the wild recesses of the Valle de Eriste.

Day 1: Benasque to Refugio de Estós

Benasque is growing. This medieval village, with its crowded narrow streets, is an historic place now being developed to attract a sudden influx of tourists in both summer and winter. Happily that development is being guided by an overall plan, so that the essential character of the place will not be swamped or destroyed– the fate of so many similar small villages in the Alps. As a result of this blossoming, a number of shops selling good quality mountaineering equipment have opened in Benasque in recent years. Benasque is also an important centre for trekkers needing to restock with food, maps, camping gaz, films and other necessities for the hills. There are restaurants, bars and hotels, and on the outskirts of the village, two or three well-appointed campsites.

The Posets circuit begins with a short stroll on a tarmac road. It doesn't take long to reach the mouth of the Estós Valley, but on a sun-bright morning there is a sense of urgency about one's stride as the thought of a peaceful, traffic-free, fragrant valley draws you on. The entrance to the Estós is through a narrow defile that gives no hint of the beautiful pastures, woods and hillsides that lie ahead, but as the track leads out of the little gorge and across the stream, so the valley unfolds. The way is clear and you gain height easily. Box trees line the track. There are wild raspberries too, and plenty of flowers. Across the stream pastures sweep up to patches of self-sown woodland, and higher beyond, to craggy peaks. But ahead the mountains are growing. They form the international frontier, and up there are some splendid high passes—among the highest and most remote in all of the Pyrénées—Port d'Oô and Portillon d'Oô, unseen and unguessed from the valley itself.

After a short distance a narrow path breaks away from the track and disappears into the shrubs to the left. This is the path which leads up to the lovely hidden valley of Batisielles where a collection of tarns lies in the midst of some harsh granite aiguilles. Ignore this path, however, and continue along the track which takes you deeper into the valley.

Above: **In the Estós Valley views are invariably dominated by the frontier peaks.**

Above right: **These cascades can be heard long before they're seen, as they come crashing through the woods.**

The valley curves; there is a fine waterfall bursting through the trees. The track leads on and comes to the Turmo *cabane* with the valley opening ahead. Packe stayed here on his early explorations, and it's amusing to read his comments:

> 'The Cabane de Turmes is a rude stone cabane on the right bank of the stream, but the weather must be very bad indeed before you are driven to take shelter in such a smoke-grimed, filthy den.'

There is, of course, no need to do so today for the F.E.M. *(Federacion Espanola de Montanismo)* has built a large and comfortable hut about half an hour's walk beyond. From here there are lovely views down-valley and off towards the mass of the Maladeta rising above the unseen Esera.

Day 2: Estós to Viadós

The first two days of this circuit are easy days. It would be possible for a fit party to combine them into one long effort, but both valleys deserve to be walked slowly. Rise with the sun anyway, and capture that unique Estós light as it shafts into the valley to sparkle in the clear winding stream, to wash the mountains with its soft rays and then to beam in solar cartwheels among the pines.

The crossing of the Col (or Puerto) de Gistain is not unduly arduous, and will take about an hour and a half from the hut. The path, though not particularly wide, is clear

enough, and when it fades across open grassland there are a few small cairns to guide you. The final slopes to it are of scree and rock, and the pass itself is a broad saddle offering long views east to the Maladeta, and west into the falling depression that will take you to the valley of the Cinqueta. But if you have the energy, wander up the steepish slopes to the north to reach an insignificant bald summit that extends your western horizon considerably. Way off you can see Monte Perdido and Pic du Marboré above Gavarnie, and nearer to hand, an unusual view of the Pico de Posets.

Waymarks take you down to the Cinqueta stream, which you meet in a green cleavage of the hills below the Puerto de Aigues-Tortes, another of those hidden frontier crossings, but one that is an easier proposition than the traverse of either the Port or Portillon d'Oo.

The Editorial Alpina map (1985 edition) shows a path heading down-valley on the left bank of the stream. The true route, however, crosses to the right bank, and all signs indicate this is the way to go. So cross the stream as soon as you reach it, go up the grassy slope on the far side and bear left along the trail. The route has altered slightly in recent years, but is still clear and without difficulty, although rather steep in places. There is one short slab that used to be potentially dangerous, but the path now climbs above it for safety.

Wandering down to Viadós the great West Face of Posets looms high overhead. Below, the stream rushes through its narrow bed lined here and there with trees, but its song drifts in the breeze. Coming down here one lovely summer's afternoon the song of the stream was joined by other music, and we saw a lone figure sitting in the shade of a pine down by the Cinqueta playing a flute. It was just the kind of music that belonged to that landscape; a flute, the stream, the buzzing of ten thousand crickets. The Cinqueta Concerto.

The barns, or granges, of Viadós only come into sight as you round the slope of hillside just before reaching them. They make a welcome sight, attractive and colourful, and bring to an otherwise deserted valley the human scale. One seems to have stepped back in time.

Time and again I find myself drawn back to Viadós. Its magic never seems to fade, and seated on a hard bench in the dining room of the *refugio* as night settles on the mountains outside, there comes a deep sense of belonging. They serve a rough red wine out of a barrel at Viadós. The innocent will be fooled by its potency. The wine snob will sneer at its flavour. But after a hard day's climbing, or a sun-warm crossing of a lonely pass, that wine is a powerful antidote to insomnia. By the time the earthenware jug has been emptied a couple of times, the stars shining on Posets will have become no less than searchlights of the moon. And you wake in the morning with a tongue as fat as a pine cone and your mouth feeling as though you'd been gargling with disinfectant. That is one of the simple charms of Viadós!

Day 3: Viadós to Benasque

This is by far the longest and most demanding of the three days it takes to complete the Posets circuit. The crossing of Collado de Eriste (2970m/9744ft) is not difficult, but the route is not always clearly defined. In inclement weather the col is not a place to be caught out, and the descent as far as the Angel Orus hut could become fraught with problems in poor visibility. But in good weather—ah, now that's a different story.

You can virtually see the col from Viadós. Looking up the Millares Valley the long south ridge of the Posets is clearly seen sloping down towards the lower crest of the Picos de Eriste. Where the two fold into each other would seem a likely place for a col to be. And so it is. Reaching it will require about 3–3^1/2 hours.

From the Viadós hut you go down to the barns and find the narrow path which heads through the meadows to the Cinqueta stream. This is crossed by way of a footbridge, and you then climb through sparse pine woods into the Valle de Millares, which opens its pastures in welcome. Flowers dazzle these pastures from spring until autumn, and on a warm morning the special fragrance of Spain is drawn from the grasses. Way above the mountains are gaunt and sterile, but the lower reaches of the valley are full of the riches of abundant vegetation. These contrasts contribute to the day's bounty.

The route soon becomes a steep haul as you wind on zig-zags over scree and boulders. It then eases for a while and you begin to think the passage of the col will not be so demanding after all—when suddenly a waymark jerks you out of your comfortable reverie, and you have to leave the easy path to go straight up a long steep spur to the left of a prominent rocky crown not marked on the map. When you come above this you enter a wilderness of boulders; a scrapyard of unwanted mountain debris. There should be cairns to guide you through this unruly landscape, but they are few and far between and you merely follow intuition—and the compass—to work a route to a false saddle which leads to the next upward section.

A steep slope of snow and scree finally brings you to the col and another wild view. This is all grey country. Savage, uncompromising country. Far off beckons the Maladeta.

You then travel steeply down, with neither path nor cairn to guide you, until you swing leftwards into a deep rocky bowl containing the Lago Llardaneta. Above to the north rises Pico de Posets, half-hidden from here by Diente de Llardana, on which there are one or two fine rock climbing routes. In fact as you descend towards the Eriste Valley you come to a grand climbers' playground of bristling aiguilles and monstrous slabs. There's no shortage of adventurous routes to explore on this side of the massif, and it can only be the lengthy approach that limits their popularity.

One of the classic southern routes to the summit of Pico de Posets comes by way of the Eriste Valley and up to the ridge of the Espalda. Not long after you leave the shores of Lago Llardaneta a line of cairns will bring you to this approach path, thereby easing the route down to the hut. Keep your eyes open for isard round here. In this high and lonely corner there lives a sprightly herd, though you're not likely to see them from close range.

Coming to the Llardaneta stream, cross to the right bank and be led by cairns down a bewildering complex of boulders below the

Above: **The granges, or barns, of Viadós occupy an idyllic position below the West Face of Pic des Posets.**

Above right: **This pine-log bridge takes the walker across the Estós stream up-valley from the *refuge*.**

Aguja del Forcau, eventually arriving at the Refugi Angel Orus Ruiz (2100m/6890ft), about five hours from Viadós.

Continuing down you will soon be among vegetation once more. Now this *is* a transformation. One moment you're dancing from rock to rock with little to relieve the tedium of raw granite, the next you're diving into a lush shrubbery to gorge yourself with bilberries, wild raspberries, strawberries or blackberries, depending on the season. Then into woods and beside the river on a clear path. I came down here when autumn hung in the trees; yellows and golds splashed amongst the leaves. There were birches and beeches and jays screeching from them. It was just like home. There were little pastoral glades, red squirrels scuffing dead leaves on the ground, beams of sunshine making puddles of light across the path. Going

down the Eriste valley I was blissfully happy, for the walk had taken on the character of the river and the trees. The river had calm pools and laughing cascades. The trees had an air of luxury about them after the hours of boulders, slabs and scree. No longer was it a hostile environment. It was warm and friendly. The Eriste Valley had won me over.

A concrete bridge—so out of character—takes you across to the left bank of the river by the large Cascada de Espiantosa which comes pouring from the western hillside, and from here down to Eriste you're on a wide bulldozed track that makes a slow descent out of the mouth of the valley and into the Esera which crosses at right-angles. It is then just a slow plod along the main valley road to Benasque, comforted only by the memories of a splendid three-day trek.

WALK 17: Classic Crossings No. 2—Port d'Oô

Location: Central Pyrénées, north of Pico de Posets. Port d'Oô links the French Val d'Astau with the Vallee de Estós in Spain. Val d'Astau (or Vallée d'Oô) is easily reached from Luchon, along the route to the Col de Peyresourde.
Distance: 13kms (8 miles) Granges d'Astau to Refugio de Estós.
Height Gain: 1769 metres (5804 feet).
Height Loss: 1073 metres (3520 feet).
Time Required: About 9 hours walking time plus rests. Allow 2 days.
Type of Walk: An arduous, but very rewarding route. Good paths for about two thirds of the approach to the pass, but thereafter only cairns—rather sparse in places. Nasty, shifting screes lead to Port d'Oô, and the descent is almost as tiring as the ascent. However, it is a visually spectacular walk with many contrasting features to enjoy.
Start: Oô (France).

Finish: Valle de Estós (Spain).
Accommodation: Mountain huts on both sides of the pass. On the French side, Refuge d'Espingo (CAF); on the Spanish side, Refugio de Estós (FEM).
Maps: IGN Carte de Randonnées No. 5: *Luchon* 1:50,000. Editorial Alpina: *Posets* 1:25,000.
Guidebooks: *Walks and Climbs in the Pyrénées* by Kev Reynolds (Cicerone Press). *Pyrénées Central* by Arthur Battagel (Gastons/West Col).

From the Val d'Astau to the Valle de Estós

The frontier ridge of mountains which forms the northern wall of the Estós Valley maintains an altitude of around 3000 metres (9843ft) between Pic de Clarabide and Pic de Boum—a distance of about nine kilometres (5¹/₂ miles).

Above: **A cold beer is very welcome on a hot day and the views from Refuge d'Espingo make a rest here an added bonus.**

Right: **Val d'Arrouge juts away to the side of Refuge d'Espingo and is worth exploring if you've a spare day.**

Along that remote stretch are to be found the highest passes of all: Col Supérieur de Literole, Col des Crabioules, Col Inférieur de Literole, Portillon d'Oô and Port d'Oô, each one only a fraction lower than the peaks themselves. Each one provides a challenge. None could be termed an easy stroll, and few are crossed by more than a handful of climbers each year.

Yet Port d'Oô, at 2908 metres (9541ft), a mere depression along the ridge between Pic Jean Arlaud and Cap du Seil de la Baque, ranks as one of the most stimulating and rewarding crossings to be made in the Pyrénées. It is a strenuous route (Packe called it a toilsome scramble) both going up on the French side and coming down in Spain, and by the time you reach the soft Estós pastures you'll know you've had a day out. But what a day!

As long ago as 1787 Port d'Oô was known to have been used as a crossing point, no doubt by the ubiquitous hunter of isard, for when Ramond de Carbonnières made the passage he found a few cairns leading to it. Be that as it may, there is no path as such even today over the upper part of the route, and in misty conditions the Port could be a very elusive goal. It is the sort of crossing that calls for clear weather, for its major attraction is not simply a physical trek across a high and wild ridge, but a visual experience, full of contrasts and variety.

When we crossed it one late summer we enjoyed magnificent clear skies and an over-zealous sun. There is practically no shade anywhere, and we scorched our way for hour after hour in an oven-like temperature, with the heat basking down overhead and reflecting back from the rocks to give us double-exposure.

Ramond, on the other hand, complained that on his crossing 'the heavens were pregnant with tempests' and throughout his journey he and his guides were forced to battle against violent winds that numbed them with cold. Even so, this hardy politician and mountain explorer went, in one day, from the village of Oô, over the Port and down into the Estós Valley, and from there continued as far as the Esera and finally down to Benasque—an epic journey. It took him fourteen hours, and this coming only a day after another mammoth walk of 17 hours! A hard man, our Ramond. My suggestion is for a somewhat less frenetic pace, with an overnight stop in the C.A.F's Refuge d'Espingo prior to making the crossing.

The Route

The crossing of Port d'Oô is usually made en route to further walks or climbs on the Spanish side, a passage rarely taken for itself. It's a stern introduction.

Luchon is at the railhead from Paris (via Toulouse) and is the most convenient place to aim for if approaching the central portion of the range by public transport. From there it is advisable to take a taxi (or hitch-hike along the route of the Col de Peyresourde) as far as either the village of Oô or the Granges d'Astau.

Those with their own transport may drive as far as the Granges d'Astau, which are found at the end of the narrow road cutting south from Oô. There should be sufficient room for parking here.

From the granges a clear path (GR10) heads south to Lac d'Oô, then climbs above its eastern shoreline to Refuge d'Espingo. GR10 cuts away north-eastwards shortly before the hut is reached. Continuing from the hut the path goes to Lac Saussat, climbs beyond the lake and then forks. The left branch goes to Lac du Portillon and the Portillon d'Oô, while the right branch, now cairned, climbs on to pass Lac Glacé, over screes and up to the Port d'Oô.

The descent from the pass to the Estós Valley is very steep. Guided by a rather hit-and-miss line of cairns go straight down through a boulder-field, pass a small tarn and wind through one or two grassy gullies, the

Above: **The Pyrénées in the nineteenth century. Lac de Portillon d'Oô. This illustration adorned Charles Packe's** Guide to the Pyrénées **published in 1862.**

Above: **The contradictory nature of both sides of the frontier, as seen from Port d'Oô. Icefields on the French side, bare rock on the Spanish.**

trail becoming more evident the lower you go, until you reach the Refugio de Estós.

The Walk

From the start, the walk is of considerable interest, for the Granges (or barns) d'Astau occupy a pastoral site with woods and rough meadows nearby. Streams come dashing from the unseen Lac d'Oô in the south, from Val de Médassoles in the south-east, and from Val d'Esquierry in the west. The whole region is noted for its wild flowers, in fact the valleys of Esquierry and Médassoles are celebrated as the *Jardin des Pyrénées,* and Packe's *Guide* lists 116 of the plants to be found in the neighbourhood of the lake. (Not bad for a guidebook 'Especially Intended for the Use of Mountaineers'!)

The path works its way easily through the woods, and after about an hour you reach Lac d'Oô to be greeted with a lovely romantic scene. The lake, circular and stocked with trout, lies trapped in a deep mountain bowl. Showering into it on the far side is a splendid, much-photographed waterfall, and the upper rim of the rocky bowl is clad with trees. By contrast, the northern end of the lake is blocked by a small dam, and on its edge there is a café that does a brisk trade with the many visitors who wander here throughout the summer, repeating an excursion that has been noted, literally, for centuries. Lac d'Oô was a popular tourist haunt certainly over two

hundred years ago, for in 1787 Ramond remarked that it was 'an object of curiosity to those persons who pass the summer season at Bagnères de Luchon'.

Above the eastern side of the lake the path steepens somewhat, and on our crossing, overladen with climbing and camping gear and enough food to last a fortnight, we were soon perspiring badly. There is some shade for a brief spell, but it's never enough when the sun is at full strength. Only the ever-lovely views— and the promise of even better to come— motivated us to continue.

It is a well-used path, and deserves to be so, for above Lac d'Oô a glorious panorama is revealed. You go through a groove of a saddle where the GR10 path breaks away to the left, and continuing ahead find Refuge d'Espingo standing on a hillside bluff a little below to the right, overlooking an idyllic cirque of mountains. Immediately below the hut, spread in a green mattress of turf, Lac d'Espingo sparkles in the sunshine. The *refuge* is a great place to relax and spend a night before tackling the crossing of the Port d'Oô. When we were there, a great mixed flock of sheep and goats were grazing down by the lake, and beside the shepherd's *cabane,* a mule was tethered. To the west we gazed into an enchanting-looking Val d'Arrouge, at the head of which rose jagged peaks; Mail Mouillat, Pic d'Arrouge and Pic de Hourgade. Lovely peaks, challenging peaks, and the ridge they created worked its way in a wall to the south-east where its main peaks, Pic Belloc and Pic des Spijoles, lay misted in the brilliant light. The whole cirque was tempered and flooded by light, illuminating the rock texture which contrasted and complemented the sweep of grassland and the rich blue of the lake. In that bowl of mountain laid out before Refuge d'Espingo, we witnessed the very essence of the Pyrénées.

The path continues to slope down to another lake, Lac Saussat, that has grassy hummocks at one end and a grassy flood-plain at the other. Mountains crowd in to the east, while in the south a steep, rocky wall threatens to close the valley completely. Running alongside Lac Saussat the path is paved with flat slabs of stone and above it the way is so well-engineered it creates the illusion that it will all be like this. Reality soon proves otherwise, for shortly before coming to a bridge which takes the path across a stream and up to Lac du Portillon, a cairn on the right indicates the Port d'Oô route and you wind up the hillside, round bands of rock and over a boulder field with a line of cairns to lead the way. It's a steep haul, and it seems like an eternity before you top the rocky barrier beyond which lies the green pool of Lac Glacé, with its flotilla of little icebergs floating in it.

We sat atop this rocky barrier and took stock of our surroundings. We had left behind a mountain idyll and traded it for a true wilderness. But what a wilderness! To the north-east the walls of Pic Quayrat (3060m/ 10,039ft) showed clearly their great potential for hard rock-climbing; they teased us, and demanded a return. Pic Lézat was its neighbour, a little higher, but partially hidden from view. Beside us to the west rose more enticing crags; those of Pic des Spijoles (3065m/ 10,056ft) with sufficient routes on them to satisfy the appetite of most crag-rats for a long time. South of Lac Glacé we looked at the curving Seil de la Baque glacier that hung round the rim of the rock wall, marking the international frontier like an off-white cravat, and knew we'd have to work our way up to the edge of it soon. It was an innocent-looking sheet with little life remaining.

There is a half-frozen pond above Lac Glacé which feeds the lake with a clear stream; the last opportunity to top-up water bottles until some way down from the pass in Spain. You cross the stream and then scramble over rocky terraces and up shallow gullies, to emerge onto a high rolling desert of barren ice-scraped rock, with the frontier ridge now in full view above

and the snow col under Pic des Gourgs Blancs (which enables the Gourgs Blancs valley to be reached), visible in the near distance.

We descended into a shallow depression, crossed a dying tongue of glacier and came to the foot of a long scree slope. The way heads up the screes. A misery of slipping and sliding, of dust and grit in your boots, of three paces to gain one and a half. But in such a manner you reach the slight dip in the ridge which is Port d'Oô. And what a relief it is to be there.

From the Port Spanish slopes plunge into more wilderness. The Estós Valley is no more than a hinted gulf, a great hollow 1100 metres deep (3609ft), between the frontier ridge and the great block of Pico de Posets opposite. But there are some interesting sights looking eastwards along the ridge, where the contrasts between the French slopes and those that fall into Spain are acute.

We dropped down on the Spanish side, picking our way gingerly over scree-covered terraces, then wove a route through a veritable maze of boulders—some as big as garages. It was like a furnace within that maze. No breeze stirred and the huge rocks had caught the sun's heat and trapped it there. At one point I slipped and fell between two towering blocks, and found myself trapped like an upturned turtle, held down by the weight of my rucksack that had become wedged among the rocks. Far below could be heard the sound of running water.

It's not an easy descent.

Below the boulder-field you veer towards a tarn, then break away along a line of cairns that lead down a series of vegetated gullies, over grassy bluffs, through stream beds and elbow-deep thistles until at last you round a spur and find the Estós hut a short stroll away. By the time you reach it you'll have a raging thirst and bruised toes. But before the aches subside and are replaced with a great sense of delight with the crossing, spare a thought for Ramond de Carbonnières who had no hut to collapse in, but who carried on walking for a few more hours, all the way down to Benasque.

Note: To create a four-day circuit and return to France by an alternative route, walk down through the Estós Valley to the Esera, which you reach a short distance above Benasque. Then head up-valley, into the upper sanctuary of the Esera, and cross the classic Port de Venasque to the Hospice de France, and from there you can easily reach Luchon through the Valleé de la Pique.

WALK 18: The Four Passes Walk

Above: **Although Pic de Sauvegarde is a very popular summit, Pic de la Mine on the other side of Port de Venasque invites few to its crest. The views, however, are as fine as those from Sauvegarde.**

Location: Central Pyrénées, to the south-east of Luchon. The first pass, Port de Venasque, links the Vallée de la Pique with that of the Esera.
Distance: 14kms (8¹/₂ miles).
Height Gain/Loss: 1085 metres (3560ft).
Time Required: 6-7 hours. (Add 1¹/₂ hours for the inclusion of Pic de Sauvegarde.)
Type of Walk: Reasonably strenuous, especially the climb to the Port de Venasque. Note that this walk should not be attempted before the end of June on account of avalanche danger in normal years. In full summer it is a safe and enjoyable circuit suitable for most competent mountain walkers.
Base: Bagnères de Luchon.
Start/Finish: Hospice de France.
Accommodation: Camping *sauvage* recommended in the Vallée de la Fréche. There is a spartan unmanned *refuge* below the Port de Venasque, on the French side. No facilities other than sleeping platforms and a fireplace.

Maps: IGN Carte de Randonnées No. 5: *Luchon* 1:50,000.

In Full View of the Maladeta

In the first edition of his *Guide to the Pyrénées*, published in 1862, Charles Packe rated this walk highly and recommended it as one of the first expeditions to be taken by the visitor to Luchon. A walker and mountaineer of considerable stamina, Packe suggested treating it as a long day's round-trip from the town (a circuit of 37 kms/23 miles), although he did make some allowances, recommending that 'Ladies who wish to avoid fatigue may take a carriage as far as the Hospice de Luchon, to await them on their return.'

It is a walk that gives some splendid, much-lauded views of the Maladeta massif, as well as an assortment of long vistas to far-off regions visited elsewhere in this book. The

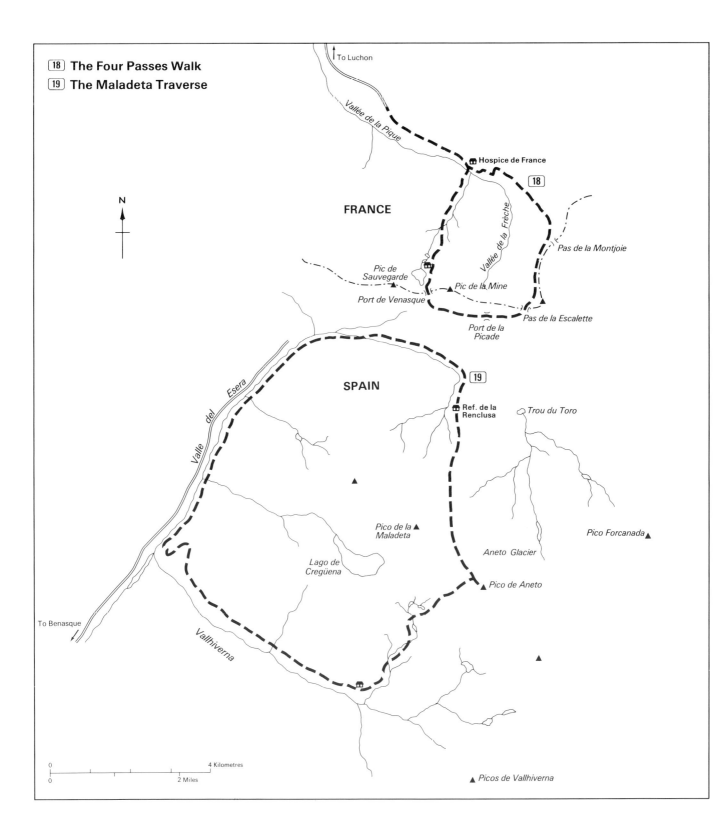

N

To Luchon

Vallée de la Pique

Hospice de France

18

FRANCE

Vallée de la Frèche

Pas de la Montjoie

Pic de Sauvegarde

Pic de la Mine

Port de Venasque

Pas de la Escalette

Port de la Picade

SPAIN

19

Ref. de la Renclusa

Trou du Toro

Esera

Valle del

Pico de la Maladeta

Pico Forcanada

Aneto Glacier

Lago de Cregüena

To Benasque

Pico de Aneto

Vallhiverna

0   4 Kilometres

0   2 Miles

Picos de Vallhiverna

passes themselves, though very different in character, are not particularly difficult or arduous, but they are no less rewarding for that. I've visited each of them on a number of occasions over the years, and have never been disappointed by the experience. On snow and ice, with crampons biting and the rocks towering over the Port de Venasque sheathed with verglas, the mountains take on a stature more akin to the Himalaya than the Pyrénées. In June flowers burst through the melting snows near Port de la Picade and Pas de l'Escalette with a rare extravagance, while in full summer you gaze over landscapes that melt in a sun-drawn veil of haze. Every season has its own particular appeal, but spring and early summer are especially fraught with avalanche danger on this circuit, and no-one should consider attempting it before the end of June at the earliest.

The Route

From Luchon take the D125 road through the Vallée de la Pique towards the Hospice de France. This road was cut by landslip in the seventies about 7.5 kilometres (4^1/$_2$ miles) from Luchon, but a footpath continuation has been made to avoid it. From the Hospice follow the mule-track heading south up to the Port de Venasque and pass through it onto the Spanish side. Descend a short distance towards the Esera Valley, then bear left and go through the easy saddle of the Port de la Picade. Skirt the left-hand slopes of a shallow bowl beyond the Port, and return to France by way of the narrow Pas de l'Escalette. The route now crosses below the Somet (or Pico) de l'Escalette, then follows closely to the frontier ridge as far as the Pas de la Montjoie before making a steady descent to the Hospice seen ahead and below in the valley.

The Walk

Having experienced the road walk from Luchon to the Hospice de France in the past, I would strongly advocate taking a taxi as far as the landslip, thus saving a rather tedious and 'sole-destroying' stretch of tarmac. Not that the woods of the Valley de la Pique are tedious; indeed they are fine woods, and at certain times of the year the road is lined with wild raspberries for the picking. But I believe it is better to save your energies for the climb up to the first pass of the day.

The Hospice de France (Packe's Hospice de Luchon) is an ancient, historic building near the head of the wooded valley which projects south-eastward from Luchon's fashionable boulevardes. Dating from the eleventh century, it was used for hundreds of years as a staging post for mule-trains trading between France and Spain. (On the Spanish side there's another, similar building—though long-since derelict—in the Esera Valley below the Maladeta massif, which served the same purpose.) It's a cause for deep regret that after nine centuries of use the Hospice de France has begun to fall into disrepair since the cutting of the road from Luchon which has effectively destroyed its tourist trade. However, the building has not always been weather-tight—as Ramond de Carbonnières discovered in 1787 when he was forced to spend a couple of storm-bound nights there. 'Rather than be absolutely in the mire,' he wrote, 'I mounted to the loft; to this, however, there were no windows, and the rain was pouring through the roof on all sides, the slates of which were continually lifted or blown away by the hurricane.'

Since there is no accommodation here I would recommend camping, so before setting out on the walk, wander a little farther up-valley beyond the Hospice (the upper reaches of the valley are known as the Vallée de la Frèche) and choose a suitable site for the tent. By pitching the tent first you are then saved the effort of carrying unnecessary weight on the circuit.

In front of the Hospice de France you cross a stream by way of a footbridge and enter a narrow valley that rises steeply ahead. A clear mule path leads through this, initially on the western side, and soon begins to rise with a series of regular zig-zags. Several times I've staggered up here under an overweight climbing sack; the first time it was to find unstable snow lying low down, and when it became necessary to cross to the east side of the valley, we were forced to wade thigh-deep through stone-pitted drifts before we found a surface hard enough to kick steps into.

Eventually we came to a small corrie containing a trio of tarns, mostly frozen. Beside one of these we found the little Refuge du Port de Venasque, a spartan unmanned hut with room for perhaps ten people on its communal sleeping platforms. As we arrived an avalanche came peeling from the direction of the Port. Unnerved, we spent an hour at the hut watching the mountains shed their late-winter burden, then accepted that we'd come at the wrong time of year and would have to back down again and leave the crossing into Spain for another visit.

Above: **Late-summer view of the Maladeta massif from the Port de Venasque.**

Other visits were made. In summer the crossing is undertaken without incident and it is sheer pleasure all the way. But on one or two occasions I've had to spend a bitter night in the hut (climbing in through the window as snowdrifts blocked the doorway) in order to make an early crossing while the snow and ice-coated slopes above were still frozen and safe. But I've also been caught out and cowered inside the hut as an avalanche actually rolled right over the flat roof!

'The tourist who makes the excursion on a warm day in August, with ample stock of provisions, can scarcely realise the dangers and rigours of this journey when undertaken in the winter or in the early spring.' (Packe)

The Port itself comes as a welcome surprise, for it remains virtually hidden until the very last moment. The path sneaks up from the tarns and along the foot of the steep, broken crags of Pic de la Mine. Then it dodges round the base of a rocky spur and zig-zags tightly among the shadows to emerge at the narrow wedge of the pass (2448m/8031ft). France lies behind you and all of Spain ahead. The mountainside falls steeply at your feet. Deep below lie the pastures and streams of the Esera Valley. But rising from it on the other side is the massive granite block of the Maladeta. It is a view almost guaranteed to catch your breath, and practically everyone who has written about this crossing has remarked in ecstatic terms about it. 'The mist cleared away so as to let me have a complete view of this giant mountain,' wrote J.D. Forbes in 1835, 'with its prodigious glaciers, which seem to me to rival those of Mont Blanc, and to vie with the ice-fields of Grindelwald.'

The Maladeta's 'prodigious glaciers' are certainly no match for those of Mont Blanc or Grindelwald today. They are mere glacial draperies, fast shrinking to expose wild and rocky little cirques and basins. But the view remains a memorable one and well worth the effort involved in reaching the pass. But even better is the view from the summit of Pic de Sauvegarde (2738m/8983ft), the easy mountain rising above the pass to the right (west). There is a path winding up to it from just below the Port de Venasque, and it's worth making the diversion for the extensive panorama that includes, not just the mass of Spanish peaks, but also many on the French side too, and the green forested foothills off to the north.

The path to Pic de Sauvegarde goes up the south side below the frontier ridge and was made as a direct consequence of the death of Archdeacon Hardwick, a companion of Packe's, who slipped and fell halfway up here on 17 August 1859. Today this path is well-worn and it takes about 45 minutes from pass to summit.

There is, however, a more sporting route to be made along the very crest of the ridge (rope advised) for those with scrambling experience; a route Keith Sweeting and I made in snow and ice one early June. Most of the ridge was tackled without the need to belay each other, but near the summit we were forced out onto the face, from which we aimed directly for the top. Finding the summit guarded by a large lip of cornice, we had to cut a tunnel through it with our ice axes before we could say we had actually reached our goal. But as we did so the mists thickened around the peak and denied us the views we'd been seeking!

To continue The Four Passes Walk it's necessary to descend from the pass to a grassy shelf above the rocks of the Peña Blanca. From here you traverse eastward with the broad, obvious saddle of Port de la Picade (2470m/8104ft) ahead, and wander up the slopes to reach it. This pass lies in the lateral ridge that divides the Esera from the Pomero Valley (which in turn sweeps down into the Vall de l'Artiga de Lin), and from the slopes leading to it you have views matching, and even competing with, those from the Port de Venasque.

Dumping our rucksacks we slumped on a rock projecting from the snow and gazed beyond the Maladeta, beyond the trench of the Esera, to the snow-coated giant of the Posets massif rising out of the hinted Estós Valley. There were knobbly peaks of the frontier ridge stretching out to the west; others that contained the valleys of Literola and Remuñe, while nearer to hand in the south-east stood that most individual of the Escaleta's mountains, the Forcanada. Not even Aneto could rival the personality of that forked summit.

Port de la Picade forms a boundary not just between the Esera and Pomero valleys, but also between Aragon and Catalonia. The Catalonian flanks melt into a shallow scooped basin. On the narrow eastern side of this the Collado de l'Infern leads to the rich, natural flower gardens of the Pomero Valley, one of the lesser-known wonders of this corner of the Pyrénées and a valley well worth visiting as part of another circuit that goes to the head of the Vall de l'Artiga de Lin, across Col dels Aranesos below the Forcanada, and down into the Esera Valley.

Resuming the walk again, cross the northern slopes of the basin below Port de la Picade and then climb to the Pas de l'Escalette (2396m/7861ft) where you regain the frontier ridge once more. This section of the ridge, however, is quite unlike the one containing Sauvegarde, Port de Venasque and Pic de la Mine. It is far gentler, without distinctive peaks, and before long you're wandering along a green crest (the Crête de Crabidès) heading north, with the Vallée de la Frèche appearing most attractive below. On the Spanish side slopes fall away to the Artiga de Lin, while ahead you gaze beyond the shaft of Vall d'Aran to a criss-cross network of ridge and peak and more hinted valleys.

The final pass of the walk does not have to be crossed. Pas de la Montjoie (2069m/6788ft) is marked with a frontier stone, and as you reach this you will find a clear path leading from it, steadily descending the grassy hillside walling the Vallée de la Frèche. Coming down here once in late June, snow was lying in great drifts, but as the valley drew nearer, I found the lower slopes were covered, not in snow, but in carpets of narcissi. Their fragrance was drawn by the sun that fought to clear the clouds, the sun that had taunted me since the Pas de l'Escalette. By the time I reached the Hospice de France, summer had come with full glory.

WALK 19: The Maladeta Traverse

Location: In the heart of the range, on the Spanish side of the frontier. The Maladeta stands at the head of the long Valle del Esera which separates it from the frontier ridge, and may be reached by road from Benasque.
Distance: 28 kms (17 miles).
Time Required: 2 days.
Type of Walk: Strenuous, demanding a knowledge and understanding of crevassed glaciers. Rope, ice axe and crampons must be taken for the crossing of two glaciers. Some scrambling involved. It is a scenically spectacular route.
Base: Benasque.
Start: Refuge de la Renclusa, on the northern slopes of the Maladeta.
Accommodation: Mountain hut (Renclusa) prior to setting out. There is a hut in the Vallhiverna which sleeps about twenty.
Map: Editorial Alpina: *Maladeta—Aneto* 1:25,000.
Guidebook: *Walks and Climbs in the Pyrénées* by Kev Reynolds (Cicerone Press).

Over the Summit of the Pyrénées

The Maladeta massif rises as a huge ice-draped block of granite above the Valle del Esera; one of the biggest mountain lumps in the Pyrénées with the highest summit of them all, Pico de Aneto—Néthou to the French—(3404m/ 11,168ft) rising as a shapely cone out of its glacier. (Maladeta comes from Mala Eta, or Más Alta, which means 'the highest'.) 'All our attention was taken up by a very majestic summit,' wrote Ramond de Carbonnières on his visit to the Esera in 1787, 'seen in all its grandeur, covered with eternal snows, surrounded with large bands of ice, and overtopping every thing. It is the Maladetta *[sic]*, a mountain reputed inaccessible.'

Inaccessible, it is not, of course, and Ramond himself attempted to prove the fallibility of this reputation when he climbed to

Above: **Returning from the Maladeta Traverse, a rough track leads above the Rio Esera with views to peaks which form the frontier with France.**

the lofty western ridge and stood: 'Alone, and in a spot which the foot of man had never trodden . . . I seemed to command the world.'

Little more than a century later two British climbers, Harold Spender and Llewellyn Smith, came into the Esera on a long trek across the Pyrénées. Spender was impressed: 'The combined group, seeming to form one mountain,' he wrote, 'gives a great impression of size and breadth . . . there is no break in the long rock ridge which here and there rises to summits—the Albe, the Maladetta [sic] the Néthou, the Moulières, and the Pouméro . . . the whole group together, so strong, so massive, so solitary.' (This 'long rock ridge' of the massif proper extends for a distance of 7 kilometres (4½ miles) without once dropping below 3000 metres/9843ft.)

The Rio Esera creates a moat round the Maladeta to north and west. On its eastern side the mountain plunges in steep ravines to the valley of the Noguera Ribagorzana, while its southern flanks fall away into the Vallhiverna whose streams flow west to join the Esera. In many respects the Esera and Vallhiverna have much in common. Both are extraordinarily rich in wild flowers in early summer. In both valleys their streams are born of melting snow and ice; both are caressed by indolent Spanish breezes, have tiny collections of tarns hidden in their upper recesses, have the overwhelming fragrance of aromatic plants drawn out by the sun and are soft, idyllic oases overshadowed by the Maladeta's otherwise grim crests and fast-shrinking glaciers.

It is a pity that a road has been scored into the upper reaches of the Esera. For those of us who knew the valley before this intrusion, its existence is a cause of immense regret. Not a sentimental regret for the loss of innocence— nor indeed because one hoped to retain an elitist, almost 'private' solitude—but because the former sanctuary of the upper Esera has been violated by the thoughtless actions of some of those drawn to it by this new-found ease of access. The Esera was once a pure gem where one could find peace, solitude and untroubled beauty among some of the finest mountain scenery in all of Europe. Vehicular access, of course, has changed all that and the wilderness aspect has gone completely. However, there are still remote corners of the Maladeta massif where pools lie almost ripple-free and one can sit upon a rock and allow the mountains to work their benign influence. (Those with a true feeling for the spirit of the mountains will surely find it in the flower-strewn pastures of the Esera and on the bold form of high ridges and summits that overlook it.)

This route gives an opportunity to sample both valley gentility and high mountain savagery; a north-south traverse of the Maladeta massif, with the chance to reach the summit of Aneto as a short diversion. There are crevassed glaciers to negotiate and sections of scrambling on rock (not rock climbing as such) with a considerable amount of exposure beneath your boots. But while the glaciers are modest by comparison with those of the Alps, they should not be treated lightly and every normal precaution should be taken when crossing them. This means the correct use of rope, ice axe and crampons—the only route in this book where their use is considered absolutely essential.

If your party is not adequately equipped, do not, under any circumstances, be tempted to follow this route onto the glaciers. The history of the massif is coloured by incidents where climbers have fallen into unseen crevasses—some were fortunate enough to be rescued, while others perished, their bodies lost for a hundred years and more before being turned out by glacial action. (One poor unfortunate was Pierre Barrau, the guide who, in 1817, accompanied Frederic Parrot on the first ascent of Pico Maladeta. In 1824 he was again bound for the Maladeta when he sank through a snow-bridge covering a crevasse in the glacier while unroped. His remains were not discovered until the glacier produced them in 1941.)

The Route

The normal ascents of Aneto and Maladeta are made from the Refugio de la Renclusa which is situated in a corrie below the Maladeta's glacier. This is on the northern side of the massif. From here climb south over rough boulder slopes to gain the ridge of the Cresta de los Portillones which divides the Aneto and Maladeta Glaciers. Descend from it by way of an easy gully, Portillón Superior, to reach the Aneto Glacier and cross this to an obvious snow saddle seen to the north-west of Aneto's summit. This is the Collado de Coronas. Climb Aneto from the col by way of a steep cone of snow or ice which takes you to the short stretch of exposed ridge known as the Pont de Mahomet, beyond which stands the summit cross.

Return to Collado de Coronas and cross through it to the south-west. Go straight down the Coronas Glacier and continue through the deep bowl of the Valle de Coronas, passing a few tarns, and down to the Vallhiverna. Either spend the night here in a hut situated near the Puente de Coronas, or camp in any one of a number of idyllic places.

Next day walk down the Vallhiverna to the Valle del Esera, which is reached at Plan de Senarta some distance up-stream from Benasque, and there turn right and continue along the valley into the upper reaches of the Esera again to complete the circuit.

Day 1: Valle del Esera to Vallhiverna

I have climbed Aneto on several separate occasions, under varying conditions and at different times of the year. An ascent in September is entirely different to one made in June. Even the route across the glacier is different, and the views are of another order. June sees snow lying way down into the Esera, and the climb up to the crest of the Portillón involves much kicking of steps in the pre-dawn ice-crust. As for the Aneto Glacier, that is usually well covered with snow and all crevasses bridged and barely detected. By late-summer, however, all this will have changed—unless there has been an unseasonal heavy snowfall. Then the route to the crest will be among alpenroses, and the glacier itself will be 'dry' which, although free of snow covering, usually means running with surface water!

The route suggested to the summit of Aneto is the *voie normale*. That is not to say it's the same route adopted by the first men to climb it in July 1842. They, de Franqueville a Frenchman, and Tchihatcheff a Russian, made a curious wandering detour of a route which began in a rough shelter not far from the present-day Renclusa hut. With their guides, Jean Argarot and Pierre Sanio, together with a pair of isard hunters, Bernard Ursule and Pierre Redonnet, they then climbed up to the Collado de Alba and descended on the far side to the Cregueña tarn. From here they crossed the Collado de Cregueña and went down into the Vallhiverna where they slept in a little *cabana*. Next day the party went up through the Vale de Coronas and, reaching Collado de Coronas, made the final ascent from there. (This ascent from the Vallhiverna is more or less reversed by our downward route.)

Four days later, Tchihatcheff made the second ascent from the Renclusa across the Aneto Glacier, thus pioneering the standard route taken by the vast majority of today's climbers.

The original shelter used by the pioneers as their overnight base in the Renclusa corrie, still stands today under an overhanging wall of rock on the left bank of the stream opposite the modern barn-like hut. This large modern hut will invariably be crowded during the height of the season, but there's a small, somewhat primitive annexe nearby, or—the better option—there is camping down below in the Esera. If this option is taken, obviously an additional hour will be needed for the day's trek. In any case, an early (4 a.m.) start is recommended in order to be across the Aneto Glacier before the sun has risen too high. If you spend the night in the hut, you're not likely to sleep beyond this hour anyway, for the guardian rouses everyone with his cry of: '*Aneto, las cuetro; las cuetro!*' (It's four o'clock! It's four o'clock!).

The ascent route begins a short distance from the Renclusa, and heads south up the steepening slopes of the Portillón spine following a meandering line of cairns. In the dark this is not always easy to follow, but as you approach the crest the sun should be rising to lighten the way. Now you'll be able to look across the Maladeta Glacier and the ice-scoured corries beyond it, and over the shadowed valley to the frontier ridge. Far off the foothills pale into a milky light. But standing on the crest you see Aneto's glacier take on the stain of sunrise. The first sighting of the summit comes from this point too. Far better than this, though, is the view off to the double-pronged Forconada in the east, and the sea of peaks beyond the Noguera Ribagorzana. Lost among that tangle of summits are the Besiberri peaks and those of Travessani, as well as the confusion of rocky spikes and ridges of the Encantados.

Cresta de los Portillones is a wonderful belvedere and a major watershed, separating as it does the Maladeta and Aneto Glaciers. And here's an added curiosity. The waters which flow from the Maladeta Glacier, *west of the Portillón*, flow south as the Esera out of the mountains to the Ebro basin. From there they head eastwards to the Mediterranean. Aneto's glacier, on the other hand, rising as it does to the *east* of the Portillón, sends its waters down to the Plan de Aiguallut at the head of the Esera Valley, and there they plunge into the Trou de Toro and disappear. In fact these waters find an outlet to the north, in the Vall de l'Artiga de Lin, where they flow down to the Vall d'Aran as the Garonne. Then the river

Right: **Icy pool below the Aneto Glacier. The summit is rather foreshortened from here.**

which disappeared when it drained through the ice in August 1857.

Collado de Coronas allows a view through the ridge to the big Posets massif rising above the Esera and Estos valleys. It's a surprise view and a very fine one, but as there is still a little more work to do before reaching the summit, it's best not to dally too long here. Those views will hopefully still be clear on the downward route.

The steep cone of snow or ice which rises beyond the col may be eased with the use of crampons, but calf muscles will still complain at the angle. Once you've overcome this there is just a scramble across the beautifully solid granite rocks of the Pont de Mahomet (Puente de Mahoma) to the summit, marked by crucifix and Virgin. This short ridge section once enjoyed a certain notoriety, but in truth there is nothing very difficult about it unless the rocks are sheathed in verglas. Then the exposure takes on a new dimension. Packe wrote in his *Guide*:

> 'This bit is the most trying to the nerves of the whole expedition; and as you bestride this narrow ledge, crossing it on hands and feet, with the clouds floating around you, you feel verily suspended in mid air.'

As the highest point in the Pyrénées, Aneto's summit offers a vast view, but it is not particularly inspiring, for it lacks any major feature to draw the eye. There is a bewildering mass of distant peaks and hinted valleys, a gleam of water in a shadowed vale, a far green meadow and the darker greenery of forest. There are teardrop tarns, too far away to have character, and the beckoning gulf of the Vallhiverna to the south.

Sometimes I've basked on the summit in brilliant sunshine, butterflies drifting past—even at 3404 metres (11,168ft). Sometimes there have been great banks of cumulus piped into distant valleys, individual summits rising from a sea of froth. Once though, on the day Keith Sweeting and I made this traverse, a dirty, threatening grey scum of storm cloud was blown our way by a cold wind, and we beat a hasty retreat from Aneto's crown—though not fast enough to avoid its temper soon after.

Tearing yourself away from the summit return to the Collado de Coronas and pass through it. The Glacier de Coronas is spread below, a small apron of ice, steep at the top but easing lower down. On either side of it, craggy ridges stretch out to contain a hanging valley and mark the extent of the glacier's former

Left: **On the Aneto Glacier.**

heads west, out to the lowlands, watering the vineyards of Bordeaux before emptying into the Atlantic!

The route from the hut will have brought you onto the crest near the Portillón Inferior, a temptingly easy gully leading down the eastern side of the rocky spine. You should resist the temptation to descend this, as it will only make for a longer and more difficult approach to the glacier. Instead bear right and wander along the ridge, crossing a minor summit and following cairns until you come to another gully, Portillón Superior. In the early part of the season this is often rimed with ice and may require some care to negotiate, but later, as summer proceeds, so it becomes a descent route of little significance.

By the time you reach the edge of the glacier it will be obvious whether or not it is snow covered. If it is, then rope the party together and proceed directly across the glacier, making a rising line towards the Collado de Coronas. There will almost certainly be a well-trodden track leading across, but normal safety precautions should still be adopted.

If, however, the glacier is 'dry', continue along the base of the Portillón towards Collado Maldito, then cut along the top of the icefield under the main ridge to avoid the major crevasses—but taking care not to stray too close to the edge of the bergschrund. Near the col there was once, so Packe tells us, a lake width. Stomping down the glacier, Sweeting and I were caught by the storm we'd seen approaching from the top of Aneto. It was not a happy descent. Strong winds and rapidly diminishing visibility were by no means welcome, but they were of minor importance compared with the tongues of lightning that licked at the rocks bordering our glacier, while crashing thunder drums burst all about us.

A trail of cairns leads from the glacier snout to a few small tarns, and you plunge from them through the hanging valley, very steeply in places, passing from a barren world of rock and old snow patches to dwarf pine and alpenroses. There's a strong sense of wilderness in this descent that is relieved only when you go through the lower reaches of forest and into the Vallhiverna itself. Suddenly the world smiles again.

There was no real hut here when we made our first traverse, just a simple shelter offering a roof for the night and a fireplace. As it was still raining hard when we arrived we gave up the idea of a stream-side bivouac and set up home for the night inside. A pair of muleteers also came in to dodge the rain and, huddled round our fire, they shared with us their dry, several-days-old bread which they softened with wine squirted from goat-skin containers.

Day 2: Vallhiverna to the Upper Esera

The Vallhiverna deserves more than a cursory visit. Given sufficient time and energy there are more tarns to explore up in the Llosas cirque at its head, and a journey onto the summit of the Picos de Vallhiverna for a fresh view of the Maladeta makes an entertaining day's outing. There are many interesting corners to poke into; cascades to gaze on, flowers to enjoy, wild fruits to pick.

The Maladeta massif is unquestionably Charles Packe country, the Vallhiverna one of his favourite valleys. This wealthy Leicestershire squire had a passion for the Pyrénées rivalled only by that of his friend, the great mountaineer-eccentric Count Henry Russell. In the summer of 1865 Packe spent 31 days around the Maladeta—mostly based in the Vallhiverna—taking measurements and making calculations from numerous vantage points in order to draw up the first decent map of the region. Russell describes how, with neither predecessors nor books to guide him, he 'conscientiously explored and mapped . . . no less than 1000 square kilometres (386 square miles), where none but chamois hunters

Right: **Leaving the summit of Aneto involves scrambling over the granite blocks of the Pont de Mahomet. Pico Maladeta is the peak just right of centre of the photograph.**

had trodden before him'.

Packe made the first descent of the Vallhiverna gorge which opens into the Esera. Today a track avoids this and leads along the hillside above it. The walk down the valley is gentle and extremely pleasant with the sun shining and birds flitting among the pines. In early summer several of the low cliffs walling the track are a-dazzle with *Ramonda myconi*, a delicate and very pretty little primrose-like flower that is one of more than a hundred plants endemic to the Pyrénées. Later, as summer works its way towards autumn, valley pastures are flecked with the pale purple heads of autumn crocus, and tiny pools amid these pastures add a sparkle, catching the reflection of the Picos de Vallhiverna smiling from the south-east.

By comparison the Esera teems with humanity, and you wander up-stream along the track from the Plan de Senarta on the eastern side of the valley, past the gaunt buildings of Banos de Benasque and a Civil Guard post and, round the curve of the valley where the ancient Hospital (Hospice) de Benasque stands in ruins. The track leads on, over the stream in the Plan d'Estan where there used to be tarns but alas are no more, and up among clumps of dwarf pine with the swelling mass of Maladeta rising above your right shoulder.

Gazing up at it one is likely to become nostalgic for the lost tranquillity of high places.

WALK 20: Luchon to Andorra

Location: Eastern central Pyrénées; France, Spain and Andorra.
Distance: 132kms (82 miles).
Time Required: 9 days.
Type of Walk: Strenuous with a fair amount of height gain and loss each day. Much of the route is poorly waymarked and without paths, and some passes require a little scrambling. Best tackled as a backpacking expedition. Essential to carry food supplies for several days at a time.
Start: Bagnères de Luchon.
Finish: El Serrat, Andorra.
Accommodation: Mountain huts, one or two hotels. Camping or bivouacking necessary at the end of some stages.
Maps: IGN Cartes de Randonnées Nos. 5, 6 & 7 1:50,000. Editorial Alpina: *Maladeta-Aneto* 1:25,000, *La Vall d'Aran, Pica d'Estats-Mont Roig* and *Andorra* at 1:40,000.
Guidebooks: *Walks and Climbs in the Pyrénées* by Kev Reynolds (Cicerone Press). *Pyrénées High Level Route* by Georges Véron (Gastons-West Col).

A Grand Walk Through a Mountain Wilderness

Of all sections of the Pyrénéan High Route, this stretch is undoubtedly the hardest. On Day Two the highest pass of the classic traverse of the range from the Atlantic to the Mediterranean has to be crossed. On a clear summer's day this may not be particularly difficult to find or negotiate, but should visibility be limited, or verglas be lying on the rocks (not unusual at this altitude, even in late summer), then the Coll de Mulleres assumes a sinister profile and becomes a much more serious obstacle than most novice mountain trekkers would care to experience.

There are other hard days. Long days with remote passes to tackle, one after another in close and challenging succession far from habitation. There are high exposed ridges and deep forest-clad ravines. There are broad sloping hillsides chequered with rock slabs and

Above: **Estany Tort de Rius occupies a wonderful landscape of stone and water; very much a zone of silence.**

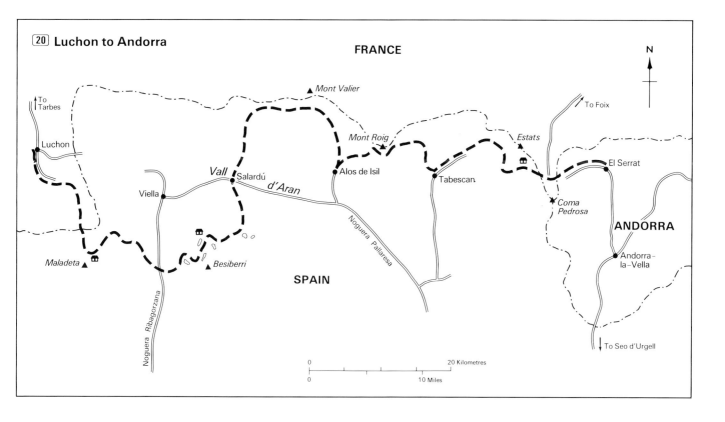

FRANCE

N

To Tarbes

Luchon

To Foix

Mont Valier

Mont Roig

Estats

To Seo d'Urgell

Vall

Salardú

d'Aran

Alos de Isil

El Serrat

Viella

Noguera Pallaresa

Tabescan

Coma Pedrosa

ANDORRA

Maladeta

Besiberri

SPAIN

Andorra-la-Vella

Noguera Ribagorzana

0   20 Kilometres

0   10 Miles

poor grass with only a vague scattering of cairns to indicate the onward route. Since the maps of the area leave much to be desired, it is necessary to have a good eye for the country, to be able to read the land and understand the intricacies of a wilderness environment.

It's a backpacker's route. There are huts along the way, but insufficient to enable each night to be spent beneath a roof. There are just two small villages between Luchon and Andorra, and as their food stores carry only a limited stock, supplies for several days must be carried from the start.

But it is a rewarding journey, for the scenery is among the most spectacular of the whole mountain chain, and the trekker gains a deeper understanding, not only of the Pyrénées, but of himself as he overcomes each natural obstacle set in his path. The journey through the wilderness country between Luchon and Andorra is one of *the* classic walks, not only of the Pyrénées, but of Europe.

The Route

It begins in the very heart of the range by crossing out of France and into the realms of the Maladeta massif on the Spanish side; from forested valleys to views of glaciers, small snowfields and high jagged crests. Heading eastward the Mulleres ridge is crossed and a long descent made to the valley of the Noguera Ribagorzana. Then comes a stage of tarns and granite peaks to the north-west of the Encantados region, before tackling a real wilderness that eventually leads to the Vall d'Aran, that geographical anomaly where the two axes of the Pyrénées overlap.

Between the Maladeta and Vall d'Aran the frontier makes a sharp northward turn, then resumes its roughly eastward trend at Pic de Sacaube overlooking the Pont du Roi. The frontier, though not the watershed, follows the ridge linking the peaks that form the northern wall of Vall d'Aran, and having left the village of Salardú, our route wanders below this frontier line, then crosses several transverse ridges in superb, challenging and isolated country, before sampling a brief taste of the splendours of the valley of Rio Cardos, the head of which opens to lush meadows and woodland glades with clear, running streams.

From the head of the Rio Cardos a path takes you up towards the range's easternmost 3000 metre peaks, and traverses another region of solitude before dropping into the Vall Ferrera, the last valley on the trek through

Spain. Beyond Port de Bouet the route dips to a French enclave, then up and over the last pass into Andorra.

Days 1 and 2: Luchon to the Noguera Ribagorzana

The morning train arrives in Bagnères de Luchon in time for a late breakfast at a boulevard café. Tree-clad mountains rise on three sides of the town, invariably spiralling mists or squeezing rain from within them. I've lost count of the wet days I've spent in Luchon over the past couple of decades, but it's a town that has its attractions despite the rain, including a covered market and plenty of food stores in which to stock up for the wilderness days ahead.

It's not unusual to see mountain trekkers heading out of town with long sticks of French bread projecting from their rucksacks and pockets bulging with fruit and cheese and dried meats. Not unusual, perhaps, but it's still a source of amusement to the procession of spa patients wandering delicately beneath their black umbrellas, with handkerchiefs or scarves clasped over their mouths. (If it's a choice of spa waters and mud baths or the clarity of a mountain stream and the fragrance of aromatic plants, I know where I'd rather be heading!).

There is little enjoyment to be gained from walking the long kilometres of tarmac through the Vallée de la Pique above Luchon, so I'd recommend the extravagance of hiring a taxi as far as the end of the road. As explained elsewhere, this road used to go as far as the Hospice de France, but landslips put paid to that and the route is now barred two thirds of the way along. But it is still worthwhile taking a taxi as far as you can and walking the remainder of the route by a combination of diverted forest path and old roadway.

The route from the Hospice de France to the Port de Venasque is one of the best known in this corner of the Pyrénées (*see* Walk 18). Once the avalanches of late spring/early summer have finished pouring from the walling peaks, the path is clear and straightforward—if rather steep in places. There is an unmanned *refuge* just below the pass. It's a very basic shelter, however, and in summer one would not give this meagre hovel a second glance, but rather continue straight past to the Port de Venasque (2448m/8031ft) which reveals the glory of Spain's high peaks hovering on the far side of the Esera's deep trench.

Between the Port de Venasque and the great bulk of Maladeta the gentle stepped pastures of the Esera entice with their superb wild campsites among dwarf pines and myriads of alpine flowers. On the northern slopes of the Maladeta you can just make out the barn-like Refugio de la Renclusa, base for climbs on the high surrounding peaks, and the starting point for the Maladeta Traverse (Walk 19).

Descending from the pass, make towards the head of the Esera's valley where, just beyond the Trou de Toro, there's a level plain with streams winding across it. Above this to the right stands Pico de Aneto (Néthou to the French), but half-left ahead, above the next step of valley, the Valleta de la Escaleta, stands the double-pronged Forcanada (2881m/9452ft). Despite its modest height it dominates the rough boulder-pocked grasslands of the Escaleta, and our route leads towards it following a line of cairns beside several small tarns. The way becomes steadily more rugged until at last there is practically no more vegetation and only an ice-scratched glacial pavement leading to the very crest of mountains running south from the Forcanada. In clear weather conditions you can gaze westward across the shoulder of Pico de Barrancs to the ice-draped northern slopes of Aneto and Maladeta beyond, and speculate how many more decades are left before those glaciers give way to a similar landscape to the one you are now crossing.

Coll de Mulleres (2928m/9606ft) is not an obvious pass, but merely the lowest part of the ridge leading between Cap de Toro and Tuc de Mulleres. On the eastern side lies a steep descent over broken crags onto a true wilderness of boulders, screes and diced rocks. More steep bands of cliffs lie threateningly below, and in poor visibility the traverse of this region could be hazardous to the uninitiated. Far below lie several tarns, but below these are grass slopes once more, then trees and fragrant shrubs, sheep grazing, streams and little cascades, and at last, meadowlands open to the sun. There is only one unwelcome intrusion into this pleasing land of sudden soft shadows, and that is the ugly concrete snout of the Viella tunnel which gives road access between the Noguera Ribagorzana and Vall d'Aran. Better by far to pitch a tent just short of the valley itself, with only the stream and high mountains for company. But for those who prefer a roof overhead, there is the ancient inn of the Hospice (or Hospital) de Viella standing near the tunnel's snout where a night's lodging may be arranged.

Above: **From the slopes leading to Col de Calverante a good view looks down beyond the laden trekker to the Calverante lakes.**

Days 3 and 4: Noguera Ribagorzana to Salardú

The two days' walking from the Viella tunnel to Salardú in the Vall d'Aran are among the very best possible among these mountains. They're hard enough days for the laden backpacker, but they're scenically magnificent, and sufficiently tempting in themselves to extend into three or even four days to maximise the experience. Yet for all their

glories they are not stages to treat casually, for there are several passes to traverse and some rugged and trackless countryside to labour through. In fine, clear conditions the journey will be a very different undertaking to one tackled in mist or storm.

Leaving the Ribagorzana behind there follows a gentle amble through beechwoods into the rock-pitted meadows of the Vall de Conangles, then up to Port de Rius (2315m/7595ft), the day's first pass where one gains a fine view back towards the Mulleres ridge crossed yesterday, and the snows of the Maladeta beyond that. But ahead, facing north-east, there lies Estany de Rius, a gleaming tarn with granite rocks rising directly from the water. A path heads along its left-hand shoreline, then southward over a hummock of rock and poor grass to another landscape of tarns, white granite boulders, slabs and trim but modest peaks jutting all around.

The walk through this region of peace and tranquillity is a sheer delight, but there's a rise at the far end to another pass, Collado de l'Estany de Mar, seen at the end of the northern spur of Besiberri Nord. On reaching this pass a fresh valley system spreads itself far below. Yet another tarn lies a little more than 200 metres (656ft) beneath the col, and a steep drop is hinted at its far end. Rising from that is the big block of Montardo d'Aran with misted blue sierras forming a distant backcloth.

Down then to Estany de Mar on a steeply winding path, across a level marshland, jumping one or two streams, round the lake by projecting cliffs and over rocky bluffs to its northern end. Then down once more, this time to the dammed Estany de la Restanca to find the little Refugi de la Restanca nestling above it.

Next day is another long one, with a steep haul straight after breakfast to reach Port de Güellicrestada, a saddle below Montardo d'Aran, which is frequently climbed directly from the pass. Güellicrestada has no rough descent on its eastern side, but an easy stroll down to a grassy plateau and a broad opening country littered with tarns and boulders like sleeping hippopotami, with huge views off to the Agulles de Travessani in the south, and the long ridges of Besiberri and Tumeneja in the south-west. It is all such deserted, splendid country; an outlier of the Sierra de los Encantados—the Enchanted Mountains.

Almost due east of Port de Güellicrestada, and about an hour's walking away without

benefit of a path, is the brief saddle and watershed of Port de Caldes (2550m/8366ft). Below this lie yet more tarns at the northern end of the Circ de Colomers, a wild collection of peaks making a rim to the Aigües Tortes-San Mauricio National Park. On this northern side of the ridge all streams flow to the Vall d'Aran and by way of the Garonne to the Atlantic. On the southern side the mountain slopes all drain towards the Ebro and the Mediterranean.

Out of the Colomers cirque a narrow path leads into the long pastoral valley of Aiguamotx which will deliver the trekker into Salardú, but the thirteen kilometre stretch of track through the valley, coming as it does at the end of the day, ensures that one arrives in Salardú footsore and weary and more than

ready to settle the dust in one of the village's bars.

Days 5 to 7: Salardú to Pla de Boavi

Salardú is torn between ancient and modern. Typical of many of the villages on the Spanish side of the mountains it has its narrow alleyways, its grey stone buildings and time-weathered doors. It also has long views down through the valley and over a tangle of far-off ridges to the snows of the Maladeta. But the modern world is slowly infiltrating and nearby hills are being adorned with ski tows. Salardú has responded so far with one or two breeze-block hotels, although there is hut-style accommodation in the main street, and a short distance up-valley the *Centre Excursionista de*

Above: **Estany de Baborte is lodged in a remote hanging valley.**

Catalunya (CEC) has provided the Chalet Juli Soler i Santaló with room for more than a hundred in its dormitories.

Above the village a broad grassy dome rises for 800 metres (2625ft) to Serra de Comalada. To the east of this runs a long swathe of pasture and forest, gently sloping to the north from the broad saddle of Pla de Beret. Several streams ooze into this marshy saddle, and from its humble cradle comes the Riu Noguera Pallaresa to flow in a curious northward loop before veering clockwise round a large block of mountain and then rushing south in search of the Ebro.

Leaving Salardú the route heads up to Pla de Beret from which point there are alternative ways of reaching the pretty little hamlet of Alos de Isil. The easiest is to follow the Noguera Pallaresa for more than 30 kilometres (18½ miles) along a broad track, passing about halfway along it the ruined hamlet of Montgarri with its *Sanctuari* dating from 1117. It is a surprisingly interesting valley route, though not as restful as might be presumed. There are opportunities to gather wild raspberries or strawberries growing beside the track, and at certain times of the year there are plenty of flowers and fragrant shrubs to brighten the way.

The other route from Pla de Beret is considerably more taxing for it entails crossing the eastern wall of the valley by way of the Basibé tarns and the Marimanya ridge (2660m/8727ft). This is a fair-weather only stage, preferably without heavy loads, but in good conditions it makes a splendid day's trekking with views over a large patch of rolling country.

From Alos de Isil a very early start should be made to attempt the long, hard crossing of the ridges that splay out from Mont Roig (Mont Rouch to the French). There are three passes to negotiate in country as wild and remote as any yet experienced. Paths are in short supply, although in their absence occasional cairns or paint flashes will be a welcome guide. It is by no means a stage to consider lightly and should be avoided by the inexperienced. Settled weather is essential, for these high ridges are not the place to be caught by a storm, and should the clouds descend problems with route finding will doubtless occur. In the unhappy event of an accident you're a long way from assistance; a long way from anywhere. But given fitness, good conditions and experience it is a magnificent day's mountain travel that will remain firm in the treasury of wild country memories.

The first pass of the day is that of Col de Curios (2475m/8120ft), shown as Col de Cornella on some maps. Reached through a bowl of scree and boulder debris, this col is little more than a narrow V cut from the south-west ridge of Mont Roig. A dramatic little pass, it gives a sudden surprise view onto a hanging valley bearing a brace of tarns with the soft ridge of Sierra de Mitjana opposite. A steep stone-filled gully leads down to the tarns, then you mount grass slopes to Col de Calverante (2420m/7940ft)—sometimes shown as Col de Curios on certain maps to add a touch of confusion!

Through this col an easy slope leads to a solitary tarn trapped in a remote cup of mountainside, soft turf at its edges and a curving ridge walling it in a horseshoe above. Cairns trace a route for twenty minutes or so up to that horseshoe to find the third and final pass of the day, the upper Col de Calverante (2610m/8563ft) which is not named at all on some maps, but which enjoys a vast panorama over a bewilderingly complex maze of ridge, peak and hinted valley. Steeply below to the east lies Estany Major, and having descended to its natural rock-slab embankment, yet more tarns will be seen in a string to the north.

Down clean slabs of glacier-smoothed boulders, alongside streams that dance in spray, passing one tarn after another below the looming East Face of Mont Roig, you come at last to grass and shrubs and trees, with the warm fragrance of Spain rising to greet you, and the harsh electric buzzing of innumerable insects all around.

The deep valley of the Roia de Mollas is dense with forest and the faint path leading into it has a habit of disappearing under rampant foliage. But eventually a track is located which leads comfortably to the little farmstead of Cuanca; a bewitching place of old stone walls and briars on the bank of a noisy stream. Beyond it a broadening farm track runs clearly all the way to Tabescan where a metalled road announces civilisation.

Civilisation at Tabescan consists of one or two small hotels and bar/restaurants, food stores and an ugly electricity station. After the high wild country traversed since Salardú it comes as something of a shock, but up-valley, two hours or so away, lie the idyllic park-like meadows of Pla de Boavi sliced by streams and with silver birch, spruce and neat shrubs growing in what seems to be landscaped order. It makes an obvious pitch for a small tent.

Days 8 and 9: Pla de Boavi to Andorra

All major difficulties of the route should now be over. Given clear weather the remaining two days of mountain travel are reasonably straightforward, even though they pass through yet more remote country without habitation other than the occasional shepherd's hut and the climbers' *refuge* (Refugi de Vall Ferrera) on the slopes of Pic d'Areste. There are some awkward sections, it is true, but although they are not especially difficult, the days are certainly not without charm or interest. The countryside now takes on a different appearance to that of the earlier route. It has a more lavish vegetation with deserted pasturelands and forests darkening the lower hillsides and valleys. The rock of the mountains has a reddish-ochre sheen to it, and when you come across a hay barn its uneven stone walls seem to melt in a camouflage against the hill on which it is perched.

On leaving Pla de Boavi there is a climb of over 1000 metres (3281ft) to tackle before reaching the first pass. Happily for most of the way there is a path to follow, and the ascent is not unduly taxing so long as you make a reasonably early start to avoid the worst of the heat. It is only later that the path disappears.

Heading into the Sellente Valley there is forest shade at first, then streams to cross, a level pasture with more streams converging, and finally a sweeping zig-zag path which climbs to a higher pastureland with the ruins of a former *refuge* standing at its northern entrance. The path then fades. Reached about 3½ hours from Pla de Boavi, Coll de Sellente (2485m/8153ft) is the key to the grass, rock and tarn-filled scoop of the Circ de Baborte—one of several little cirques in this isolated and largely untrodden quarter. Rising a short distance away to the north-east are the 3000 metre peaks of Sotllo, Estats and Montcalm on whose northern slopes are found the very last glacial vestiges of the range. Across their summits run the frontier ridge again, and below these peaks on both sides the country for once has more similarities than differences.

In the Baborte cirque a number of little pools are linked by clear winding streams, but leading to its lip, Estany de Baborte is a larger tarn of character and sufficient size to dominate the cup of hillside in which it is trapped. As you approach from the north-west, you see beyond its mirror levels to the empty gulf of distance, with far-off sierras hovering above the hint of the Val Ferrera's great moat. The scramble over rocky bluffs and along steep slopes on the tarn's northern shore adds a certain spice to the day. (High on a spur of hillside above the tarn there sits a small metal emergency bivouac hut, Refugi del Cinquantenari, otherwise known as Refugi de Baborte. It has sufficient room for about nine occupants.)

Vall Ferrera comes into view. A long deep trench, heavily forested but with open pastures in its bed, lies 500 metres or so below (1600ft). For some time there appears to be no path leading into it, but after passing a shepherd's hut occupying a shelf of rough grazing land, a trail heads into the forest and battles a way down to the river.

The frontier ridge runs roughly north-south from the heights above Pla de Boavi as far as Andorra. Having reached the bed of Vall Ferrera it is then necessary for the trekker to aim eastwards in order to gain one of the passes, or *Ports,* that allow escape from Spain. There are two or three to choose from, but the most obvious is that of Port de Bouet which is reached by way of the marshy steps of hillside above Pla de Bouet. This is lovely rolling hill country; soft and gentle mountains with open moorland-like slopes of cropped grass leading to other little cirques that entice for future visits. Circ de Baiau is particularly full of promise. Beyond its ridge stands Andorra. Above it to the south rises Coma Pedrosa, the highest summit of that tiny country, from which a tremendous panorama is revealed.

But to the Port de Bouet one must forsake the attractions of neighbouring peaks, and concentrate fully on the job in hand. That is rewarding enough, for the pass looks down onto the valley of Vicdessos, a narrow French enclave across which rise more Andorran mountains. Andorra blocks that valley and closes its eastern side, and on this final stage of the walk from Luchon you turn your back at last on Spain, trespass briefly over France and take a winding trail up the mountainside to find that historic pass, Port de Rat. Beyond it lies Andorra and a long unhappy road of concrete through the Valira del Nord to the capital, Andorra-la-Vella, a modern hell of noise and traffic fumes. After the peace, solitude and day-long beauty of the Pyrénéan heartland, Andorra's brazen excesses come as a hideous echo of all one's worst nightmares.

I recommend spending a night in El Serrat and either walking on eastwards next day, across the grain of the country to Val d'Inclés or l'Hospitalet, or taking a bus to Andorra-la-Vella and another from there out to France and the train home. Home with your memories of a truly classic walk.

WALK 21: The Tour of the Agulles de Travessani

Above: **Above Estany Major de Colomers the path leads through a gentle vale of soft turf and indolent streams.**

Location: In the western section of the *Parque Nacional de Aigües Tortes i Sant Maurici,* south of the Vall d'Aran and east of the valley of the Noguera Ribagorzana. Approached through the valley of the Noguera de Tor, beyond Caldas de Bohi.

Distance: 12kms (7¹/₂ miles).

Time Required: 7¹/₂-8 hours.

Type of Walk: Fairly strenuous and demanding in terms of route-finding. There are long periods without the benefit of a path and cairns are not always obvious. It is very rough under foot for much of the way, but the views are always extremely grand. This is a fine-weather route, not to be attempted if there is threat of poor visibility. A map and compass will be essential items of equipment.

Base: Refugi Ventosa i Calvell (C.E.C).

Map: Editorial Alpina: *Montardo* 1:25,000.

From Tarn to Tarn in a Wilderness Land

South of the Vall d'Aran, and bordered to the west by the valley of the Noguera Ribagorzana, and to the east by the Noguera Pallarésa, there lies a vast region of granite mountains spattered with tarns of all shapes and sizes. It is a bewildering, bewitching land; a complex terrain whose geography is sometimes difficult to untangle. Long jagged ridges splay out in all directions to confuse the direction of rivers, while many of the numerous little lakes appear to have no outflow at all.

Much of this great spread of country is included in the *Parque Nacional de Aigües Tortes i Sant Maurici*—the second of Spain's Pyrénéan National Parks, and one that has an

enormous appeal for those who love a semi-wilderness area. The best-known corner of this National Park is that around the Sant Maurici lake, where the beautiful twin Encantats peaks rise out of the forests. There is road access from the village of Espot, yet it has to be said that this access has seriously devalued a once-delightful patch of rugged mountain country. However, the western sector of the Park remains very much the domain of the hardened walker and climber. Roads merely nibble at the outlying regions, and from their head there's very little to hint at the glories hidden above. This certainly reduces the number of visitors, while the very harshness of the land helps to leave much of it trail-free and gloriously 'empty'.

There are some splendid peaks here of considerable appeal to those of us who love to spend long hours of solitude grappling with the intricacies of mountains that never make the pages of the popular climbing magazines. There are no reputations to be made among these little-known summits, faces and ridges,

yet the sport they offer is 'among the finest in all the Pyrénées. Experienced mountain walkers will also find much to reward a visit.

The Besiberri ridge is a lengthy wall containing numerous individual summits, overlooking a real Genesis country of stark granite boulders, slips of snow and glistening tarns. There is very little vegetation and no pasture to speak of in this battleground of nature. But what a wonderland it is!

To the north-east of Besiberri a spine of peaks stands out like the backbone of a dinosaur turned to stone. These peaks are known as the Agulles (or aiguilles) de Travessani; a bristling crest culminating in Pic de Travessani (2755m/9039ft). Between Besiberri and the Agulles lies a high plateau, stepped by past glaciations and with a collection of about twenty tarns trapped by huge granite slabs like stranded, bleached whales.

To the east of Travessani is the Colomers amphitheatre. This too, is a high granite plateau, similarly stepped by long-forgotten glaciers and with another generous spattering

Above: **This strange-looking hut has been superseded by the well-appointed Refugi Ventosa i Calvell.**

Right: **From the Travessani tarns you can see towards the Port de Colomers.**

of tarns—even more numerous than those to the west. The waters from these flow northwards into the Vall d'Aran, and through that valley to join the Garonne which in turn heads out to the Atlantic near Bordeaux. All the waters draining the Besiberri area west of the Agulles de Travessani flow south to the Ebro basin, and from there to the Mediterranean. Crossing this watershed, to north and south of the Travessani needles, are two passes; Port de Caldes and Port de Colomers. By linking the two, a magnificent, challenging circuit can be achieved—but it is not for those whose requirements include soft grassy valleys and clear footpaths. This is a demanding walk of raw grandeur.

The Route

A road leads north through the valley of the Noguera de Tor, which in turn branches away from the Noguera Ribagorzana near Pont de Suert. It continues beyond the fashionable spa of Caldas de Bohi and ends at the Cavallers dam where a path goes along the eastern side of the dammed lake, into the rough boulder-strewn Riu Mallo pastures, and on to reach a fine hut; Refugi Ventosa i Calvell, owned by the *Centre Excursionniste de Catalogne* (the Catalan Alpine Club). This makes an ideal base for walks and climbs in the area.

From the hut the route heads northward in the shadow of the Agulles de Travessani, then bears east to cross Port de Caldes, from which point a longish descent is made to Estany Major de Colomers, on whose bank stands another hut. Now you head south, going from one tarn to another, gradually rising higher above the complexities of a wild valley system towards the broad head of an amphitheatre, then west on an easy ascent to Port de Colomers.

The descent from this pass is long and sometimes a little confusing. It takes you from one level to another, from one tarn to the next, trading jumbled boulders for a narrow lick of pasture, and from there to more bald granite slopes until eventually you reach the spongy margins of Estany Negre. A short steep climb leads back to the hut. Allow about $7^1/_2$–8 hours for the circuit.

The Walk

As with a number of walks described in this book, this outing is best begun earlier than one would normally consider necessary for a route of this length and one that does not entail a glacier crossing. An early start enables you to catch the magical light radiating from behind

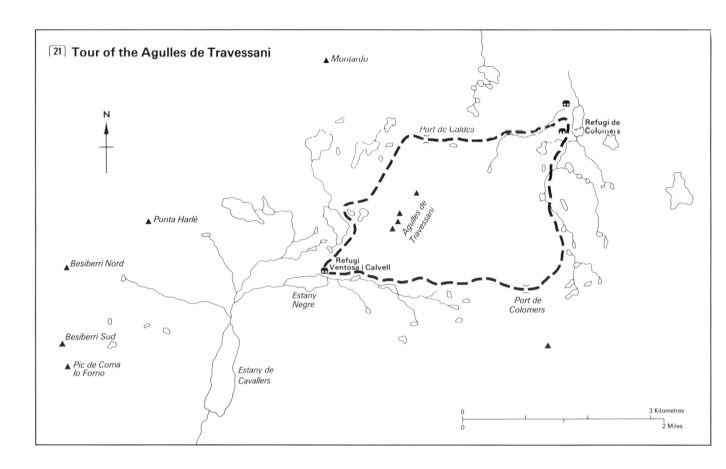

the Travessani pinnacles, reflecting in the still waters of the many tarns, and bathing the Besiberri ridge in its soft and liquid glow. Better too, to start early to allow time to stray off-route in order to study a cascade or to watch isard or marmots or vultures circling on huge outstretched wings. Better to start early and fill the day with memories for tomorrow, than to rush through this untamed land without time to absorb its many attributes.

One such early morning, quite recently, three of us drifted from one tarnside to another in a daze of wonder. We had discovered a magic land and were heady with it. There were tarns and pools and larger lakes everywhere; some banked by high grassy hillocks, some walled with granite. The Agulles rose as jagged teeth against the light. Besiberri's extensive ridge looked superb off to the west—especially Pic Harlé and Pa de Sucre; a challenging, wild and magnificent wall of peaks. There were cows grazing on the steep slopes banking the southern end of the Estanys de Travessani, and higher still, horses untended on a wild stretch of pastureland. But peace was in the air. Peace and an incredible stillness, broken only by the occasional 'plop' as a frog landed in a pool.

To begin with there is a path leading up to the first cluster of tarns known as the Estanys de Travessani. It's an encouraging start, but do not be fooled into thinking you'll be on footpath all day, for before long the trail vanishes and you follow instead a meandering line of cairns. This can be confusing, for there are several such lines of cairns leading in a variety of directions! It is important, therefore, to note that the Port de Caldes lies to the north-east of the first tarns, and you should regularly check your direction of travel with the compass. Cairns will lead all the way to the pass, and as they do, so the landscape unfolds, and there are splendid views back to the south and the west where you can attempt to count—and name—all the little lakes that come into sight. As ever, the Besiberri ridge dominates the view, while at the head of this valley system Montardo makes a swaggering challenge to be taken seriously. (Although it is as high as a number of other peaks around, it offers a very easy ascent from the south-east and is probably the most popular mountain— by number of ascents—in the area.)

Wandering up towards Port de Caldes you cross a series of granite ledges, knolls and minor ridges, still following neat little cairns. Then you see the unmistakable twisted outline of Estany de les Mangades below to the left, with the smaller Estany del Port de Caldes above it, and you then bear right with the obvious col seen just ahead.

Once on the Port de Caldes (2550m/8366ft) a blue wash of ridges that enclose the Colomers wilderness beckon from the east. In that fascinating new vista more tarns wink in the sunshine and promise a continuation of good things to come. This pass is crossed on the Pyrénéan High Route, having come from the Refugio de la Restanca to the west, but although I had only crossed it a few years previously, when I stood here on this circuit my mind went blank and I couldn't remember any of it! (Strange how changing circumstances can produce alternative scenes in memory.) I spread out my map and took several compass bearings to make absolutely certain I was where I'd hoped to be, and it was not until a little later, on the descent from the pass, that suddenly the jig-saw began to fall into place.

Descending from the pass you go down to the left of the tarn that lies a little below it in a stony hanging valley, then more steeply to join a clear stream dancing in from the right. Soon it leads into a narrow vale of soft turf punctuated by a few brave pines, with the stream running delightfully through, then down to Estany Major de Colomers (2085m/ 6841ft). Instead of following a slender trail down to the northern end of the lake, cut away to the right towards the *refuge* standing above it. Sheep are often brought here for the night, and the smell will make you hasten away towards the higher country again.

There is a vague route along the western side of the lake, though some way above it, and this eventually leads up to a higher, unnamed tarn set in a large grassy basin out of sight of the Colomers lake. A path, which could almost be a mule trail, takes you higher, from one level to the next, heading south and following the line of a stream which links a number of tarns set in the Colomers cirque. The path soon disappears and a few cairns direct you further south into a veritable desert of stone. There is suddenly very little vegetation, just a fuzz of spiky yellow grass poking between the rocks. It's as though the last Ice Age has just departed, leaving behind only the rocks that formed a bed for the glaciers. It is a landscape of stone and water—splendid beneath a clear blue sky, but

extremely oppressive, I would imagine, under threatening storm clouds, while in mist one would be hard-put to find the correct route.

The map shows only a selection of the tarns that exist in this cirque, and as there's a distinct shortage of guiding cairns, you have to rely on experience and observation to find the route to Port de Colomers. What you must look for is a shallow scoop of a 'gully' coming from the mountains on the right. A few cairns will be found leading along the southern shoulder of this 'gully' towards a hint of a pass. As you gain height, so the pass becomes more obvious, and the route then zig-zags up a stony depression which takes you directly to Port de Colomers (2591m/8501ft) itself.

Feeling very fit after having spent nearly six weeks in the mountains that summer, I virtually ran up to the pass and was brought to a sudden halt by the tremendous view that greeted me there. This was wilderness country *par excellence*, a wonderful, untamed, impressive land. A big land that time had passed by.

Immediately to the west the slope dropped away to more tarns far, far below, trapped by the savage mountain walls. But it was Besiberri that drew my eyes, for it displayed a form of uncompromising harshness. Yet in its very harshness there was great beauty and a richness of texture, with an array of gendarmes and individual summits bristling beneath a glowering sky.

Down you go from the pass, now on a path once more. It leads into a surprise—a high, level stretch of pastureland, with the twist of an ox-bow stream winding through where frogs leap away from the threat of Vibram soles. A fjord-like tarn lies at the end of this pasture, with the continuing path leading along its edge and then disappearing to leave you to work out your own descent of a steep rocky slope. There are more tarns, more confusing slopes and more splendid, intimate views into corries that cut into the mountains to your left.

At last, after a wearisome, yet magnificent descent, you reach the level of Estany Negre (2127m/6978ft)—another fjord-like lake which lies directly below the Refugi Ventosa i Calvell. One last steepish climb on the broadest path of the whole circuit will take you to it. But as you watch evening draw over the mountains outside the hut, it's likely that you'll already be planning other routes among those countless wild acres. That is one of its gifts, and one of its dangers.

WALK 22: The Carlit Lakes Walk

Location: To the north-east of Andorra. Best reached by road over the Col de Puymorens. It is possible to get to the Carlit region by public transport: either by train via Paris-Toulouse-Ax-les-Thermes-La Tour de Carol (the Paris-Toulouse-Barcelona line), or from Perpignan to Villefranche where you catch the classic *petit train jaune* to La Tour de Carol.
Distance: 39 kms (24 miles).
Time Required: 2 days.
Type of Walk: A moderate-grade walk over a variety of terrain. The ascent of Pic Carlit should create no difficulties, although the gully used is rather steep. The descent is also steep at first, but easier lower down. Paths are mostly very good and clearly defined. In places cairns are followed in lieu of a proper trail. In poor visibility care should be taken when following these cairns—especially on the approach to Pic Carlit and in the upper reaches of the Gave de la Têt.
Base: Porté-Puymorens or Porta.

Accommodation: Auberge and hotel at Lac des Bouillouses. This is, however, a recommended backpacking tour.
Map: IGN Carte de Randonnées No. 7: *Cardagne-Capcir* 1:50,000.
Guidebook: *Walks and Climbs in the Pyrénées* by Kev Reynolds (Cicerone Press).

Exploring the Carlit Heartland

When you stand on the summit of Pic Carlit (2921m/9583ft) all the eastern view is littered with tarns and the distant mountains fall away as insignificant forest-clad hills. It's a lovely view, and there are no neighbouring peaks competing with it. You stand there, on the last of the so-called High Pyrénées, and hold the Eastern Pyrénées at bay.

The Carlit massif is a region of modest peaks rising from a high plateau of granite. It is a magnificent walking area that offers numerous

Above: **An overnight drop in temperature brought a surprise snowfall to the Carlit in September.**

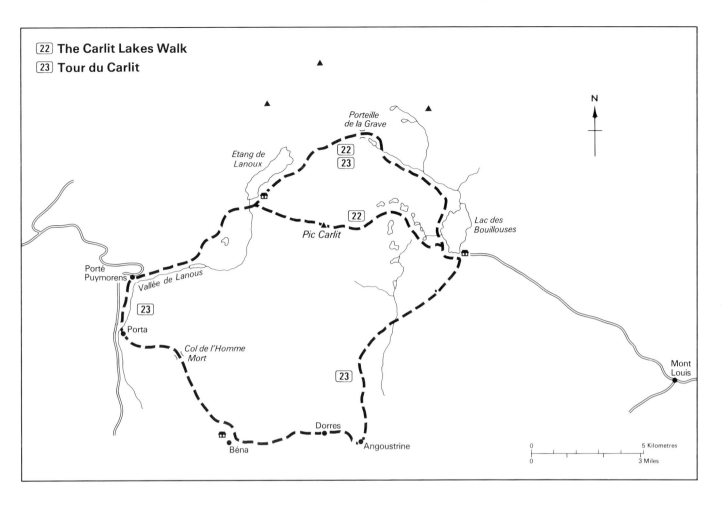

22 The Carlit Lakes Walk
23 Tour du Carlit

circuits and traverses, and with so many permutations available it would satisfy perfectly a holiday based on one of the outlying villages, while backpackers could happily wander from valley to valley for days at a time on a concentrated exploration. Few of the summits would attract the attention of a rock climber, but there are a number that offer low-key ascents for competent hill walkers. This walk crosses over the highest of them all.

South of the Carlit lies the delightful valley of the Cerdagne, the basin of a former glacial lake and the only broad, flat-bottomed valley in all the Pyrénées. To the west flow the valleys of Carol and Ariège, linked by the Col de Puymorens, and to the east, by the Capcir, the valley of the Aude which flows northward from Col de la Quillane above Mont-Louis. The northern boundary is roughly indicated by the Vallée d'Orlu which stretches out to Ax-les-Thermes.

So much for the outlying areas. The 'heartland' of the massif has one or two valleys with

an almost moorland quality about them, bounded by strangely smooth-sided mountains reminiscent, in texture and colouring, of parts of Wales. Elsewhere the British hill walker is reminded of the Highlands of Scotland, especially when gazing out from a high vantage point to a landscape dominated by a patchwork of lakes.

In certain respects the Carlit is unique in Pyrénéan terms. Admittedly there are plenty of other granite areas with a high preponderance of lakes. But there is something rather special about these. They seem, somehow, almost landscaped, as though they belong to the grounds of an aristocrat's estate. Some are almost too perfect, too neat, with their little bank-lined shrubberies and scattered dwarf pine, and a distant view of conical peaks. But this is how the last Ice Age deemed the land to be, and Time has been the only gardener here.

Part of the region is a designated Nature Reserve. Herds of isard are to be seen roaming round the higher peaks, and mouflon—rare wild sheep with huge horns—have been introduced here in recent years from Corsica. Being separated from the main Pyrénéan peaks by Andorra's island-like intrusion, the Carlit massif has managed to create its own peculiar atmosphere, and anyone working their way through all the routes in this book, will come to discover for themselves the truth of this observation. The Carlit is different.

The Route

This two-day walk begins at the village of Porté-Puymorens which nestles a short distance below the Col de Puymorens on the road to Spain. First you head east along the Lanous Valley, then on a traversing path high above it to reach the large barrage at the Etang de Lanoux. You break away from this to reach the base of Pic Carlit, then climb the mountain by way of a steep but easy gully that takes you within a few metres of the summit. Continuing, you descend eastwards on a path which leads beside several of the tarns seen from Pic Carlit, and on to the southern end of the large Lac des Bouillouses where accommodation is possible at the Auberge du Carlit, or at the hotel run by the Touring Club de France.

The second day's walk heads north along the western shore of Lac des Bouillouses, on the route of the GR10. At the far end of the lake you continue for a short distance before branching off to the left, and enter a lengthy stretch of broad valley which you follow almost to its head. Cross the Porteille de la Grave, and descend towards Etang de Lanoux. Without going down to the lakeside you break away from GR10 and head south-westward above it on a path which leads to the simple, unguarded Refuge La Guimbarde. From there you take the path along the hillside above the Lanous valley, and down to Porté once more.

Porté has hotels and a campsite, and there is another hotel and a *gîte d'étape* a short distance down-valley at Porta. But this outing would also make a fine backpacking expedition, with numerous idyllic sites for wild camping scattered along the route.

Day 1: Porté-Puymorens to Lac des Bouillouses

Porté is a huddle of ancient stone buildings cowering almost beneath the Puymorens road, but to the east stretches the lovely Lanous Valley, at the head of which stand the peaks and ridges that protect Pic Carlit's western flanks. The valley is lively with broom and birch, and about 3 kilometres along it there's a

lake that is very popular with anglers. Another, Etang de Font-Vive, is found a little higher, in a green bowl of hillside.

A quiet lane projects into the valley. It extends a short distance beyond the first lake and serves a works cableway that goes up to the barrage at the southern end of Etang de Lanoux. Motorists could use this road and park in an unmade lay-by at a point almost level with the western end of the first lake. Otherwise it is a gentle stroll for walkers along an easy gradient.

Opposite the lay-by a narrow path climbs steeply up the hillside through a scratchy mass of broom and heather, with finches darting round you and piping all the while. Ten minutes later you emerge onto a slightly broader trail running along the hillside, and bear right on it. This leads on a rising traverse all the way to the dammed lake, crossing little streams, climbing over projecting bluffs, and with a view overlooking the soft blue of Etang de Fonte-Vive. Sometimes the path is narrow and crumbling, sometimes wide enough, you'd think, to take a Land Rover. It's a pleasant walk on a bright morning, but on approaching the high concrete wall of the dam, you'll be longing for some of nature's harmony. Man's attempt to tame the wilderness by harnessing the power of water is seldom environmentally satisfying, and even though the great barrage has stood here for decades, the site is still cluttered and untidy.

It is preferable to cross the stream below the dam on a footbridge. Follow the track round to the left, then break away on a path heading east into a rough rising countryside. This will bring you across a green ridge along a line of cairns, and into full view of Pic Carlit, with Etang de Fourats lying a little below. From here the route of ascent is clearly evident.

There is a Y-shaped gully rising towards a slight indent below the summit. The path leads to the lower end of the stem of this Y, then zig-zags steeply up it to take the right fork leading to the little col.

The first time I made this ascent, visibility was perfect and the path could be seen from a distance. But on the next occasion the mountain itself was invisible, lost in the mists, and I saw nothing of it at all until I was actually in the gully. I went up treading clouds, but came onto the pass and emerged from them, disturbing a ptarmigan wearing its winter plumage as I did so. Behind me to the west those clouds were slowly shifting, but on the eastern side of the mountain I could see way

Above: **Etang du Vive is one of the loveliest tarns near Lac des Bouillouses, with views up to Pic Carlit.**

beyond Capcir. That night it snowed. It was early September and the Mediterranean was not far off. So be warned. The calendar, and southerly latitudes, are no absolute guarantees of sunshine.

Having reached a point so near the summit, it is convenient to leave your rucksack at the col and scramble the last few metres to the top. But note that the actual summit is found just south of the col, not to the north where a larger cairn is seen.

The descent route is obvious, and the path visible way off as it wends among the tarns. First you cut down a slope of scree, then follow waymarks over a spiky, shattered rib and onto an easy path that takes you down to a miniature garden-like landscape of tarns and streams, dwarf pine and alpenroses, juniper and heather mattresses and many tiny flowers in the grass. Off to the south the big open country slopes out to a hint of the Cerdagne, but this is lacking in interest by comparison with the immediate landscape. This after all, is a very special region, and each lake you come to has its own unique personality. Perhaps the finest of them all is Etang du Vive where you gaze north across its silent levels to the shapely cone of Pic Péric. A delectable spot, but there are so many idyllic little vignettes that you could spend many contented hours wandering from one image of loveliness to another. It is almost with a sense of regret that you come to Lac des Bouillouses—another dammed lake—and overnight accommodation.

Day 2: Lac des Bouillouses to Porté–Puymorens

Lac des Bouillouses is a popular destination for anglers, walkers and family picnic parties since it lies at the end of a road coming out of the Cerdagne at Font-Romeu and Mont-Louis. Many parties make the ascent of Carlit from here, the normal 'tourist route'. But the further you walk from the roadhead, the less people you will find and it will not be long before you have the heartland pretty much to yourself again. This stage of the walk, however, will be quite unlike the previous day's trek. There will be fewer lakes and there's no summit to reach, but instead, a long valley with a broad saddle at its head, followed by a descending traverse of yet another lengthy valley above Etang de Lanoux. A different day's walk, but no less interesting.

There is a clear, well-trodden path to lead you along the western shore of Lac des Bouillouses, mostly among pine trees and a few rough boulders. If the lake is full it adds colour to the scene, but late in the year the water level may well have dropped to expose tide marks round its edges, and it then wears a rather sad face.

At the far end of the lake the hills subside. They become less imposing, less challenging. Their attitude is benign, courteous even. But then you bear left—still on GR10—and enter the valley of the Grave de la Têt.

The Têt is one of *the* rivers of the Eastern Pyrénées. It rises at the head of this moorland-like valley and flows down in gentle curves, all unassuming and shy. But when it escapes from Bouillouses it drains the south-eastern slopes of the massif, skirts the fortified town of Mont-Louis and then drops into a great furrow it has made on the way to the Mediterranean. Below Mont-Louis the Têt's valley is severe, wooded and wild, but later there's much cultivation, with orchards on the hillsides. All that, however, is a far cry from the upper valley of the Grave de la Têt.

The path though faint in places, is not difficult to find. It leads through the initial gentility of the valley and then begins to rise towards its head by way of short, grassy steps. It's a charming walk among modest hills that rise 3-400 metres above you, but the valley itself has an average altitude of more than 2000 metres (6562ft), so the mountains are not as small as they appear.

Near the head of the valley the path bears left and you gain more height, walking into an upper level where a small tarn occupies a soft-turf pastureland. Watch out for cairns to guide you across the stream that comes from it and then begin a short ascent to the pass. Porteille de la Grave (2426m/7959ft) is a long, broad, grassy saddle, only 250 metres below Pic de la Grave. Down on its western side, almost filling the valley, is Etang de Lanoux; to the south, confusing slopes lead up to Pic Carlit.

Still on the route of GR10 go down the western slopes towards the lake, but then break away from the main path where it forks, and head off along the hillside above the left bank. It's an interesting traverse path that leads you over various knolls and round to the unmanned Guimbarde hut. This little *refuge* could be a romantic shelter, for it occupies a splendid site on a bluff near the southern end of the lake. But it has been vandalised in recent years and now only the most desperate of walkers would seek a night's shelter there. In a storm, yes. Otherwise it would be better to bivouac.

It will only take a few minutes to wander from the hut to the broad path leading from the dam down to the Lanous Valley. The Carlit Lakes Walk is almost over, for the way down to Porté-Puymorens is along the same path used at the start of the circuit, although an alternative descent could be made via Etang de Font-Vive, and from there into the Vallée de Lanous on the anglers' path. Either way, you should be in the unsophisticated village of Porté within a couple of hours, and ready to work out your next long walk.

Why not try the Tour du Carlit whilst in the area?

Right: **Pic Carlit looks down on one of many tarns leading to the larger Lac des Bouillouses**.

WALK 23: The Tour du Carlit

Above: **Porta, a small village on the road to the Cerdagne, has** *gîte* **accommodation for walkers on the Tour du Carlit.**

Location: North of the Cerdagne, and to the north-east of Andorra. Reached by car from Mont-Louis (14 kms to Lac des Bouillouses). By public transport: *petit train jaune* from Ville-franche to Mont-Louis, or by train on the Paris-Toulouse-Barcelona line as far as La Tour de Carol, and then by the *petit train jaune* to Mont-Louis.

Distance: 45 kms (28 miles).

Time Required: 3 days.

Type of Walk: Constantly varied, with an easy-to-moderate grade. There are no major climbs nor difficulties. Waymarking is to be found on most sections.

Base: Mont-Louis or Lac des Bouillouses.

Start/Finish: Lac des Bouillouses.

Accommodation: *Gîtes d'étape* at Porta and Béna; auberge or TCF hotel at Bouillouses.

Map: IGN Carte de Randonnées No. 7: *Cerdagne-Capcir* 1:50,000.

Guidebooks: *Walks and Climbs in the Pyrénées* by Kev Reynolds (Cicerone Press).
Detours Pyrénées No. 3: *Pyrénées de l'Est* (Randonnées Pyrénéennes).

An Extended Tour of the Carlit Massif

The Carlit massif wears two faces. In the heart of the region, its mountains thrust out of an elevated plateau of granite and, as already discovered on the Carlit Lakes Walk, this plateau is liberally coloured with tarns and streams and one or two larger lakes held in check by huge concrete barrages.

Its other face looks to the sun. Gazing over the warm expanse of the Cerdagne, its hill slopes ease down to this unique broad swathe among aromatic plants and outstanding granite tors. Buzzards circle lazily overhead. Horses graze unattended. Tiny hamlets squat almost hidden from the world in tight valley crevices along the spring line, marking the upper limit of summer pasture.

One face is distinctly highland in character—even though it may well have a personality quite distinct from other areas of the Pyrénées—while the other is soft and pastoral, a landscape that once belonged to a spartan peasant agriculture, now largely deserted.

This extended tour, taken over three days, has been devised by the French walkers' organisation, *Randonnées Pyrénéennes*, and waymarked in part by them. It is a delightful circuit that will take you through a section of the Pyrénées that is almost unknown outside a small handful of enthusiasts, but it is an area well worth exploring and one that will repay you with glorious views quite unlike anything experienced elsewhere in these mountains.

Accommodation along the route is in *gîtes d'étape*, while there is a choice of auberge or hotel at Lac des Bouillouses where the circuit begins and ends.

The Route

Starting at the dammed Lac des Bouillouses the walk heads north along the western side of the lake, on the path of GR10. (This first stage is identical to that taken on the last day of the Carlit Lakes Walk.) At the far end of the lake it then heads north-westward through the valley of the Grave de la Têt, over Porteille de la Grave and down to the southern end of Etang de Lanoux. Then, following the waymarks of GR7, (or, as an alternative, take a slight variation by dropping into the valley of Lanous), descend to the village of Porté-Puymorens on the Puymorens-Cerdagne road. From Porté the route crosses the road and goes down to Porta, an attractive stone village with overnight accommodation in either *gîte d'étape* or hotel. This stage will occupy about 8 hours of walking.

Day Two leads out of Porta on a climb up the hillside that forms the eastern wall of the Vallée du Carol, and leads to the unhappily-named Col de l'Homme Mort (2300m/7546ft). A descent is then made into a small river valley heading south-east, then over a spur to a second valley that brings you to the tiny hamlet of Béna with its magnificent views overlooking the expanse of the Cerdagne. Although this stage requires no more than five hours of walking, an overnight here is highly recommended in the *gîte d'étape*.

For the final stage of the circuit, the waymarked trail leads eastward through two more hamlets, then over Col de Jouell and down to the attractive village of Dorres. From here an easy descent is made to Angoustrine, which is visited briefly before the route heads north along a well-tracked valley to Bouillouses.

Day 1: Lac des Bouillouses to Porta

Early in summer the pasturelands around Lac des Bouillouses are bright with gentians, alpenroses and dwarf azalea. Wild flowers drift everywhere; in woodland glades, along the margins of so many tarns, even making cushions over the rocks themselves. Later, as summer draws on, herds of horses are brought out of the Cerdagne to graze here on the broad expanse of unfenced country shown on the map as the *Désert du Carlit*. But Lac des Bouillouses mostly attracts anglers. (The French are extremely keen on fishing, and in so many regions of the Pyrénées one comes across a trout stream or a lake, far from habitation, with one or more anglers thigh-deep in the water, twitching the surface with an artificial fly. Being accessible by road, Lac des Bouillouses attracts its fair share.)

Lac des Bouillouses is reached by road from Mont-Louis near the Col de la Perche in the Cerdagne. It's a pleasant, interesting drive that winds through woods and up to the so-called *Désert du Carlit*, with Pic Carlit rising over the shoulders of other neighbourhood mountains. Since this first day will occupy about eight hours of walking, excluding rest stops, it is advisable to make an early start.

Initially the GR10 path leads comfortably along the west bank of the lake, hugging a waymarked course on the edge of pinewoods, fragrant when morning's warmth draws scent from the trees. Ahead rises Pic Péric (2810m/9219ft), an attractive, conical mountain with an easy route to its summit, and one which stands midway on a north-south traverse of the massif. Seen in the early morning this makes a fine start to the day.

At the far end of the lake you wander into a moorland-like terrain where the path forks. If you were tempted to take the right-hand branch, you'd be led across to Etang de la Balmette under the rising slopes of Pic du Pam, then on to Les Angles, a ski resort in the valley of Capcir. This region is even more untypical of the Pyrénées than that of the Carlit or Cerdagne, and is worth lingering in—especially in winter when its wide plains and forests make for ideal cross-country ski excursions.

But our circuit takes the left branch and continues along the GR10 rising over a sill which leads into the valley of the Grave de la Têt. This is pleasant walking country, almost 'home-from-home' for British hill walkers in its texture and colouring. It's a valley that rises

Above: **Etang de Font-Vive lies below the Carlit Massif.**

in gentle steps, the path always remaining to the left of the stream until shortly before the final slope up to the pass at its head—Porteille de la Grave (2426m/7959ft)—where you cross the stream below a tarn, and shortly afterwards work a route among screes.

From the grassy saddle of the Porteille, GR10 cuts down to the northern end of Etang de Lanoux, then continues westward over Porteille de Lanous and down to L'Hospitalet. The Tour du Carlit follows this path for a short distance, then breaks away to head south then south-west on a lengthy traverse of the southern slopes well above the lake. This is a fine stretch of path and it leads to the unmanned Refuge de la Guimbarde before descending into the Lanous Valley and on to Porté-Puymorens.

Leaving Porté you are faced with grinding traffic on the Puymorens road, but you cross over and descend by path and track, keeping company with the Carol river as far as Porta, which squats a little above the road on the eastern side again.

Porta is a pleasant, stone-built village, tight around its narrow alleyways and rich in vernacular architecture. There's a *gîte d'étape*

here with room for 16 trekkers, and a small hotel set beside the main road. Behind the village rise wooded hills. On the far side of the valley the hillslopes reach up to the borders of Andorra. Somehow it all seems a far cry from Bouillouses.

Day 2: Porta to Béna

This stage is the shortest of the tour, yet it leads to some magnificent panoramas, has a real sense of isolation and mystery about it, and gives the opportunity to study a unique mountain landscape without being pressured by time. In summer this can be a dry stage, so make sure you fill water bottles before leaving Porta.

Leaving the village follow a path heading south up the hillside towards the forest that lines the valley, and enter it to rise south-eastwards in zig-zags, climbing the spur that projects west from Pic de Comaou. There will be nearly 800 metres of height to gain (2625ft) on this, which is quite enough to start the day, but in about two and a half hours from Porta you leave forest shade and come to the high pastures that lead to Col de l'Homme Mort

(2300m/7546ft) to gain a fresh appreciation of this corner of the mountains. A big, rolling, empty country spreads off to the east where numerous streams flow south to the Cerdagne, draining the Carlit slopes.

From here to the hamlet of Béna the walking is nearly all downhill. You begin by dropping into the valley drained by the Salit stream and then wander through it until the stream bears southward round the insignificant lump of Pic de Béna. Here you branch off to the left to skirt the slopes of the peak, with wonderful wide views into the Cerdagne and with bald, Spanish hills on the far side drawing your concentration and demanding one photographic halt after another. It is a remarkable panorama; certainly one of the very finest in all of the Eastern Pyrénées.

Béna is tiny. A small collection of half-forgotten farm buildings perched away from the world, and with a splendid *gîte* in which to spend the night. It is one of those utterly memorable sites that demands a return—again and again.

Day 3: Béna to Lac des Bouillouses

Tucked in a tight little vale to the east of Béna lie the hamlets of Fanès and Brangoly. Like Béna their reason for existence has been superseded by a modern world that has little call for the subsistence farming that justified their existence for centuries, and it seems that only the purchase of holiday homes by wealthy townsfolk from non-mountain France has saved them from total desertion and dereliction. Wandering through there is an air of timelessness; the scratching of hens, the rough tangle of briars, the undisturbed dust on the track, all combine to create an impression of unreality. It is difficult to pinpoint an age. The few cracked buildings could belong to any since the Middle Ages. Save for electricity cables, the external view is one that modernity has simply passed by.

A track takes you away from Béna through a rough landscape of granite tors and pasture, and down into that valley cleavage with Fanès seen below. When we came down here one crisp September day with snow on the Carlit peaks above, there were cows in a walled meadow. One had only just calved and we watched for several minutes as the still-sticky calf tried gallantly to stand on its pin legs while the mother licked her clean and nuzzled her towards the right end of her body for milk. (Next morning snow was lower down the hillsides and I wondered how the calf would fare, being born so close to an early winter.)

The track continues from Fanès to Brangoly. Trees overhang the route, and a stream flows below. Rabbits may be seen down by the stream, and there will be buzzards overhead. Brangoly is bigger than both Béna and Fanès—but only just. It boasts a church, though if it holds services the priest must surely come a long way to conduct them. However, on the far side of the Col de Jouell, which is crossed half an hour after leaving the hamlet, you come down to Dorres, a substantial village and one of the showpieces of the Cerdagne. In this neat and charming granite village there stands a fine church with three bells. There's also a restaurant and hotel, and more splendid views across the broad valley to the Puigmal.

The continuing waymarked route takes you down the road to Les Escaldes, but shortly after this rather unlovely collection of spa buildings you break away on a track that rounds the hillside and brings you to the edge of Angoustrine.

Angoustrine is on the Bourg-Madame to Font-Romeu road, a short distance from Llivia, that curious anomaly of a small town that is politically Spanish, yet entirely surrounded by French territory—an enclave whose status is due to a grammatical nicety. This former capital of the Cerdagne remained in Spanish control when thirty-three villages were ceded to France. Llivia, being classed as a *town*, was not included in the arrangement!

A wooded valley cuts north behind Angoustrine, with a track leading through it. Our route wanders along this valley with more granite tors standing above the river on the right. The hills here are modest hills, becoming more bare as the valley rises and curves north-eastwards. The route skirts below Puig del Cap de l'Homme where two valleys join, and you continue along the Angoustrine stream into a changing landscape. The country opens out. Granite peaks jut from a high plateau, and there ahead rises the dam holding back the waters of Lac des Bouillouses. It's an intrusion, but it helps put perspective into a walk that has displayed so well the two faces of the Carlit.

I can't help feeling there will be aspects of this walk that will come rising from the well of memory, like a cork in a bowl of water, to niggle away until a return is organised. The Carlit and the Cerdagne have certainly called me back on several occasions, and no doubt will do so again.

WALK 24: The Pyrénéan High Route

Above: **In the centre of the range the route leads through the Esera Valley. Here the walker crosses Plan d'Estan where two or three tarns once lay. They have since disappeared.**

Distance: The basic distance is about 400kms (250 miles), but the High Route will probably double that—depending on the precise route and alternatives taken.

Time Required: 7-8 weeks.

Type of Walk: Demanding and varied, through much deserted and spectacular country. Snow will probably be encountered on certain high passes throughout the summer. Ice axes should be taken. An ability to read map and compass is absolutely essential. It is a route for experienced trekkers only.

Start: Hendaye-Plage (Atlantic coast).

Finish: Banyuls-sur-Mer (Mediterranean).

Accommodation: A variety of mountain huts and *cabanes*, but there are several stages without shelter at all. Trekkers should carry either a tent or bivouac equipment.

Maps: IGN Carte de Randonnées Nos. 1-11 all at 1:50,000. In addition, certain Editorial Alpina maps will be required for some Spanish sections—depending on alternatives or variations chosen (see guidebooks for details).

Guidebooks: *Pyrénées High Level Route* by Georges Véron (Gastons/West Col). *Walks and Climbs in the Pyrénées* by Kev Reynolds (Cicerone Press) for Lescun to Andorra sections.

Along the Frontier Ridge

In selecting the walks for inclusion in this book I found myself confronted by a dilemma. Without question the High Route is *the* classic walk of the Pyrénées, and as such it naturally came top of my list. But I had already written about it in Walt Unsworth's *Classic Walks of the World* (Oxford Illustrated Press, 1985) and was loath to duplicate that chapter here. Besides, this book is primarily aimed at the majority of walkers and lovers of mountains who are unlikely to have either the time or dedication required to tackle a route of its length, so I decided to break the main, central section, into three separate stages, each one manageable within the compass of a fortnight's holiday. These stages have been written in greater detail than was possible in an essay covering the complete High Route, and are included as *Highlights of the National Park, Gavarnie to Luchon,* and *Luchon to Andorra.* That still leaves me with a fair amount of ground uncovered.

A compromise solution is to outline the High Route in a more condensed form. This chapter, then, will hopefully draw the attention of ambitious long-distance mountain walkers to this most challenging and rewarding of Pyrénéan expeditions. The High Route is indeed a gem of a route that deserves to be better known.

First of all, the nuts and bolts of the route. From Hendaye on the Atlantic coast to Banyuls-sur-Mer on the Mediterranean is a distance of more than 400 kilometres (250 miles). The High Route will, of course, double that distance, so the walker will need to set aside a minimum of seven weeks in order to tackle its complete length. The main route is divided into some forty-five day stages, but allowances should be made for rest days, bad-weather days, days for restocking with supplies—and the odd day for getting lost! In addition to the main route there are also alternatives and variations to avoid certain difficulties, or to explore a region otherwise bypassed. There are as many as fifty such alternatives.

The High Route is a more serious proposition than the GR10, described elsewhere. Some sections call for basic mountaineering skills. There will be a few days when scrambling pitches are unavoidable. Other days when an ice axe will be a necessary aid. There are lofty passes to cross where snow lies trapped for much of the summer. There are long days on exposed ridges where a weather-eye will constantly be alert for warning signs of approaching storm; other stages when you will be many hours without any possibility of finding water or shelter (from storm or an overpowering sun). Although waymarking has been carried out for the vast majority of the route, there will be regions without any path at all, and only a vague scattering of cairns to create a considerable amount of confusion in poor visibility. Navigational skills are a prerequisite for anyone setting out on this walk. But for all this, it is basically within the capabilities of any strong hill walker who has had all-weather experience of roaming the mountains of Britain.

As for accommodation on the way, there are mountain huts scattered along much of the route, some with guardians in residence during high summer, but others that are unmanned and offering only minimal facilities. Yet there will be stages without any hope of finding overnight shelter at the end of the day. In such cases the walker will be faced with camping or beneath-the-stars bivouacking.

The majority of the main High Route, as devised by members of the French Alpine Club and the Randonnées Pyrénéennes organisation, follows the frontier crest wherever it can, but favours the northern slopes where the ridges demand it. Now and again it strays onto Spanish territory, and I am firmly convinced that it is this straying from one side of the international frontier to the other that enables the long-distance hill walker to gain a more complete picture of the range than would otherwise be possible. The very essence of the Pyrénées can then be experienced, and it is this which gives the High Route its quality.

Through the Basque Lands (10-11 days)

For a short stretch on some days of this trek the High Route shares the same path as that of the GR10. In the Basque country it begins that way, wandering from Hendaye to Col d'Ibardin on the borders with Spain. La Rhûne (900m/2953ft) dominates a landscape of bracken and broom-carpeted hills, and the summit is visited on the first full day's walking. It's a crowded mountain top, busy with television masts and tourists who have arrived by rack-railway from Col de St Ignace. But on a clear day the views are impressive for they cover a huge area, including not only the immediate Basque lands, but also the far-distant forest of Les Landes—a sea of green matched by the sparkle of its Atlantic neighbour.

An alternative first day's stage would be to follow GR10 as far as the village of Sare where there are restaurants and hotels, for the High Route itself goes up to Col Lizuniaga where accommodation is uncertain. (There are shepherd's huts nearby, but you cannot rely on using them.) Continuing, the route trespasses into Spain for much of the day, but returns to French territory again at Dancharia where the frontier actually divides the community in two by way of the river which is taken to be the border. Not far away is Ainhoa, one of the

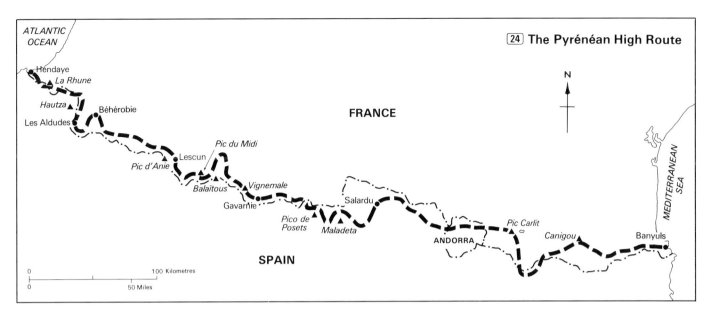

prettiest of all Basque villages and one that is visited by GR10.

From Dancharia to Bidarray is an easy six-hour day, but from Bidarray a longer trek is in store. Longer, but the best so far. There are dramatic cliffs, broad views and several summits to cross. Pic d'Iparla (1044m/3425ft) is the loftiest of all, and its ridges form one of the highlights of this stage, although they should be avoided in poor weather. A day later there comes an opportunity to climb to the summit of Hautza (1306m/4285ft) on a short diversion from the route. A lovely panorama is the reward—given fine weather. Unfortunately the Basque country is prone to mists and rain, as witnessed by the lush vegetation, and should the early stages of your journey be dogged by poor conditions, the alternatives offered in the guidebook should be adopted. It is so easy to become disorientated in bad visibility, especially where sheep trails compound the mystery of the onward path. And sheep trails are very much a feature of the hill country of the west.

The international frontier is a constant companion almost throughout the Basque lands, yet this is invariably only indicated by an occasional marker stone. But roads are crossed, passes leading from France to Spain are briefly trodden and passports should be kept in a handy rucksack pocket in the unlikely event of your being challenged by a frontier guard.

Carrying a tent provides a certain degree of freedom on several stages, especially where a search for accommodation would otherwise necessitate the loss of hard-won height. One such stage is that which leads from the pretty village of Les Aldudes. Without a readiness to either camp or bivouac, the trekker has to descend to Béhérobie at the end of a very long day. With a tent, of course, it is possible to find a suitable pitch, thus enabling you to have a shorter, less strenuous day.

The stage between Béhérobie and Col Bagargui via the summit of Occabé is shared with the GR10, but an alternative is offered for the second half of the day with the crossing of Col de Burdincurutcheta, a traverse of the flanks of Mendibels, and the opportunity to visit the top of Pic de Escaliers. (Many of these Basque names can tie the tongue in knots. Try, for example, Arthanolatzégagnia, Achourterrigagna or Chardékagagna—each one a peak traversed on the route. Entering the so-called High Pyrénées near Pic d'Anie comes as a welcome relief—if only for the ease of pronouncing the names of places en route!)

The High Pyrénées (4 weeks)

There are two ways to pass from the Basque lands to the High Pyrénées. The first, and easier way, heads through a remarkable limestone plateau along a line of cairns and waymarks, crosses Col des Anies, allows a diversion to be made (for those not overburdened with a heavy rucksack) to the summit of Pic d'Anie, and finally brings you to the foot of the Aiguilles d'Ansabère. The alternative, via Col d'Anaye, is potentially hazardous in poor visibility and should on no account be considered by inexperienced trekkers—even in perfect weather conditions. It takes you over a truly wild landscape, totally devoid of paths, water or shelter, but is considered by some to be the very best way of entering the spectacular Lescun/Ansabère region.

From the limestone pinnacles of Ansabère the route goes over the ridge into Spain for a spell, then regains French slopes with a belvedere of a path leading to Refuge d'Arlet, with Pic du Midi d'Ossau beckoning from the east. Two days later you cross Col d'Ayous and come into full, glorious view of this Pyrénéan symbol.

Next in line comes the big granite massif of Balaïtous. The standard route round this is described in Walk 4, while one alternative is to avoid Arrémoulit and Port du Lavedan and instead make a wider loop north by visiting the dammed Lac d'Artouse, crossing the col of the same name and dropping to Refuge Migouélou, and then rejoining the normal route next day in the pastures north of Balaïtous. Another option is to skirt the mountain to the south, having crossed Col de Palas, working round to Col de La Fache which leads into the Marcadau Valley.

From Marcadau to the Vignemale's wonderful North Face, and from there to the Cirque de Gavarnie it is all highly photogenic and memorable trekking. Then the long stage east from Barroude to Rioumajou, a day of full commitment, is another of those only to be undertaken in good conditions.

Various options are available for the walk from Rioumajou to Viadós, and again the route splits north of Pico de Posets. One way is to return to France in order to explore the Aygues-Tortes (not to be confused with the Aigües-Tortes in Spain much farther east), while the other remains in Spain for the descent of the lovely Estós Valley.

Beyond the Maladeta, now well into the second half of the High Route, the Vall d'Aran is crossed, and this is seen very much as a major watershed of the walk. After this there are almost two distinct High Routes. One steadfastly maintains its position on the south side of the frontier, while the other traverses the French slopes, only now and again sending a link across the ridge to offer the possibility of changing landscapes. Both are worthy routes, and it is no clear-cut decision which to choose, but by the time the Carlit massif has been reached to the east of Andorra, that choice has been resolved and one major line remains to be

taken to the coast.

The Eastern Pyrénées (7-8 days)

Leaving the Carlit region at Lac des Bouillouses, the High Route crosses the Cerdagne plain to the hamlet of Eyne tucked against the lower slopes of the rolling southerly mountains. It then goes through the exquisite Vallée d'Eyne where, in early summer, the meadows are extravagant with bloom, climbs to a col and roams the frontier ridge heading east before descending into the cirque of Ull de Ter in Spain. There is a CEC hut here in which to spend a night before tackling the large plateaux of Pla de Calm Agre and Pla Guilhem.

This is Catalonia where sudden storms can be violent, if short-lived, in summer, and one should always keep alert to any change in the weather. Here, as elsewhere on the High Route, an early start to each day is desirable.

After Mariailles you cross the Canigou massif with those lovely views off to the Mediterranean. From here it would appear to be all downhill to Banyuls, but there are still four more days of trekking to face before the sea is finally reached. Four days in which to wind down steadily, each stage being a little less demanding than the one before. The main problem in the Eastern Pyrénées is not so much the terrain, but the heat. In full summer, trekking can be an exhausting business, and those who prefer to tackle the High Route as a series of walking holidays, rather than as a whole, would be advised to consider late May or June for this eastern section. At that time, the temperature will not only be more agreeable, the atmosphere clear and sparkling, but the valley meadows and hillsides will be in full flower, and the orchards of the Vallespir covered with blossom.

The final day of this epic journey is an experience to savour. There are the views; not of big mountains and trim glaciers, but of a dazzling coastline and the Roussillon plain where Perpignan represents a form of commerce totally foreign to the solitary farms and hay barns passed on so many stages of the long walk.

You come down out of the hills and walk ahead on concrete streets to the sea. And as you stand there with the water lapping against your legs you'll be tormented by a kaleidoscope of impressions that will take weeks to sift into some semblance of order. But by then you'll be planning your next trip.

For trekkers are incurable dreamers.

Middle Mountain Tours

Practically every walk in this book hugs the higher mountains. These, after all, are the cream of Pyrénéan outings, providing routes through the finest scenery and nudging the more dramatic peaks. But there are other circuits too. A little lower, perhaps, in most cases, but these 'middle-mountain' tours—all in France—are still extremely rewarding. Yet space is limited and it is not possible to devote a whole chapter to every walk that demands attention, so the following brief route outlines must suffice. The Randonnées Pyrénéennes organisation has published a series of guidebooks to these circuits, under the general title of *Detours Pyrénéens*, and more precise details of the walks will be found there.

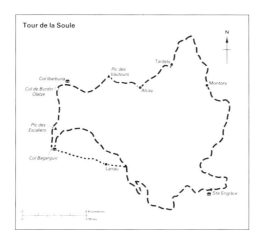

Tour de la Soule

Location: Western Pyrénées, in the Basque country.
Distance: 68 kms (42 miles).
Time Required: 6 days.
Start/Finish: Tardets.
Accommodation: *Gîtes d'étape*.
Map: IGN Carte de Randonnées No.2: *Pays Basque Est* 1:50,000.
Guidebook: Detours Pyrénéens No.1: *Pyrénées Occidentales*.

This tour picks out some of the best features of the Pays de la Soule, and follows a stretch of GR10. The village of Tardets-Sorholus, which marks the start of the circuit, is a charming place and the folk-lore centre of the region. From here the route makes a clockwise tour, first visiting the Chapelle de la Madeleine, a

place of local pilgrimage, then south via the cols of Sustary and d'Erretzu to the village of Montory. Ste-Engrâce is the destination for the second stage, and from this former shepherds' village the tour continues through forests to the finest of all the gorges in the Basque country, the Gorges de Kakouéta.

There then follows a climb of 900 metres (2953ft), initially above the gorges, to Col d'Anhaou and from there to another splendid gorge, that of Holzarté (otherwise known as the Crevasses d'Holcarté). Logibar lies a little to the north, and marks the end of Stage Three.

From Logibar there is the option of heading west to Larrau in the great Iraty forest and making the ascent of Pic d'Orhy (2017m/6617ft) via Col Bagarguic. Otherwise the standard tour goes north-westward in a long loop before finding the way to the col where a *gîte* is situated. The final two stages return to Tardets by way of Col de Burdin Olatze, Col Ibarburia and the summit of Pic des Vautours (1072m/3517ft).

Tour de la Vallée d'Aure

Location: To the east of the Néouvielle massif.
Distance: 31 kms (19 miles).
Time Required: 2-3 days.
Start/Finish: Azet.
Accommodation: *Gîtes d'étape*.
Map: IGN Carte de Randonnées No.5: *Luchon-Aure-Louron* 1:50,000.
Guidebook: Detours Pyrénéens No.2: *Pyrénées Centrales*.

This walk samples a typically French Pyrénéan valley just far enough out of the mainstream mountains to be wooded and gentle, almost like foothill country. It's not foothill country though, but a medium-scale landscape, a true middle-mountain area. Off to the south and the west larger peaks rise over intermediate crests, and above St Lary the hills have been tamed for skiing. Much of this tour wanders through woodlands. Some of it treads bare green ridges. There are small villages in the valley and on the hillsides, and quiet farms being worked, giving the whole scene a distinctly pastoral flavour.

The village of Azet is on the eastern hillslopes above St Lary, and setting out from

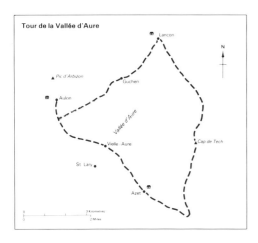

Tour de la Vallée d'Aure

here you head uphill along GR10 to gain the ridge that divides the Vallée d'Aure from Vallée du Louron. Once on the ridge the route leads in a northerly direction along the crest with fine views to the Néouvielle peaks in the west. The highest point on the ridge is Cap de Tech (1678m/5505ft) and this is reached about three hours after setting out from Azet. This is the halfway point on the first day's walk, and the afternoon's route takes you further along the ridge before descending on a forest track to Lancon, a little village on a spur overlooking the confluence of the Louron and Neste d'Aure, with an impressive view of Pic d'Arbizon.

From Lancon the circuit requires only a short, 4-hour stage to Aulon at the foot of Pic d'Arbizon. Initially the way drops to the Vallée d'Aure at Grézian, crosses the river to Guchen on the left bank, then climbs through forest into a quiet back-country valley before sloping down to the village and its *gîte*. On the final stage to Azet you must retrace the route back to the forested slopes opposite Aulon, climb through them to the ridge at Pla du Castillon, then head straight down on the far side to Vieille-Aure. Cross the river and the main valley road, then follow GR10 uphill to Azet.

Tour du Capcir

Location: East of the Carlit region.
Distance: 45kms (28 miles).
Time Required: 4 days.
Start/Finish: Matemale.
Accommodation: *Gîte d'étape* and unmanned mountain huts.
Maps: IGN Carte de Randonnées No. 8: *Cerdagne-Capcir* 1:50,000.
Guidebook: Detours Pyrénéens No. 3: *Pyrénées de l'Est.*

Capcir, the upper valley of the Aude, is not at all like the rest of the Pyrénées represented in this book. It is a region of 'low' spreading hills and broad-based valleys. A region of heavy forest and pastureland—ideal ski-touring country, in fact. But it is also a fine region for walking tours.

Having stated that the hills are 'low', perhaps this should be explained, for there are summits well in excess of 2000 metres (6562ft). But the hills rise from a regularly high plateau (there are villages well above the 1500 metre mark), so their tops seem less impressive than otherwise one might suspect. Yet none of this detracts from Capcir's appeal. It is like a great green basin facing north and bounded on either side by extensive pine forests. In this basin lies the Matemale reservoir, with the village from which it takes its name squatting below the dam. The Tour of Capcir starts here.

Making a slow, steady traverse of the eastern hillside, the way rises to Col de Sansa on a forest road, crosses through and continues on the eastern side of the ridge to pass beneath the peak of Madrès (2469m/8100ft). An unmanned hut, Refuge de Nohèdes, makes a simple base for the night, and is found a little below a second ridge to the south-east of Madrès.

On leaving the hut the circuit suggests going up and over the summit, with a steepish descent thereafter to the valley, and the dammed lake of Puyvalador. You then head into the Val de Galbe, at whose entrance a *gîte* will be found in the little hamlet of Espousouille. The tour continues through the valley, then swings to the south to cross the shoulder of Pic de la Montagnette to the tarn-strewn plateau of Camporells. From the hut here at 2240 metres (7349ft) the final stage of the walk is practically all downhill. It crosses a region of tarn, forest and pasture, and passes Lac d'Aude, source of one of the most important rivers in this corner of France.

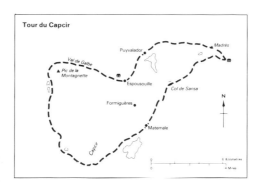

Tour du Capcir